USING
ALDUS
PAGEMAKER

U S I N G
A L D U S
P A G E M A K E R

Publish it Yourself!

R O G E R   C.   P A R K E R

BANTAM BOOKS
TORONTO • NEW YORK • LONDON • SYDNEY • AUCKLAND

A Bantam Book / October, 1987
USING ALDUS PAGEMAKER: PUBLISH IT YOURSELF!

ISBN 0-553-34407-2

PRINTED IN THE UNITED STATES OF AMERICA

B 0 9 8 7 6 5 4 3 2 1

Contents

1

An Introduction to Desktop Publishing

The Importance of Visual Persuasion

Everyone in business, from self-employed entrepreneurs to Fortune 1000 corporate executives, can benefit from the ability of desktop publishing software programs like Aldus PageMaker to help them effectively communicate in print.

Print communications are an essential part of person-to-person and business-to-business communications. Individuals and businesses succeed to the extent that they effectively sell, or persuade, others. Most of this selling is done on paper through the mail or as tangible "leave behinds" following face-to-face meetings.

Print communications are powerful because they are tangible. The spoken word begins to lose effectiveness the moment it's spoken. But print communications have a life of their own. They can be read as quickly or slowly as desired. They can be read over and over again. They can be shared with others.

Print communications take place at all levels. They begin at the resume stage, when individuals attempt to convince prospective employers that they should be hired. At the entrepreneurial level, print communications take place when business owners communicate with prospects, clients, and customers using advertisements, brochures, and newsletters. And, at the corporate level, "selling in print" takes place when executives prepare presentations and annual reports designed to convince senior management and stockholders to approve their expansion plans and marketing strategies.

Words Are Not Enough

Print communications require more than strong arguments and well-chosen words. The effectiveness of print communications is based on appearance as well as content. **A strong message can be torpedoed by a poor visual presentation.** Desktop publishing programs like Aldus PageMaker can help you communicate more effectively by improving the appearance of your print communications and helping you prepare them as quickly and cost-effectively as possible.

Graphic excellence is a necessity, not a luxury. People **do** choose books by their covers. Good-looking documents invite readership. Visually-appealing documents increase your ability to quickly and effectively communicate your ideas, recommendations, and selling messages to your readers.

In the past, the ability to prepare good-looking print communications was limited to those who had access to specialized tools plus training and experience in the graphic arts. Since the tools of graphic communications were expensive and extensive training was needed to master them, only a few individuals could cultivate their latent graphic talents and abilities.

If you didn't have the tools, training and time, you had to hire others—which increased costs and caused delays—or do without. This is a tragedy because many individuals have natural graphic abilities which could be developed; with a little effort. The rewards for making the effort are both economic and spiritual.

Limited Only by Your Imagination

It is important to note that desktop publishing consists of more than just preparing brochures and newsletters. Desktop publishing is appropriate for any print communications that have to look good as well as be produced on-time and at minimalm cost. Desktop publishing is therefore appropriate for simple projects such as business cards, purchase orders and invoices, as well as for sophisticated projects such as annual reports, brochures, newsletters, newspapers, magazines and—even—books.

The page layouts for this book, for example, were prepared with Aldus PageMaker on the same desktop computer used to write the copy. The camera-ready mechanicals were delivered to the publisher ready to be printed.

The following is a brief review of some of the types of print communications you can prepare with desktop publishing:

Annual reports	Magazines
Books	Newsletters
Brochures	Newspapers
Business cards	Newspaper advertisements
Business plans	Newspaper inserts
Catalogs	Posters
Data sheets	Presentations
Financing proposals	Price Lists

Product literature	Software documentation
Proposals	Training ManualsProposals
Signs	Resumes

DESKTOP PUBLISHING VERSUS WORD PROCESSING

Word processing software has been around since the earliest days of personal computing. Word processing replaces strikeouts and retyping with on-screen revisions. Word processing programs permit you to create, edit and revise your words on the screen of your personal computer. When revisions need to be made, instead of retyping the page—or the entire manuscript if your revisions change page numbering—you simply correct your words and print out a fresh error-free copy with updated page numbers.

Desktop publishing adds a visual, or graphic, dimension to your work. Instead of concerning itself primarily with content, desktop publishing is more concerned with appearance. Here is a summary of the ways desktop publishing moves beyond word processing.

Ease of Use and Flexibility

Desktop publishing's power comes from its ease of use. This ease of use is based on desktop publishing's highly visual nature. Desktop publishing gives you immediate visual feedback at every step you take. Although many word processors can perform some of the desktop publishing functions described below, you often have to work harder to accomplish the same results, because you usually can't see what you're doing as you do it.

This is especially true in the areas of selecting and changing typefaces and typesizes, working with multiple columns, and adding graphic elements such as rules, boxes, shaded backgrounds and reverses (white type that appears against a black background).

It's important to note that desktop publishing with Aldus PageMaker brings the capabilities described below to a wide range of personal computers. Some of these features were previously available to personal computer users, but only on the Apple Macintosh. With Aldus PageMaker, however, you can do the same things on computers made by Compaq, DEC, IBM, Hewlett-Packard, Wang and other MS-DOS compatibles such as the Leading Edge Model "D." This means that you can take full advantage of desktop publishing's capabilities, even if you don't own an Apple Macintosh. This preserves your investment in your current computer, although you may need to add a color monitor or accelerator board.

Multiple Type Sizes

Most current word processing programs permit you to control the appearance of your document. Yet, most word processing programs offer only a limited ability to choose different typefaces, adjust type size, and select normal, bold-face, and italic type. In many cases, in fact, you do not get an accurate on-screen representation of what the printed page will look like.

On most MS- and PC-DOS computers, for example, you can control character size and style, but *see* only one typeface on the screen.

The term used to describe the visual nature of desktop publishing is WYSIWYG . WYSIWYG is short for "What you see is what you get."

Multiple Columns

Many word processing programs permit you to work with multiple columns. Yet, there is often a catch to this. Often, you can see only one column at a time on the screen of your computer—the column you're working on. Parallel columns are often visible only when you print your document. This seriously limits your ability to design your pages for maximum visual appeal.

In addition, conventional word processors are often very slow when used in multiple-column mode. Add a word in the first column, and you're forced to wait for the changes caused by the new word to "ripple through" the other columns.

Desktop publishing programs, however, excel at multiple column work. You can simultaneously view all columns as they will be printed. Your work goes faster, too, because desktop publishing normally involves placing previously-written copy into the multiple columns of your document.

Rules, Boxes, Reverses and Shades

Some word processors give you limited power to draw lines or to box-in paragraphs. Usually, however, auxiliary programs are needed if you want to apply a shaded background to the boxes. These backgrounds are necessary for creating reversed type (white type against a black background) or to create callouts or sidebars highlighted with a grey background. Finally, with most word-processing programs, it is often difficult to revise these boxes after they have been drawn.

Desktop publishing programs like Aldus PageMaker permit you to add page borders as well as vertical lines between columns, or to separate topics within a column by horizontal lines. You can add rectangles, squares, circles, or ovals of any size, and fill them with black or various shades of grey.

Mixing Text and Graphics

Your ability to communicate effectively often depends on enhancing your presentation with graphics from other programs. Graphics include graphs and charts prepared by spreadsheet programs such as Microsoft Excel and Lotus 1-2-3, illustrations prepared by paint and draw-type graphics programs, and scanned images derived from photographs.

Desktop publishing programs permit you to create a document

assembled from numerous text and graphics files. Equally important, desktop publishing programs usually go beyond word processing programs in their ability to show you what you're doing as you crop, enlarge, or reduce graphics images.

Page Size

Most word processing programs limit you to working with standard letter size or legal size paper. Desktop publishing programs like Aldus PageMaker permit you to work on documents of any size. You can create documents as small as business cards or as large as 17 by 22-inch newspaper pages.

You have total and complete freedom to define the size of your document. It's as easy to create a $5^1/_2$ by $4^1/_4$ inch fold-over brochure as it is to create an 11 by 17-inch tabloid-sized newspaper advertisement or insert.

Refined Appearance

Another way desktop publishing programs move beyond word processing programs is the way they offer typographic details that can greatly improve the appearance of your publication. For example, most word processing programs limit you to the same double and single apostrophes and quotation marks, regardless of whether they're used at the beginning or end of a quotation.

Desktop publishing programs, however, offer separate "opening" and "closing" quotes and apostrophes, which are visible on the screen when they're used. Indeed, some desktop publishing programs automatcially insert correctly-angled "open" and "closing" apostrophes and quotes depending on their location in the sentence. In addition, desktop publishing programs permit you to use true one-em dashes—unbroken horizontal lines—instead of two short dashes.

These small details can go a long way toward earning your reader's attention and respect—even before he begins to read your words.

Who Needs It?

Desktop publishing can profitably be put to use by virtually everyone who has an idea to sell to someone else in print. This includes a broad spectrum of users, including—but not limited to:

- Recent college graduates preparing their first resumes, or upward-bound professionals who want to keep their resumes up to date.

- Consultants and entrepreneurs preparing business plans or financing proposals.

- Self-employed professionals, or service firms, making new business presentations.

- Retailers laying out newspaper advertisements and newspaper inserts.

- Corporate executives trying to convince Senior Management, and stockholders, of their latest marketing plans and departmental reorganizations.

- Businesses of all types that need brochures and newsletters to keep in close contact with their customers.

In each case, desktop publishing can contribute to the individual's success by permitting better-looking print communications to be prepared in less time and at lower cost. With Aldus PageMaker and your present personal computer, the power is always there when you need it . . . even the night before the project is due.

WHAT CAN YOU DO WITH DESKTOP PUBLISHING?

Here are a few of the reasons you might want to become involved with desktop publishing. Although these reasons are separated for clarity, they are closely related.

1. Cutting Costs

Desktop publishing with Aldus PageMaker eliminates the expenses and delays involved in setting type and mechanical pasteup. Traditionally, the following process is used to produce a typset page ready to be delivered to a commercial printer for duplication.

1) Typewritten or word-processed copy is re-entered into a typesetter.

2) Typeset galleys are produced. Galleys are sheets of set type that have to be cut apart and then pasted together by hand as they will appear on the printed page.

3) The type is pasted up by hand, attached to cardboard using hot wax or rubber cement.

Often, revisions have to be made. The copy may be too long or too short. Or human error may have introduced typographical errors. This means the process has to be repeated. New type has to be re-entered into the typesetter and fresh type produced for pasteup.

A one- or two-word change at the beginning of an article often has a ripple effect that changes line endings and paragraph spacing throughout several pages. Add a sentence to Page One, and you might have to re-set and re-paste-up the next twenty pages!

Desktop publishing with Aldus PageMaker saves money by:

a) Eliminating the re-entering of word-processed text.

b) Permitting you to set your own type and prepare your own mechanicals, using your own—or a rented—laser printer or phototypesetter.

Because of the time and money savings, desktop publishing permits you to prepare projects you otherwise couldn't afford to do. Limited-distribution newsletters and brochures which would be not be economically feasible if prepared using traditional typesetting and paste-up methods become practical when you set the type yourself and prepare your own electronic paste ups.

2. Added Control

Desktop publishing gives individuals like yourself control over all aspects of print production. It permits people with patience and a willingness to master PageMaker to acquire skills that would normally take years to master. This means writers can design and produce their own books, and newsletter editors can do their own paste-up without leaving their computer. Entrepreneurs can produce their own advertising when and in the exact way they need it, and executives can fine-tune their own presentations.

Individuals who have an idea of what they want their finished project to look like can create the project by themselves, without the frustrations, costs, and delays involved in hiring others to translate their ideas into reality. Deadline management becomes easier as more work can be done by fewer people.

Communications problems disappear, because the creative individual with the idea can produce the final project himself. Desktop publishing's immediate visual feedback helps you build on your good ideas and to eliminate unsatisfactory solutions as your project takes shape.

10

3. Learning by Doing

Although desktop publishing can be justified on the basis of cost savings and added control, its most exciting aspect is its ability to strengthen individual creative abilities. By eliminating the tedious and time-consuming aspects of mechanical paste-up and production, desktop publishing gives you more time to devote to the creative aspects of print production, including:

- Manipulating typefaces and type size.

- Designing publications and maintaining a proper balance between words and graphic images.

By permitting you to to change typefaces and typesizes on the screen of your computer, desktop publishing lets you see how your finished project will look before the type is set. By printing out your work frequently, you can make sure that what you're seeing on the screen of your computer is what you'll actually get on paper. This permits you to monitor the visual appearance of your publication continuously as you prepare it.

4. Project Direction

Although a desktop publishing program such as Aldus PageMaker is usually used to prepare documents ready for duplication by a commercial printer, many users find it extremely valuable for creating rough working layouts for execution by others. Many retailers, for example, use Aldus PageMaker to prepare layouts for their local newspaper to complete. Many advertising professionals use Aldus PageMaker to prepare rough layouts for client presentations.

Even a quickly created, imperfectly executed layout produced with Aldus PageMaker has more communicating power than a rough sketch prepared with a magic marker and a yellow legal pad!

11

HOW FAR CAN DESKTOP PUBLISHING GO?

Desktop publishing with Aldus PageMaker can be what you want it to be. You can use it to develop ideas for execution by others, or you can create finished projects yourself. Desktop publishing is flexible enough to produce everything from business cards to Annual Reports. Its limitations are based on how much time you want to spend with it.

Printers

Desktop publishing's power derives largely from the new generation of non-impact laser printers pioneered by the Hewlett-Packard Laserjet and Apple LaserWriter. These revolutionary printers have changed forever the way individuals and business communicate on paper.

Until recently, there were two principal types of printers: impact and non-impact.

Non-Impact Printers

Non-impact printers were either thermal or ink-jet. Thermal printers required special heat-sensitive paper, which limited their widespread use for normal office correspondence. Ink-jet printers have never achieved great success due to their complexity and their susceptibility to problems caused by temperature, humidity and their varying performance with different types of paper.

Impact Printers

Impact printers include dot-matrix and daisy-wheel designs. Dot-matrix printers create letters and graphics from patterns of dots made by an array of pins striking paper through a conventional ribbon.

The disadvantages of dot-matrix printers include noise, relatively slow speed, and print quality. Even the best dot-matrix printers have relatively large pins. The best dot-matrix printers create characters out

12

of a grid of approximately five hundred impressions per square inch, compared to 90,000 per square inch for a laser printer. This results in zig-zag diagonal lines and relatively coarse letters that are not as finely formed as many would desire. It often makes dot-matrix printers unsuitable for high-quality office correspondence. Dot-matrix printers can mix text and graphics but they usually take a lot of time to print complicated images. The high-pitched screeching noise they make as they print can make dot-matrix devices an intrusion in an otherwise quiet office environment.

Because of their higher quality type, daisy-wheel printers used to be the preferred choice for quality correspondence. Daisy-wheel printers use rotating mechanical elements that contain a complete alphabet of fully formed characters. The element spins until the correct letter is in place, and a hammer forces the raised character against the ribbon, forming an image on the paper.

The disadvantage of daisywheel printers is that they are usually quite noisy, and—most important—the numbers and letters they can generate are limited to the particular printwheel installed. You have to stop the printer, remove the daisywheel, and install another one every time you want to change the appearance of your document by using a different typeface. Equally limiting, daisywheel printers are unable to print large characters or graphics.

Laser Printers

Laser printers eliminate many of the problems that have long been associated with other types of computer printers.

Laser printers create words and graphic images out of a grid of up to 90,000 dots per square inch (a box consisting of 300 dots per side). The process is similar to that of office copiers. Essentially, a precisely-focused beam of light controlled by your computer determines which of the 90,000 dots in any given inch will be reproduced as black. It doesn't matter whether the result desired is a small "w," a large "Q," a straight line, or part of an illustration; because the laser

13

printing process is largely non-mechanical, any size or shape character or graphic can be created.

Laser printers are fast and quiet. They are coming down in price, as the new Hewlett-Packard LaserJet II proves. The only limitation is the way the printer engines are controlled. As we shall see in Chapter Three, there are two primary types of laser printers. This influences the way characters are created, which, in turn, has a great deal of influence on the capabilities of your desktop publishing system.

When Should You Become Involved in Desktop Publishing?

Hardware and software prices continue to drop while desktop publishing capabilities expand. So, should you wait?

There are two ways to answer this. One way is to analyze the extent of your current publishing efforts. Questions to ask yourself include:

1) How much am I currently paying for outside typesetting?

2) How much am I currently paying for mechanical paste-up?

3) How much am I paying for art direction and design skills which I might be able to develop on my own, or develop in my employees?

These questions barely scratch the surface, however. What's more important are the **lost opportunities** caused by not completing projects that desktop publishing could permit you to produce cost-effectively and on time.

1) How many *extra sales would you make* if you had a better and more consistent advertising program?

2) How much *extra business* would a brochure and newsletter program create for you?

3) How much *extra business* would you enjoy if your firm had a

14

more professional image on paper, for example better-looking fact sheets, price lists, purchase orders, proposals, and business plans?

4) How much would your *income increase* if you could persuade Senior Management to adopt more of your ideas?

Finally, you should consider the hidden costs of delaying your involvement in desktop publishing while others are already becoming involved. By putting off your involvement in desktop publishing, you're allowing others to jump ahead of you, refining their skills and talents.

By becoming familiar with desktop publishing today, a year from now you'll enjoy a tremendous advantage over those who are just coming aboard. As you're refining your skills and approaching the peak of your abilities, latecomers will just be beginning their learning curve. You'll be refining your eye for graphic excellence while others are reading PageMaker's documentation for the first time.

By getting started now, you may possibly pay a few dollars more for your hardware and software than you would later on, but you'll more than make up for this in terms of revenues and savings on projects already completed as well as well as experienced gained.

You'll also enjoy the intangible benefits and satisfactions of being able to say: "I published it myself!"

2

A PageMaker Perspective

What Makes Aldus PageMaker so Special?

Aldus PageMaker is a program designed to be used in conjunction with other programs. It is neither a word processor nor is it a graphics program. It does, however, incorporate important elements of both.

The purpose of PageMaker is to permit you to integrate and modify text and graphic images created by other programs, creating finished artwork ready for printing and distribution.

Even though PageMaker, by itself, is not intended to help you to "create," or originate, words or graphic images, it offers creative power not available in even the most sophisticated word processing and graphics programs. This creative power comes from PageMaker's ability to make the whole greater than the sum of its parts.

A great deal of PageMaker's strength comes from its ability to integrate. This helps it avoid the compromises of programs that try to be all things to all people.

Words

Aldus PageMaker makes it easy for you to transform word-processed copy into typeset copy. Essentially, PageMaker converts your personal computer into a typesetter. With PageMaker, you can . . .

- Place files created with your word processing program.

- Enter, delete, revise and move type, as well as change typeface, type size, type style and alignment (left, centered, ragged right, justified).

- Adjust letter, word, line, and paragraph spacing.

- Create multiple columns on a page.

- Wrap text around charts and graphic images.

Graphics

Aldus PageMaker permits you to add impact to your words with a variety of graphic effects.

- Draw lines or create rectangles, squares, circles, and ovals of various sizes, and fill them with a variety of line patterns or shades of grey.

- Place graphics files created with paint or draw-type graphics programs or scanned images.

- Increase or decrease the size of graphic images without changing their original proportions.

- Crop for emphasis (eliminating unnecessary details adds emphasis to important points).

- Stretch or compress graphic images non-proportionally to fit available space.

PageMaker's graphics tools make it easy to add emphasis to your ideas with lines, boxes, and background shades. You can add borders around pages, lines between columns, lines within columns and use shaded boxes to set off one part of a page from another.

PageMaker's Master Pages option permits you to add graphics images—such as borders or vertical lines between columns—that will automatically be placed on each page.

HOW PAGEMAKER OPERATES

Aldus PageMaker provides an electronic equivalent to expensive graphics tools such as phototypesetters and photostat cameras. Phototypesetters create type on paper using a photographic process. Photostat cameras are used to enlarge or reduce type or graphics images. The output of these devices must be pasted into position manually. The traditional "tools of the trade" include razor knives, wax or rubber cement, T-squares, and large working surfaces.

Aldus PageMaker replaces the traditional drawing board with its electronic equivalent. PageMaker has "magnetic" snap-to guides that eliminate the painstaking mechanical aspects of graphic production. PageMaker permits you to manipulate words and graphics images on the screen of your personal computer. There, you can set type, resize graphic images, and paste up ads, books, brochures, and newsletters. Since the work is done electronically, lines of type are always perfectly parallel to each other and columns are always perfectly aligned.

By simplifying the mechanical aspects of typesetting and mechanical pasteup, PageMaker permits you to devote more time to project planning, writing better copy, and designing better-looking pieces. By developing your own skills, you gain independence, save money, save time, and—in many cases—improve both the quality of the finished project and your ability to produce better projects in the future.

Preview Number One

As an introduction to how PageMaker operates, let's consider a typical "before" and "after" scenario. This example will familiarize you with PageMaker's capabilities and ease of use.

Figure 2-1 shows an advertisement for a typical business. The ad looks alright, except that the headline is too small in proportion to the white space surrounding it. Because of its small size, the headline lacks impact. (It's almost as if the ad were ashamed of its headline.)

The obvious solution is to increase the size of the headline. Without PageMaker, you'd have a choice of doing this in one of two ways:

Figure 2-1

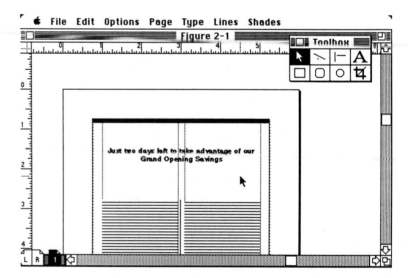

- You could photographically increase the size of the type used in the headline with a stat camera.

- You could reset the type in a larger size.

If you had a darkroom equipped with a photostat camera, typically costing between $5000 and $10,000, here's what you'd have to do:

1) Remove your artwork from your drawing table and take it to the photostat camera.

2) Photographically enlarge the headline

3) Return the artwork to your drawing table.

4) Realign your artwork to the drawing table

5) Peel up the old type.

6) Paste down the enlarged version.

If your calculation was a bit off, and you inadvertently enlarged the headline too much or not enough, you would have to repeat the process until you got it right.

If you had your own typesetter, a piece of equipment costing $10,000 to $25,000, you could reset the type.

Few individuals, however, have access to a photostat camera nd typesetter. As a result, most of us have to depend on others. This is both expensive and time-consuming. Although enlarging the type might require only five to ten minutes of actual work, *in most cases, it would involve delays of at least a day, and possibly more*. If you used an outside typesetting service, for example, here's what you'd have to do:

———

1) Return to the typesetter with new type specifications.

2) Wait for the revised type to be set.

3) Return to pick up the revised type.

4) Paste the new type into place.

If you had miscalculated, and the revised type was too large or too small, you'd have to go through the process all over again, experiencing further delay.

The PageMaker way is much easier. It replaces a twenty-four to forty-eight hour wait and $25 to $50 worth of revision charges to the following six simple steps that take approximately thirty seconds and do not involve additional typesetting charges.

Note: when reading the following, don't worry if you don't fully understand each step. This preview is simply designed to provide you with an introduction to PageMaker's power and ease of use. The steps described below will be discussed in greater detail in later chapters.

1) Using the mouse connected to your computer, simply move the pointer, or arrow, on the screen of your computer (Fig. 2-2) to the large "A" in the PageMaker Toolbox and "click" by pressing the mouse button. (If you are using the PC version of PageMaker, press the left-hand button.) Note that the letter "A" is now highlighted—indicated by a white "A" against a black background.

2) Move the pointer to the headline.

3) Press the button down on the left-hand side of the headline and hold it down as you move the pointer across the headline. This is known as "dragging." Release the button at the right-hand side of the headline.

Note how the words you have selected now appear in reverse (Fig. 2-3), with white letters against a black background.

———

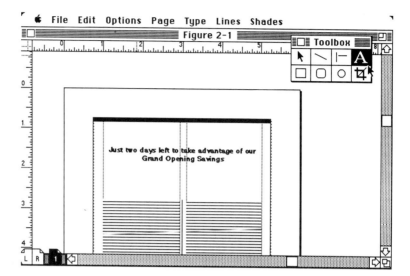

Figure 2-2

Figure 2-3

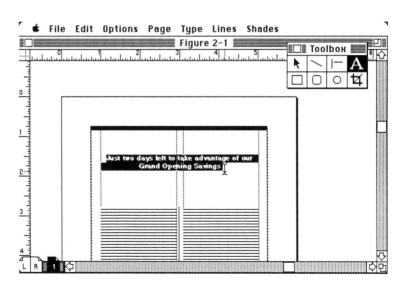

4) Move the pointer to the word "Type" in the PageMaker menu bar running across the top of your screen (Fig. 2-4). Holding the button down, drag the word "Type" down and notice how a variety of choices, or commands, presents itself. Stop at the words "Type Specs" and release the mouse button.

5) You are now presented with a second list of alternatives (Fig. 2-5). This is the Type dialog box. It shows you the current specifications of the type used in the highlighted headline. The dialog box also presents you with additional choices, such as boldface or italic type.

6) Notice how the number "24" is highlighted, (i.e., appears in white type against a black background). Move the pointer to the "Size" box and enter "30." Then move the pointer to the "OK" oval and "click."

Notice how much better the ad looks in Fig. 2-6. There are now *more appropriate relationships* among the size of the headline, the white space surrounding it, and the rest of the ad. The ad is now easier to read. It presents a better image of the company.

Figure 2-4

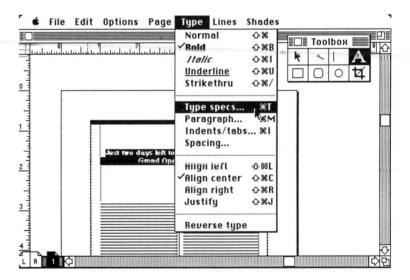

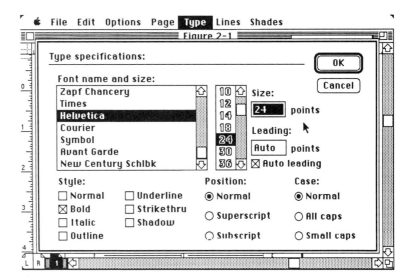

Figure 2-5

Figure 2-6

The Power to Experiment

The example just presented illustrates one of PageMaker's basic strengths: it gives you the power to experiment. Just as computerized spreadsheets such as Lotus 1-2-3 and Microsoft Excel provide you an opportunity to experiment with numbers, and word-processing programs permit you to experiment with words, PageMaker gives you the chance to experiment with the appearance of ads, brochures, newsletters and other print communications. On the screen of your computer, you can try out various ways of organizing words and images.

This power to experiment is central to effective graphic design. Most graphics designers admit that the successful solution to a given design problem is rarely the result of a burst of intuitive genius. Rather, most graphics designers arrive at the final design solution by a disciplined process of trial and error.

Using soft pencils, tissue overlays, and lots of erasers, designers try out various solutions. Each time a solution works, it is refined and used as the basis for another variation. Each time a solution doesn't work, the offending pencil sketch is erased, or a fresh new drawing created by tracing over those elements of a previous drawing showing more promise.

PageMaker speeds up this trial and error process. It permits you to do your trial and error designs on the screen of your computer in a fraction of the time previously required.

In the process of this experimentation, you improve your own capabilities. Your skills get better and better. You discover talents and abilities you never knew you had.

PageMaker is thus a tool for self-improvement. It provides you with a tool that makes it easy to build on your intuitive skills . . . skills that you probably never have had an opportunity to develop.

PageMaker's Background

Aldus PageMaker has its origins in the dedicated page makeup systems developed for large newspapers. Its heritage is in the hundred-thousand-dollar-plus computer systems used to prepare *The New York Times* and other newspapers around the world.

Paul Brainerd, the President of Aldus Corporation, married the basic features offered by dedicated page makeup systems to the capabilities of the Apple Macintosh computer and Apple LaserWriter printer. From there, it was a logical step to make PageMaker's capabilities available as well to users of MS-DOS personal computers, such as the IBM PC/AT and the Hewlett-Packard Vectra.

Indeed, Paul Brainerd is generally credited with coining the term "desktop publishing" to symbolize the fact that sophisticated page layouts can now be prepared on virtually any personal computer.

PageMaker's initial successes occurred in the graphics environment, where the program's capabilities could be plugged into existing production cycles, saving time and money. More and more, however, entrepreneurs and executives with no previous graphics experience began adopting PageMaker for their own use.

PageMaker's Latest Versions

Aldus PageMaker was originally introduced for the Apple Macintosh computer in 1985. The program was almost completely rewritten during 1986 in the process of developing a version for MS-DOS computers. Existing features were retained, but many new ones were added based on requests from PageMaker users.

In early 1987, the MS-DOS version was introduced, followed by Version 2.0 for the Macintosh. Both versions offer the same capabilities and use identical, or near-identical, commands. Indeed, 80 percent of the program code is identical for both machines.

This similarity between versions offers PageMaker users several benefits. First, PageMaker is nearly universal in its operation. Once you learn how to use it on the Apple Macintosh, you can easily move over to a IBM PC/AT, Hewlett-Packard Vectra, or any other MS-DOS computer. The same basic PageMaker commands and functions are even available on computers made by DEC, (Digital Electronics Corporation), and Wang. This means, regardless which machine you use when you begin using PageMaker, you'll immediately feel at home using it on other computers.

Equally important, because PageMaker is not machine dependent PageMaker files can be shared between Apple Macintosh and MS-DOS computers. This will become of increasing importance as local area networks containing both Apple Macintosh and MS-DOS systems become more popular.

PageMaker Version 2.0 for the Macintosh and PageMaker for the PC offer significant enhancements over previous versions. These enhancements include:

- Automatic hyphenation—the ability to split words correctly at line endings.

- A "Select All" command that makes it easy to revise entire pages and reformat stories quickly.

- Kerning to adjust letter spacing for better appearance.

- Facing-pages capability so you can work on two-pages at a time.

- Additional word, line and paragraph spacing options.

- Additional file placement and file exporting options.

- A strengthened Select tool that makes it easy to select more than one text block or graphic element for deletion, movement or revision.

Preview Number Two

As a further preview of PageMaker's ease of use, and as an introduction to several important PageMaker capabilities, see how easy it is to add a word-processed file to a PageMaker document. In this example, you'll become familiar with one of PageMaker's most important commands, its "Place" command.

Let's assume that we are working on a newsletter (Fig. 2-7) and want to add an article contained in a previously-created word-processed file.

1) Move the pointer to the "File" menu on the PageMaker screen and pull it down, revealing the various commands. Stop at "Place" and release the button.

2) You are now presented with a list of files (Fig. 2-8) that can be placed in your PageMaker document. The first available choice is highlighted, i.e., white type appears against a black background. By using the "up" and "down" vertical arrows to the right of the choices, you can scroll through the choices. (The "Place" dialog box permits you to scroll the files available on the hard or floppy

Figure 2-7

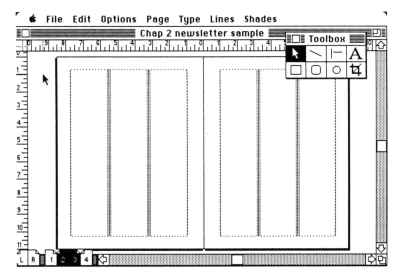

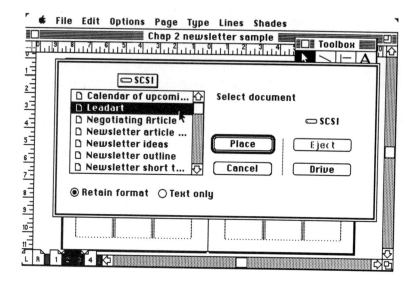

Figure 2-8

disks in your computer, or even in other computers connected through a local area network.)

3) When the name of the file you want to place is highlighted—in this case, "LEADART"—point to the "Place" oval and "click."

4) Move the pointer, which now resembles the upper left-hand corner of a printed page (Fig. 2-9), to the junction of the dotted horizontal line and the left-hand margin of the left-hand newsletter page. Click the mouse button.

See how the type "flows" down the page and stops (Fig. 2-10) when it reaches the grey rectangle that represents where a picture is going to be inserted. Note the small "+" sign at the bottom of the column.

5) Move the pointer to the "+" sign and click on it.

6) Move the pointer, which—once again—resembles the upper left hand corner of a printed page, to the dotted horizontal line at the top of the second column. Again, "click" the mouse button. Once again, observe how the type "flows" into the column, and automatically stops at the bottom of the column.

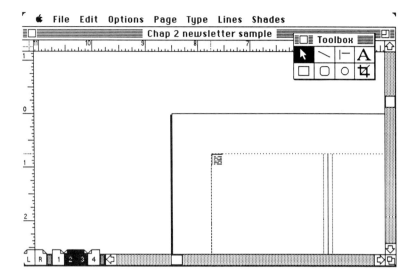

Figure 2-9

Figure 2-10

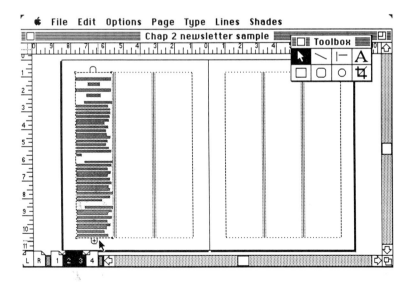

7) Repeat Steps 5 and 6 to complete the third, fourth and fifth columns.

Notice how the fifth column is shorter than the others, and that the plus sign at the bottom of the column has been replaced by a small pound—or number—sign (#). This informs you that all the text in the file has been placed (Fig. 2-11).

8) Move the pointer to the "Page" menu, and holding down the mouse button, drag the pointer down to the "Actual Size" command and release the button.

At this larger page size, you can now read the actual type that has been placed in your PageMaker document (Fig. 2-12). In the previous views, words and sentences were indicated by small "x"s. Now, however, the actual letters are visible.

This actual size view of your PageMaker screen with placed type illustrates several important PageMaker capabilities and several of the reasons PageMaker makes it easy to produce good-looking publications.

Figure 2-11

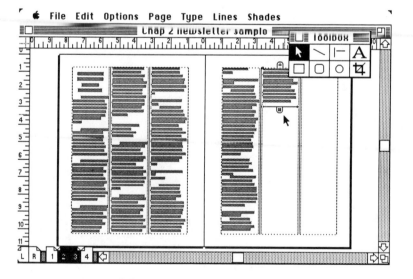

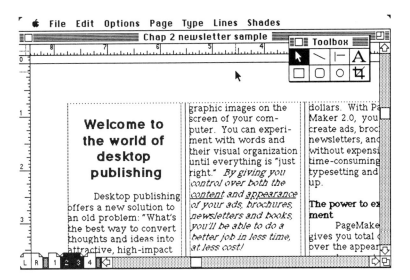

Figure 2-12

Snap-To Guides

Notice how the left-hand margins of the text you have placed in each column are accurately aligned with the column guides. Even if you didn't line up the type accurately, each line begins at the right spot. Similarly, the top and bottom lines are accurately aligned.

PageMaker's snap-to guides "magnetically" pull the type to the left-hand column guides and align the type vertically with the dotted guide lines.

The snap-to guides may be switched off when you want to align type close to, but not at, the horizontal and vertical guides. You can also turn the snap-to Guides off when you are adding vertical rules between columns.

Hyphenation

Each column is now filled with type. This is because hyphens have automatically been added at the ends of words too long to fit on a single line. This feature eliminates the unnaturally large spaces that would otherwise occur between words or at the ends of lines, as illustrated in Fig. 2-13.

PageMaker has a built-in 80,000 word hyphenation dictionary. When placing type, PageMaker automatically compares the last words in each line to the words in this dictionary, and breaks them accordingly. You have a lot of control over this operation. You can turn hyphenation off, or adjust the width of the hyphenation zone--the space in which hyphenation is permitted to take place.

Compare the hyphenated paragraph in Fig. 2-14 with the unhyphenated one. Hyphenation not only eliminates large spaces, or "rivers" of white space that can "drain" through a column, but it also permits you to increase the number of words on each page.

Master Pages

Notice how several items were already on the page when you began working on it. These included thin solid lines, or rules, between columns, the various lines and boxes defining the top and bottom margins of the page, and page numbers and words (such as publication or

Figure 2-13

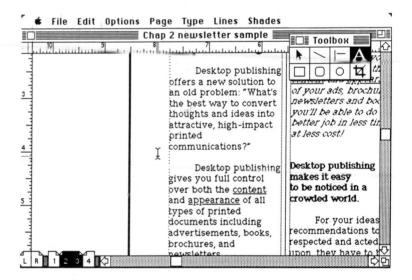

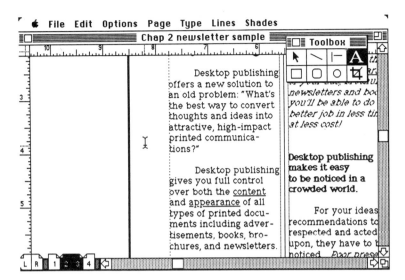

Figure 2-14

chapter titles) that were to appear on each page. There were also dotted lines indicating the width of each column as well as the starting point on the page where type began. (This is to ensure that there will be a consist amount of "air" between the top of the page and the start of each column.)

PageMaker helps you maintain page-to-page and publication-to-publication consistency by permitting you to establish *master pages*. These master pages contain column guides, and non-printing vertical and horizontal alignment guides that are automatically repeated on every page. PageMaker's master pages can also include page numbers and text such as the publication title, author's name, and chapter or subdivision information that is to print on every page.

PageMaker lets you establish separate left and right hand master pages. This allows you to include the extra inside-margin space necessary when binding pages together. It also permits you to locate page numbers at the outside of the page on both left and right hand pages, and to have different running heads appear on even- and odd-numbered ones.

Facing Pages

With PageMaker, both the left and right hand pages of your publication can be visible at one time. This is important, because in most cases, readers will be viewing both left and right hand pages together. Unless you can see both at the same time on the screen of your computer, it's possible to create pages that look all right when viewed one-at-a-time by themselves, but look positively horrible when seen side by side.

EASE OF USE

In the two examples above, you did not really need to "know" Page-Maker to use it. That's because PageMaker's commands are logically grouped in the menu bar. Commands dealing with "files," for example, are all grouped around the "File" choice on the menu bar. Commands dealing with type become visible by opening the "Type" menu bar. And commands for various page views are grouped under the "Page" menu bar.

PageMaker's pull-down menus speed up your learning curve. You don't have to memorize every command, because PageMaker's pull-down menus help you locate the command you want quickly.

On-Line Help

One of the reasons it's easy to get started using PageMaker is its unique on-line Help system. PageMaker's help system has a tree-like structure. Individual topics branch out, and are covered in greater and greater detail as you determine which you are interested in, and delve more deeply into them.

In each case, help and assistance are offered in a conversational manner. *All you have to do is know the end result you want, and PageMaker's help system will guide you to the information you need to accomplish it.* What follows is an example of how the Guidance system found in Version 2.2 for the Macintosh operates. The Help system found in PageMaker for the PC works in much the same way.

To start, return to the newsletter example and enter the help system by pulling down the Guidance command from the Apple icon at the upper left of the screen (Fig. 2-15).

You are offered three choices. Choose the third, "Getting help on specific tasks" (Fig. 2-16).

You are presented with a list of the specific tasks you might wish to execute (Fig. 2-17). Select "Creating special effects" by moving the pointer next to that line and clicking.

You are next prompted (Fig. 2-18) to be more specific n defining which task you want to learn more about. Choose "Making headlines span several columns: by clicking on the word "Here."

Immediately, you are presented with a simple, straightforward explanation of how to make a headline span several columns (Fig. 2-19).

As this illustrates, PageMaker, without interrupting your work or forcing you to refer to printed documentation, can guide you to the information you need when you need it.

Figure 2-15

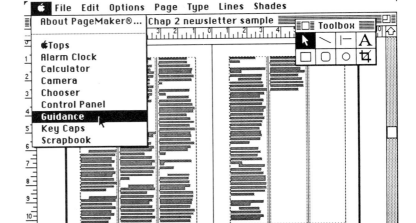

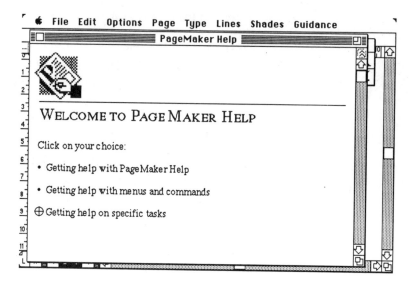

Figure 2-16

Figure 2-17

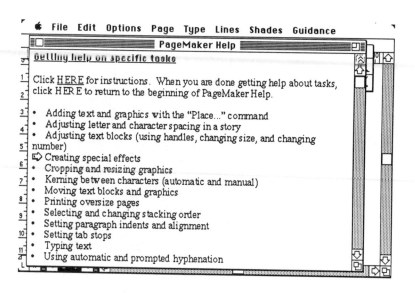

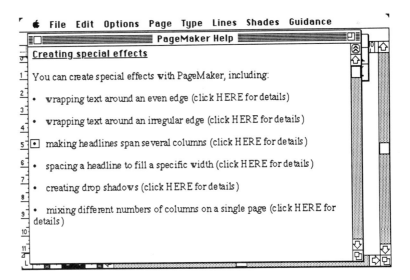

Figure 2-18

Keyboard Shortcuts

Many commands are followed by symbols and letters in the menus. These show you how to access the commands without having to remove your hands from the keyboard and use the mouse. The keyboard commands will speed up your use of PageMaker as you become more familiar with it.

For example, to move down the "Page" menu to the "Actual Size" page view, you could use one of the following keyboard shortcuts, depending on whether you were using the PC or Macintosh version of PageMaker:

■ If were using the PC version of PageMaker, Control-1 would move you to the Actual Size view.

■ If you were using the Apple Macintosh version, Command-1 would get you an Actual Size view.

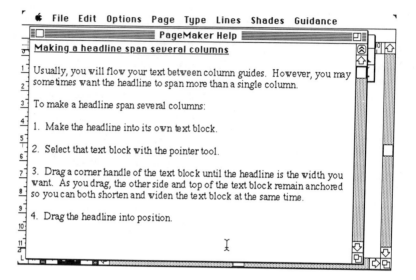

Figure 2-19

The following keyboard shortcuts help you reach the Type Specifications dialog box:

- Control-T (PC version)

- Command-T (Macintosh version)

The Place command can be accessed by:

- Control-D (PC version)

- Command-D (Macintosh version)

There is a logic to these keyboard shortcuts that makes them easy to memorize. "S" is short for "Save," "T" for "Type Specifications," "1" for "100 per cent" or Actual Size, and so forth.

You will soon appreciate PageMaker's dual mode of accessing important commands and, as you become more experienced with these commands, you'll find yourself using keyboard commands in place of the mouse and menu bar. You'll probably make this transition sooner than you expect.

Freedom from Typographical Errors

Typographical errors often creep in just when they're least appreciated—often at deadline time as last-minute revisions are being set. Because PageMaker sets type from word-processed files there is less chance for spelling errors to find their way into your publications.

Most of today's word processing programs include built-in spell-checkers, which eliminate most errors—although they cannot catch misused words such as "there" instead of "their," "it's" rather than "its," and so on. You still have to proofread your documents before printing. However, spell-checkers reduce the chances of typos creeping in and delaying your publications.

Easy Error Correction

PageMaker makes it easy to back out of any changes you make. It has an Undo feature that reverses the last action you took.

If you delete a word, for example, you can replace it using the Undo command (Fig. 2-20).

If you change the size of an illustration, for example, you can return it to its original size.

If you move a line, you can return it to its original position.

If you accidentally move a column guide, you can restore it to its intended place.

PageMaker's Undo command encourages experimentation. It allows

---

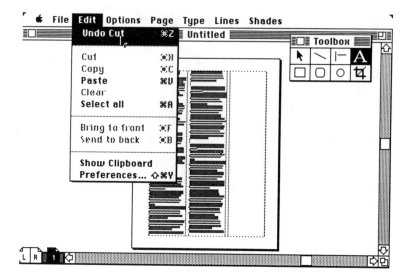

Figure 2-20

you to try out various design possibilities without the pressure of feeling that each choice has to be the right one.

The Apple Macintosh and MS-DOS versions of PageMaker also have a Revert command. This returns you to the last saved version of your document. Use it as follows:

- Save your document each time you're satisfied with the progress you've made.

- Continue to work.

- If you don't like the way your work is turning out, pull down the File menu and release the mouse button on the Revert command. Instantly, all of your recent changes will be replaced by the version of your publication you last saved.

- Continue working from that point.

Experimentation is also encouraged by the "Save As" command offered in both the Apple Macintosh and MS-DOS versions of Page-Maker. You can save more than one version of a publication allowing you, for example, to try out both two- and three-column versions of a newsletter

This would be prohibitively expensive if traditional typesetting and pasteup methods were used, but alternative layouts can be investigated economically on the screen of your computer. Your only investment is time.

PRINTING PAGEMAKER DOCUMENTS

Once you have finished preparing your PageMaker publication— whether it's an advertisement, brochure, book, newsletter or price list—you can print it out in any of three different ways. One of PageMaker's greatest virtues is that it is *output device independent*. PageMaker files can be printed, without change, at the quality level most appropriate for your publication.

a) PageMaker documents can be printed on dot-matrix printers such as the Apple ImageWriter II, IBM ProPrinter or Epson FX-80. These printers are useful for "draft"—or evaluation-quality— printing.

b) PageMaker documents can also be printed on laser printers such as the Apple LaserWriter or LaserWriter Plus, QMS PS-800 or PS-800 Plus, or other laser printers using Adobe's PostScript page description language.

PageMaker documents prepared on MS-DOS computers can also be printed on the Hewlett-Packard LaserJet Plus, LaserJet 500 Plus, or the new LaserJet Series II printers.

In most cases, laser printed output will be good enough to be used as masters for newspaper advertisements, brochures and newsletters.

c) PageMaker files can be printed on commercial phototypesetters such as the Allied Linotronic 100 and 300, which "understand" PostScript. These phototypesetters offer reproduction of the high-

est possible quality. They print PageMaker documents at a resolution of 1,200 or 2,540 dots per inch—true Annual Report quality.
The difference in print quality is illustrated in closeup in Fig. 2-
21.

PageMaker's ability to output documents on a variety of printers and
phototypesetters means that you do not need to purchase expensive
printers to produce professional-quality documents. You can use your
existing dot-matrix printer for "draft" printing, and rent time on a
laser printer or phototypesetter as needed for printing final documents.

As you become familiar with the quality, speed, and noise-free operation of laser printers, however, you're likely to want one for yourself.

Working with PageMaker

To become an experienced PageMaker user, you must follow the
following sequence of steps:

1) Start by choosing the right hardware and software.

Figure 2-21

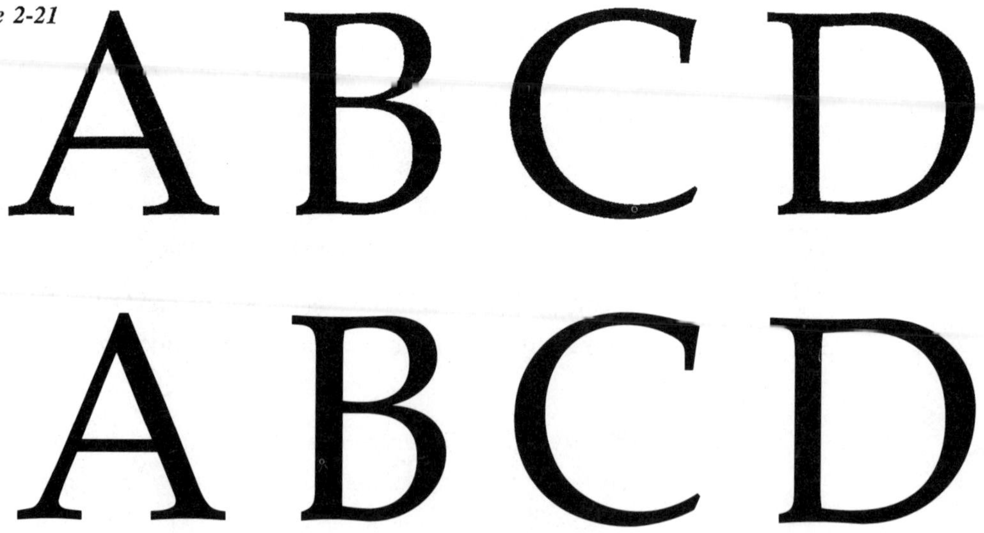

ABCD

ABCD

2) Next, become familiar with the basic PageMaker tools, and know when and how to use PageMaker's specialized commands.

3) Then, refine your writing abilities and sensitize yourself to the basic elements of graphic design.

4) Finally, learn to relate PageMaker's capabilities and your developing skills to the specific project you want to complete. You must give yourself enough time to do the job properly. You must also recognize your own limitations and understand how much work you can do yourself and how much you should delegate to others. And you should be willing to seek outside assistance when necessary.

If you are interested in using PageMaker to its fullest, you must make a conscious commitment to continuing self-improvement. After you have finished the publication you should try to find ways it could have been improved. You must be open to new ideas and willing to learn from others.

Your PageMaker skills, and those of the people with whom you work, will improve to the extent that you have a strong desire to constantly refine your talents and abilities—and theirs—so each project becomes better than the one that preceded it.

PageMaker brings tremendous page composition power to your personal computer. To utilize that power properly, however, you must supply desire and motivation.

3

Hardware and Software Considerations

What You Need to Get Started

Choosing the right hardware and software to make the most of PageMaker's power involves answering the following three questions:

1) Which computer should I choose?

2) Which software—primarily word-processing—should I choose?

3) Do I need a laser printer, and, if so, which one?

CHOOSING THE RIGHT COMPUTER

To a great extent, your choice of the Apple Macintosh or PC version of Aldus PageMaker will be deter-

---

47

mined by the type of computer you already own, or is already in use in your office.

If you already own an IBM personal computer, or one of the many MS-DOS compatibles such as those made by Compaq or Leading Edge, you'll want to choose the PC version of PageMaker.

Similarly, if you already own an Apple Macintosh computer, or there are already several Macintosh computers in your organization, you'll want the Macintosh version.

Yet, the fact that you may use a computer from one family, and whoever prepares the copy you want to set with PageMaker may use one from the other, need not mean that you be isolated in two mutually exclusive universes. The IBM and Macintosh worlds are coming closer and closer together. New methods of linking MS-DOS computers with Apple Macintosh computers have recently appeared. Programs the likes of DataViz's MacLink and local area networks such as Tangent Technologies' PC MacBridge, the Centram TOPS system and Apple's new AppleShare network make it possible for Apple Macintosh and IBM personal computers to share files, as well as peripherals such as the Apple LaserWriter printer.

Concerning the coming together of the Apple Macintosh and IBM "Big Blue" worlds, it is important to note that the Apple Macintosh 2.0 and PC versions of Aldus PageMaker use the same file structure. This means that PageMaker documents can be easily exchanged between Apple Macintosh computers and MS-DOS systems.

It is also important to emphasize that the PC and Apple Macintosh versions of PageMaker offer the same functionality. Both use the same menu-driven commands and equivalent keyboard shortcuts. With one exception—the Macintosh 2.0's file exporting function—the Macintosh and PC versions of PageMaker offer the same capabilities. All important features found on Version 2.0 (and higher) of the Apple Macintosh version of PageMaker are available in Version 1.0 (and higher) of the PC version.

Another reason for the similarity between the Macintosh and PC versions of PageMaker is that the PC version uses the Microsoft Windows program. Microsoft Windows provides an operating environment very similar to that of the Apple Macintosh. Like the Macintosh, a PC running Microsoft Windows uses a mouse and includes a "Clipboard" which makes it easy to exchange data between programs.

Like the "Quick Switch" feature found on the Apple Macintosh, Microsoft Windows permits you to switch instantly between MS-DOS programs designed to operate within it. At present, this includes several graphics programs as well as the Windows Write word processing program.

This ability to share information easily, and to switch instantly between programs can speed up your desktop publishing activities greatly. You can, for example, create a logo with a graphics program, write copy with a word processing program, and instantly place both these files into the same PageMaker document.

PC CONSIDERATIONS

One of the reasons that owners of IBM PCs and compatibles should not unquestioningly choose the PC version of PageMaker is that the PC version requires several hardware enhancements not found on every MS-DOS computer. There are reasons why it might be desirable to purchase a new system to get the most out of PageMaker.

To take full advantage of PageMaker performance, your MS-DOS computer requires the AT's Intel 80286 chip, a high-speed hard disk, an EGA graphics adapter card, a high-resolution color monitor and a mouse. It is possible to run Pagemaker on a system lacking most of these enhancements, but its performance—particularly its speed—will suffer.

The Intel '286 chip is needed to provide the processing speed necessary to execute PageMaker's sophisticated programming instructions. It takes a lot of computer power to resize type, draw lines, and

49

perform the many other sophisticated PageMaker commands. A hard disk is a prerequisite to efficient performance. Floppies provide neither speed nor the capacity PageMaker requires.

The EGA graphics card and high-resolution monitor are needed for the accurate display of type of various sizes, as well as of the placement of fine lines and graphics images. High-resolution monitors are also needed when reduced-size facing pages are displayed on the screen.

Color monitors offer an additional benefit. The colors visually separate the PageMaker document you are working on from other screen information, such as the PageMaker Toolbox, menu bar and scroll bars. Background information and status indications are easily distinguished from the document in the foreground. This visual differentiation is especially valuable during long PageMaker sessions. (Indeed, when boredom sets in during long desktop publishing sessions, you may want to reset the background colors to get a "fresh" look.)

Microsoft Mach 10 Board

As an intermediate step that can help you avoid replacing your present PC, Microsoft has introduced Mach 10 board. It speeds up the performance of IBM PC/XTs, Compaq DeskPros and other compatibles such as the Leading Edge Model "D." Running Aldus PageMaker, the Microsoft Mach 10 board offers a fifty percent speed improvement over the original PC's 8088 chip.

The Microsoft Mach 10 board also includes a port for the Microsoft Mouse. The board thus provides an upgrade path for PC owners who do not want to replace their computer with a PC/AT. An EGA color graphics card and high resolution color monitor are still desirable, of course.

In a similar way, many PC/AT owners are looking seriously at Intel's '386 board, which upgrades their '286 to faster speeds.

Second PC or Macintosh?

Although upgrading a PC to AT performance might make sense in some cases, it might make more sense to purchase a second personal computer, quite possibly an Apple Macintosh. In the process, you'd not only gain access to the Apple Macintosh's faster processing speed, based on its Motorola 68000 processor, but in the process you'd gain a second computer workstation.

This would greatly multiply the utility of both computers. You could continue to use your original PC for routine office tasks (bookkeeping, word processing, file maintenance) and use your new PC/AT or Apple Macintosh exclusively for desktop publishing. (This could help prevent delaying the preparation of payroll checks at newsletter time, and vice versa.)

Multiple computers become more and more practical as hardware costs continue to decline. Hardware costs are being driven down by increasing economies of production and increased competition at the retail level.

Use the "PC or Macintosh?" worksheet below to help you decide the PC or Apple Macintosh versions of PageMaker.

WORKSHEET
PC or Macintosh?

1) What type of computer, or computers, are already in use in your firm?

Quantity	Manufacturer	Model
_____	_____	
_____	_____	
_____	_____	

2) Is at least one of these computers an 80286 model equipped with an EGA card, high-resolution monitor, and mouse? _____

---

3) How fully do you, or your firm, utilize your present computer equipment? How many hours a week are available for new applications, (i.e. desktop publishing), on your existing computers? _____

4) Who will be in charge of desktop publishing? _____

5) Where are his offices located? _____
(It doesn't make sense for members of the Corporate Communications Department to have to visit the Accounting Department at newsletter time.)

6) Are others likely to create word processing files used in desktop publishing applications? _____

7) What type of computer will be used to create these files? _____

8) Approximately how many projects a month will be created with Aldus PageMaker? _____

9) How many hours will be required to produce these projects each month? _____

10) How difficult will it be for you, or your employees, to get up to speed using a new operating system? _____

Needless to say, before you make a final choice, you should find a computer retailer willing to let you spend time comparing the PC and the Macintosh versions of PageMaker. If possible, try to locate a retailer who has similarly-priced Macintosh and PC computers set up. That way, you can get a better idea of what your money buys in both operating environments.

You should also be guided by the computers your business associates and friends use. The availability of help and advice from others already familiar with either the PC or Macintosh world can greatly speed up your PageMaker learning curve.

MACINTOSH CONSIDERATIONS

Many individuals purchasing their first Apple Macintosh make the mistake of underbuying hardware. This often leads to initial frustration and reduced productivity. It also leads to expensive add-on purchases later.

This tendency to be "penny-wise/pound-foolish" is compounded by the tendency of many computer retailers to advertise and sell "solutions" that are—at best—only partial solutions.

Some retailers, for example, advertise "complete Macintosh desktop publishing systems" with an Apple Macintosh Plus computer, Apple LaserWriter printer and PageMaker software at what appears to be a very attractive price. But, only after you enter the store are you told that a hard disk is a virtual necessity.

A hard disk greatly enhances desktop publishing productivity on the Apple Macintosh. Programs load faster and you have immediate access to numerous software programs and data files. You can open various folders easily, looking for the specific word-processed or graphics file you want to place and—with the Apple Switcher—can easily switch between PageMaker and your favorite word processor. You can create a file and immediately place it in your PageMaker document without having to swap diskettes.

Note that the problem of aftermarket hard disks is peculiar to Apple Macintosh computers. Virtually all MS-DOS AT computer systems include a built-in high-speed hard disk.

Hard Disk Alternatives

When adding a hard disk to your Apple Macintosh, you have several alternatives available to you. You can choose either an internal or an external drive and, if you own a Macintosh Plus, you can choose a SCSI or non-SCSI one. SCSI stands for Small Computer Standard Interface, which permits faster information transfer between the computer's memory and the hard disk drive.

Internal hard disks offer several advantages. They make the most sense if you move your Macintosh frequently. If you're likely to begin a project at the office, but complete it at home, you'll enjoy the convenience of a built-in hard disk that doesn't have to be carried separately from the computer. Similarly, if several people will be sharing your Macintosh, the convenience of a built-in hard disk drive will be appreciated. It will always be available when needed.

If your Macintosh is likely to remain in one spot, however, you might want to choose an external drive. Those for the Macintosh are usually designed for placement under it, although some are intended to be placed next to it vertically.

External hard disk drives offer a bit more flexibility than internal ones. If an external hard disk should malfunction, you can still use your Macintosh while it is being repaired. But, if an internal drive develops problems, the entire computer has to go into the shop and you'll be without it for perhaps quite a while.

Another factor to take into consideration is that internal hard disk drives are manufactured by third-party vendors such as General Computer, while external ones are made by several companies, including Apple Computer. Many people will feel more comfortable with an all-Apple system.

If you own a Apple Macintosh Plus, you can choose between a conventional or a SCSI interface for your hard disk drive. Those that plug into the SCSI port of the Macintosh Plus cost a bit more, but operate faster.

WHICH MACINTOSH?

Aldus PageMaker 2.0 operates on the Apple Macintosh 512 Enhanced, the Macintosh Plus, the Macintosh SE, and the new Macintosh II. The basic 512 Enhanced includes a single 800K internal floppy disk drive. An Apple Macintosh 512 Enhanced with an external disk drive is the minimum configuration capable of doing justice to Aldus PageMaker.

Macintosh Plus

The Apple Macintosh Plus is a better choice than the 512 Enhanced version for desktop publishing and advanced word processing applications. It comes with a larger internal memory (for faster operation), an improved keyboard and the SCSI port mentioned above.

The Macintosh Plus keyboard shown in Fig. 3-1 has a separate numeric keypad and up-down/left-right cursor movement keys. You will appreciate the numeric keypad if you are going to be working with accounting programs or spreadsheets such as Microsoft Excel when you're not involved in desktop publishing.

Equally important, the numeric keypad on the Macintosh Plus keyboard has significant advantages when used for desktop publishing and word processing applications. The "4" and "6" keys on the

Figure 3-1

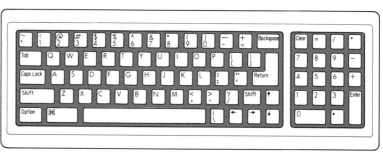

Macintosh Plus keypad quickly move the cursor through Microsoft Word documents forward and back one word at a time. The "8" and "2" keys advance the cursor up and down the document a line at a time.(Illustration—screen showing word-by-word highlighting)

Additionally, the numeric keypad can greatly speed up deleting and editing text. Simply hit the "4" or "6" key using your right hand while you hold down the "Shift" and "Command" keys using your left. This permits you to highlight words (Fig. 3-2) in front of, or behind, the cursor. Highlighted words can be quickly deleted (using the backspace key) or replaced (simply by typing in new ones).

In a similar way, the numeric keypad, used in conjunction with the Command and Option keys, expedites cursor movement through text placed in PageMaker documents.

Macintosh SE

The Macintosh SE was introduced in early 1987. It's faster than the Macintosh Plus and includes a keyboard similar in "feel" to the keyboards usually associated with MS-DOS computers. The Macin-

Figure 3-2

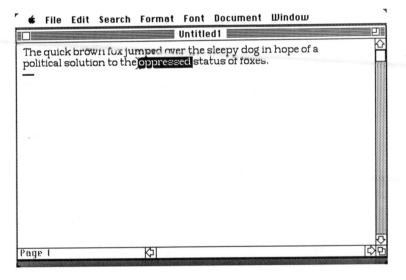

tosh SE is available with an extremely fast, very quiet internal 20 megabyte hard disk drive.

The operating speed of the Macintosh SE is approximately twenty per cent faster than that of the Macintosh Plus. In addition, the SE can transfer information to and from SCSI hard disks up to twice as quickly as the Macintosh Plus. These speed gains translate into appreciably faster PageMaker operation . . . an advantage which many desktop publishers will find it worthwhile to pay for.

The Macintosh SE has two other important features. One is that it comes with a more comfortable mouse than the others in the Macintosh family. This mouse can be plugged into either the back of the SE, or into the left or right side of the SE keyboard. This helps avoid the usual tangle of wires.

More significant, the Macintosh SE has space for a plug-in expansion board. A variety of plug-in boards have already been announced. These include boards that allow you to run MS-DOS software right on the Macintosh screen, boards for big-screen monitors, and boards that permit connection to mainframe computers.

The Macintosh SE includes the Apple Desktop Bus. This is an interface that permits connection of a graphics tablet in addition to the mouse.

The Macintosh SE is Apple's first step toward allowing users to custom-design the Macintosh which best suits their needs.

Because of its fast operation and its expansion capability, the Apple Macintosh SE represents an ideal choice for firms becoming seriously involved in desktop publishing.

Macintosh II

The Macintosh II is the fastest, most powerful Macintosh available. It includes six expansion slots, which permit you to use precisely the monitor and communications options you desire. It runs most existing

Macintosh applications up to four times faster than the Macintosh Plus. The Macintosh II does not have a built-in monitor, which makes it possible for you to choose the monochrome or color monitor best suited to your needs.

The Macintosh II will probably find its greatest acceptance in scientific and corporate environments, as well in as the most sophisticated desktop publishing applications.

CHOOSING THE RIGHT WORD PROCESSOR

Your choice of a word processor depends in part on your current involvement with personal computing. If you are already comfortable with a major word processing program, you should probably stick with what you have. But, if you're new to personal computing, you should choose the word processing program which offers the best combination of features you like combined with the best degree of PageMaker compatibility.

PageMaker for the PC, and the Apple Macintosh version of Page-Maker, work with the majority of quality word processing programs available in the Macintosh and MS-DOS environment. The extent of compatibility with PageMaker differs from program to program, however. Some word processing programs offer smoother integration with it than others.

Only word processing software is discussed in this section because word processing programs are, for most people, one of the primary reasons for purchasing a computer. Graphics programs will be covered later, as they are generally chosen to perform specific functions.

MS-DOS Word Processing Alternatives

There is a wide choice of "world-class" word processing programs available for use in the MS-DOS environment. Aldus PageMaker integrates smoothly with the "Big Ten" word processors. These include: Microsoft Word 3.1, Windows Write, XyWrite III, Multi-

Mate Advantage, WordPerfect 4.2, WordStar, DisplayWrite, Samna Word III, Volkswriter 3, and WordStar 2000.

Each program has its own personality, however, which influences how easy each is to learn and use. In addition, the programs differ primarily in the amount of formatting information retained when word-processed files are placed in PageMaker documents. All the formatting information from some programs is preserved when text created with them is placed in PageMaker documents. Other programs require text to be reformatted to a greater or lesser degree after it has been placed in a PageMaker document.

If you already using one of the above-mentioned word processors, there is little reason to change, as the learning curve involved is likely to slow down your mastery of PageMaker. If, however, you are going to be choosing your first word processing program, the following considerations are important.

Microsoft Word 3.1

There are several reasons why Microsoft Word is the preferred choice for use with PageMaker for the PC. One is that Microsoft Word 3.1—like PageMaker for the PC—is designed for use with a two-button mouse. Word's mouse interface makes it extremely easy to choose commands and select type for editing, movement, or deletion. Once you get used to being able to move quickly throughout a document with a mouse in PageMaker, you'll appreciate the same ability to go quickly to a desired character, letter, or word, or select a character, word, sentence, or paragraph, and either delete it or move it to another location.

Word also permits you to prepare fully formatted text that can be placed, without change, in PageMaker publications. Formatting information is preserved intact when Word 3.1 files are placed in PageMaker documents. This saves a great deal of time, as you can use Word to format your documents as you write them. Note, however, that Word's style sheets, which allow you to define formats with a couple of keystrokes, cannot be used by PageMaker. Word makes it easy to define:

- Typeface, i.e., Times Roman, Helvetica, etc.
- Type size from 4 points to 127 points.
- Type style, i.e., boldface, italic, boldface italics.
- Line and paragraph spacing.
- Alignment, i.e., left, centered, right.
- Justified or ragged-right.
- Tabs and indents.

You must enter information directly from the keyboard. Future versions of MS-DOS PageMaker, though, are expected to be able to accept style-sheet formatting.

Windows Write

Like Microsoft Word, Windows Write (Version 1.0) is mouse-based. And, like Word, Windows Write lets you place fully formatted paragraphs into PageMaker publications, retaining important formatting options such as typeface, type size, type style (bold, italics, underline), line length, and paragraph spacing and alignment.

Unlike Microsoft Word—and the other heavyweight word processors that PageMaker works with—Windows Write lacks a built-in spell-checker and thesaurus. Its line-spacing alternatives are limited, and it does not include indexing or outlining capability.

The primary advantage of Windows Write is that—at the present time—it is the only word processor that operates wholly within the Windows environment. This means you can easily switch back and forth between PageMaker and Windows Write. You'll appreciate this feature if you decide you have to write a three or four paragraph sidebar, or an extended caption, while working with PageMaker.

You'll likely find it easier and faster to write the extended copy with Windows Write than either:

- Writing the added text with PageMaker, or

- Leaving PageMaker, loading your favorite word processor, writing your feature, saving the file, reloading PageMaker, and placing the file.

Copy written using Windows Write can be imported quickly into PageMaker by using the Windows Clipboard—which permits fast and easy transfer of information between programs using "cut" and "paste" commands.

However, on some computers with insufficient memory, loading Windows Write may slow down PageMaker's operation.

WordPerfect 4.2

During the past few years, WordPerfect has emerged as one of the most popular word processing programs for MS-DOS computers. Unlike Microsoft Word, WordPerfect does not use a mouse interface. Rather, WordPerfect makes extensive use of the ten function keys found on the MS-DOS keyboard. Each key performs four functions, depending on whether it is: pressed by itself, or pressed in conjunction with either the Control, Shift , or Alt key. In each case, the user is presented with a menu of command choices that can be accessed by number.

WordPerfect files retain boldface, italics, and normal type when placed in PageMaker documents. However, typeface and type size information is lost, requiring refomating after entry.

Left, centered, and right alignments carry over from WordPerfect to PageMaker. However, each line of a centered headline is treated as an individual paragraph. This can cause strange type spacing.

XyWrite III

Like WordPerfect—and most of the word processing programs that follow—XyWrite III files placed in PageMaker revert to PageMaker's default typeface and type size. This means you must reformat text after you place it. Bold-face, italics, and underlined commands carry over, as do alignment (left, right, centered and justified) and indents.

MultiMate

PageMaker recognizes MultiMate font size, indents and tabs, line-spacing and most font styles. However, you have to choose the typeface and type size you desire.

WordStar

WordStar is a longtime survivor of the word processing wars. WordStar files retain limited formatting, and require extensive reformatting after placement in PageMaker files. Boldface type is one of the few formatting choices that remains unchanged.

DisplayWrite, Samna Word III, Volkswriter III, and WordStar 2000

Few formatting options are preserved when files prepared with these programs are placed in PageMaker documents. To place these files in PageMaker documents, you must go through a three step process.

- First, you must convert your text to standardized, or DCA—Document Content Architecture—files.

- You must then place the files in your PageMaker publication

- Finally, you must reformat the files, choosing the typeface, type size, and—in most cases—type style you want. You must also adjust line spacing, indents, and tabs for appropriate appeal.

Summary of Word-Processor Characteristics

	Type Face	Type Size	Type Style	Line Spacing	Alignment	Justified	Tabs and Indents
Microsoft Word	Y	Y	Y	Y	Y	Y	Y
Windows Write	Y	Y	Y	L	Y	Y	L
WordPerfect 4.2	Y	Y	Y	Y	Y	Y	Y
XyWrite 3.1	Y	Y	Y	Y	Y	Y	Y
Multimate 3.31	N	N	Y	Y	L	Y	Y
Wordstar 4.0	N	N	Y	Y	L	Y	Y
Wordstar 2000	N	N	Y	Y	L	Y	Y
Samna Word III	N	N	Y	Y	L	Y	Y
DisplayWrite III	N	N	Y	Y	L	Y	Y
VolksWriter Deluxe	L	N	Y	Y	L	Y	Y

Y = Yes   N = No   L = Limited

As the preceding chart indicates, if you are not currently committed to a word processing software program, you will probably find it useful to choose Microsoft Word 3.1 because—of all the popular programs—more Word formatting information is transferred into PageMaker documents than is the case with other word processing programs.

You'll also appreciate the way Microsoft Word uses the Mouse to edit and reformat type.

MACINTOSH WORD PROCESSING OPTIONS

There are fewer word processing choices in the Apple Macintosh environment. This is offset, however, by the greater variety of graphics programs available.

Microsoft Word 3.0

Traditionally, Microsoft Word has been the word processing program of choice for use with PageMaker in the Apple Macintosh environment. Microsoft Word's popularity has been based on its many features as well as the way most formatting information remains intact when Word files are placed in PageMaker documents.

Microsoft Word has been a steady best-seller, even though Apple Computer's MacWrite word processing program was originally included with the Macintosh at no extra cost.

Word 3.0 for the Macintosh offers the same style sheet feature found in Word 3.1 for the PC, but on the Macintosh, style sheet information is carried over into PageMaker.

The style sheets make it easy to format documents quickly and consistently. With a few keystrokes, you can define all the important visual aspects of a document's appearance—including line length and paragraph spacing, boldface and italic type, page numbering, etc. These formatting decisions are passed without change into PageMaker documents. This saves you time, as you can do a great deal of document formatting at the word processing stage.

Word 3.0's other features include: outlining capability, built-in spell-checker and hyphenation, line-numbering, compatibility with other word processors, and file linking.

Compatibility with Other Word Processing Formats

One of the major changes taking place in personal computing is the coming together of the Apple Macintosh and MS-DOS environments. More and more Apple Macintosh computers are being hooked up to MS-DOS computers through local area networks like AppleTalk. Microsoft Word takes full advantage of this confluence. Word 3.0 can easily import word-processed files from the major MS-DOS Word processing programs.

File Linking

Microsoft Word 3.0 and PageMaker Version 2.0 for the Macintosh share a feature called file linking. File linking means that editing changes made in PageMaker documents can be sent back to the original Word 3.0 document.

This eliminates possibilities for error and misunderstanding. Consider: after placing a Word file in a PageMaker document you might change a sentence or two for reasons of content or appearance. Unless your Microsoft Word files are updated to reflect these changes they will not be as up to date as the PageMaker version. File linking between Word 3.0 and PageMaker takes care of this for you.

Other Macintosh Word Processing Programs

Aldus PageMaker 2.0 is designed to work with MacWrite, Write Now, Microsoft Works, and the earlier version of Microsoft Word, Word 1.05. Unlike PC-based word processing programs, all these programs transfer most formatting information intact. This includes typefaces, type size, type style, tabs, and indents.

Thus, you are not unnecessarily handicapped if you do not choose the advanced capabilities offered by Microsoft Word 3.0.

T/Maker's Write Now emerges, therefore, as a very viable alternative to the other Macintosh word processing programs. At significantly lower cost than Microsoft Word 3.0, it includes a built-in spell-checker, which is a feature not present in other Macintosh word processing programs. Write Now can also handle longer documents than MacWrite.

WORD PROCESSING CHECKLIST

1) Do you presently use a word processor?
_____

2) Which one? _____

3) Are you satisfied with its performance?
_____

4) How compatible is it with PageMaker? When word-processed files are placed in PageMaker documents, is important formatting information retained?
_____

5) What word processors do your friends and co-workers use? _____

6) Would the productivity gains of a new word processor be offset by the time required to learn a new program?
_____

CHOOSING THE RIGHT PRINTER

The printer you select has a great deal of influence on the total cost of your desktop publishing system, as well as on the flexibility it offers.

Hewlett-Packard LaserJets and Apple LaserWriters differ in the number of typefaces and sizes you can use in your PageMaker publications.

Although the differences between the two laser-printer families are narrowing, they are still substantial.

How Letters Are Formed

There were originally two totally different methods used to create words and graphic images on a laser printer. That used by the Hewlett-Packard LaserJet involved fonts—or alphabet sets—loaded into the printer from plug-in font cartridges or downloaded from descriptions stored on disk.

Font cartridges are printed circuit boards that are plugged-into a receptacle in the front panel of the LaserJet. Each font cartridge has stored in it a selection of letters in a limited number of sizes and styles. Typically, each cartridge contains a mixture of regular, boldface, and (sometimes) italic letters and symbols in two or three sizes. The disadvantage of these font cartridges is that you are restricted to the specific letters and sizes contained on them.

Only those characters included on the font cartridge can be printed. (If you want to print italics, for example, that style must be available on the font cartridge you have loaded.)

These limitations are reflected in the PC version of PageMaker designed to work under Microsoft Windows with Hewlett-Packard LaserJet printers. When, in setting up PageMaker, you select the printer you are going to be using, PageMaker automatically limits your type options to the type faces, sizes, and styles available on the font cartridge you have specified. You are restricted to using the typefaces, type sizes, and type styles (regular, bold, italics), etc. available on the font cartridge you have installed in your printer.

Font cartridges make relatively few demands on the printer's memory, permitting the Hewlett-Packard LaserJet to be significantly less expensive than the Apple LaserWriter, even though both are based on the same Canon print engine.

Hewlett-Packard's downloadable fonts allow a bit more flexibility, although they make greater demands on the printer's memory. In addition, the downloadable fonts have to be loaded into the printer from disk at the start of each printing session. This can take several minutes. But even downloadable fonts have their limitations. Only those fonts which were loaded into the printer can be accessed.

Initially, the LaserJet was limited to printing less than a quarter-page of high-resolution (300 dots-per-inch) graphics. The Hewlett-Packard LaserJet Plus introduced in 1986 contained sufficient memory to print half-page graphics.

The new Hewlett-Packard LaserJet II is a significant improvement over the original LaserJet and LaserJet Plus. It costs less, yet offers more. Of greatest importance to desktop publishing applications, the LaserJet II series has expansion slots that can accommodate additional memory as needed. Thus, you can upgrade the printer's memory if you are going to be printing large graphic images or using a wide variety of downloadable fonts.

This approach was pioneered by an independent company, JLaser, which offered an expansion board that you plugged into your computer to increase the original LaserJet's memory enough to permit the printing of full-page graphics. The card was designed to be inserted into IBM personal computers and other MS-DOS compatibles.

Other refinements built into the new LaserJet II series include correct-order output—which eliminates the need to re-collate long documents back-to-front after they have been printed—a faster warm-up time, and a 30% reduction in weight. More character sets are included, and two font cartridges can be plugged-in at once.

Although Microsoft manufactures a MacEnhancer accessory that permits the use of Hewlett-Packard LaserJets with the Apple Macintosh, LaserJets are used primarily with MS-DOS computers. Virtually every major manufacturer of MS-DOS software now includes the printer drivers—programs that tell the software how to communicate with a printer—necessary for use with Hewlett-Packard LaserJets. In addition, several independent software publishers have available interface programs that permit LaserJet use with programs that don't directly drive it.

The PostScript Alternative

Printers such as the Apple LaserWriter use a more flexible image-processing system developed by Adobe, called PostScript. PostScript is a page description language that describes the size, shape and shading of letters and graphic elements such as lines and circles mathematically. It allows characters and graphics to be defined and then manipulated.

Adobe's PostScript system offers total flexibility. Letters, numbers, and graphic images can be any size or shape, and an infinite variety of sizes and shapes is possible. Images can be stretched, compressed or tilted into any number of variations.

As a result of this flexibility, the Apple LaserWriter quickly became the preferred choice for desktop publishing applications. The original Apple LaserWriter contained several typefaces, including Helvetica and Times Roman (Fig. 3-3). The combination of straightforward Helvetica headlines with Times Roman body copy is frequently used in book and newsletter production. Each letter can be reproduced as large or small as desired.

The original Apple LaserWriter was followed, in 1986, by the Apple LaserWriter Plus. The LaserWriter Plus has more built-in fonts (Fig. 3-4). In addition to Helvetica Light and Times Roman, Bookman, Palatino, New Century Schoolbook and extended symbol sets are included. This permits the creation of more elaborate PageMaker documents.

aA bB cC dD eE fF gG hH iI jJ
kK lL mM nN oO pP qQ rR sS
tT uU vV wW xX yY zZ 12 34
56 78 90 &¶ $¢ %# @?! §£ †‡

Figure 3-3

aA bB cC dD eE fF gG hH iI jJ
kK lL mM nN oO pP qQ rR sS
tT uU vV wW xX yY zZ 12 34
56 78 90 &¶ $¢ %# @?! §£ †‡

Figure 3-4

Helvetica Light	Times Roman
Bookman	Palatino
New Century Schoolbook	Courier

αAβBχXδΔεEφΦγΓηHιIφϑκKλΛμMνNoOπΠθΘρPσΣτTυYϖζωΩξΞψΨζZ

Until recently, Apple LaserWriters was primarily limited to use by Apple Macintosh owners. This is slowly changing, however. Several MS-DOS programs—including word processing programs such as Microsoft Word and WordPerfect 4.2— contain the printer drivers necessary for the Apple LaserWriter.

As more and more MS-DOS computers are used with Apple Laser-Writers, other programs will follow suit. Aldus PageMaker for the PC will undoubtedly arouse interest in using Apple LaserWriters and LaserWriter Pluses with MS-DOS computers.

Recently, IBM announced that it had endorsed Aldus PageMaker. IBM's dealers and direct-sales force will now be selling the Post-Script-based program. This will further legitimize Apple LaserWriters in the MS-DOS world.

There are now several manufacturers of laser printers using Post-Script. One of the earliest to appear was the QMS PS-800, which was followed shortly by the QMS PS-800 Plus. The PS-800 and PS-800 Plus offer slightly more memory than the LaserWriters, print their first pages faster, and permit larger areas of 300-dpi graphics to be printed on a page.

Hybrids

During 1986, the Hewlett-Packard LaserJet and Apple LaserWriter camps came closer together. In the summer of that year, QMS, one of the largest laser printer manufacturers in the world, began offering, through its Laser Connection subsidiary, a replacement for the main circuit board used in Hewlett-Packard LaserJet printers.

The Laser Connection board replaced the original LaserJet controller with a circuit board containing a PostScript controller. This sacrificed the LaserJet's widespread software compatibility but permitted the printer to be driven by the PostScript language. You no longer had to give up your HP LaserJet printer to take advantage of PostScript's capabilities.

71

Hewlett-Packard's Desktop Publishing Solution

In late 1986 Hewlett-Packard introduced a new factor into the equation, by coming out with its own version of PostScript. This was a page description language called DDL, for "Document Description Language." Hewlett-Packard's goal was to combine the speed of the original LaserJet printer command language with the versatility of Apple's LaserWriter.

Hewlett-Packard's DDL is similar to PostScript in several ways. Indeed, both were created by people who used to work together. Both offer infinitely variable character generation, tilting, and shading, as well as full-page graphics capabilities.

Printers using the Hewlett-Packard Document Description Language are similar to PostScript-based printers in that the basic character sets are built into the printer circuitry. However, while Helvetica and Times Roman are in a Laserwriter's memory, Hewlett-Packard's DDL characters are contained on a memory expansion board that's plugged into an MS-DOS computer.

The Hewlett-Packard Desktop Publishing Solution uses Hewlett-Packard LaserJet printers, the Hewlett-Packard Vectra AT-class personal computer and Hewlett-Packard Mouse; Microsoft Windows, and Aldus PageMaker. The complete system is sold as a specially-priced package. You can also upgrade your LaserJet II to the Hewlett-Packard Desktop Publishing Solution at any time.

Conclusion

When considering printers for desktop publishing, you first have to ask: "Do I need a laser printer at all, or can I get by with a dot-matrix one?" If your choice is a laser printer, you then have to decide between the Hewlett-Packard LaserJet and the various PostScript printers available from Apple, QMS, and others.

Hewlett-Packard LaserJets are currently in the "mainstream" of MS-

DOS computing, but they are limited in their usefulness as far as desktop publishing is concerned. Hewlett-Packard's DDL could change this, but the increasing acceptance of Adobe's PostScript presently provides a commanding lead to the Apple LaserWriters.

Printer Decision Worksheet

1) If you already own a computer, what type of printer are you using? _____

2) Can you use your current printer to output draft-quality proofs of your desktop-published documents?

_____

3) What do commercial firms in your area charge for renting time on their laser printers?
Per page $_____
Per hour $_____

4) Are these firms conveniently located? _____

5) Are they open convenient hours? _____

6) How many laser-printed pages do you think you're going to produce each month? _____

7) Other than desktop publishing, are there other ways a laser printer could increase your computer's productivity? _____
How?_____

8) Could a laser printer be shared by other computers in your firm? _____

9) How great a variety of typefaces and type sizes are you likely to need in your desktop publishing activities?

_____

10) Are you likely to need the ability to print full-page graphics on your laser printer? _____

4

A Tour of the PageMaker Screen

Becoming Familiar with PageMaker's Commands

The PageMaker screen guides you through PageMaker's command structure and provides you with a continuing status report concerning the project on which you're working. The screens for the Macintosh and PC versions of PageMaker are similar. The primary difference is in the upper-left-hand corner.

The upper-left-hand corner of the Macintosh Page-Maker screen shown in Fig. 4-1 contains the familiar Apple icon. Clicking on this symbol gives you access to the Macintosh operating system. Here, you can access the Macintosh's calendar and calculator functions. The Apple icon also permits you to access the Macintosh

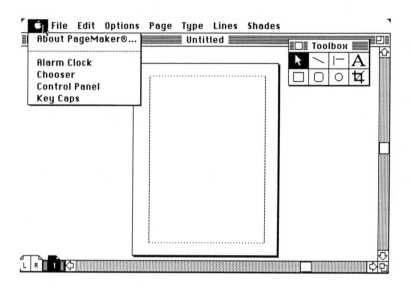

Figure 4-1

Control Panel, from which you can change printers, reallocate system memory or adjust mouse sensitivity.

Clicking on the Apple icon also provides access to PageMaker's unique guidance system of help messages. When you click on "Help" in the Apple menu a new menu bar appears, called "Guidance." This leads you through a series of interactive help screens that combine text and graphics.

Similarly, the upper-left-hand corner of the PC PageMaker screen (Fig. 4-2) offers access to the Windows operating system. You can open secondary applications—for example, word processing or graphics programs designed to run in the Windows operating environment. You can also access PageMaker's help files or Window's calendar and calculator functions.

The Windows menu also permits you to Zoom—to fill the screen with a slightly enlarged view of your PageMaker document. This eliminates the icon area at the bottom of the screen, which displays other Windows programs you have immediate access to, and lets you see a little more of your publication.

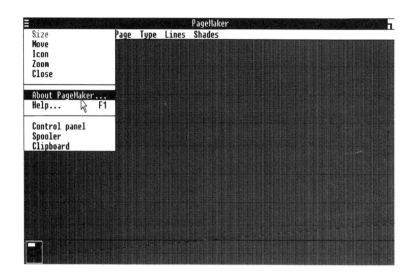

Figure 4-2

Title

The top center of the PageMaker window displays the name of the file you have opened. When you open a new file, the word "Untitled" remains visible until you save your publication for the first time. After your first save, "Untitled" is replaced by the file name you supplied.

Menu Bar

Above the title bar is the PageMaker menu bar (Fig. 4-3). Each menu option opens up to display a group of similar commands. Because of the way the commands are logically organized you will quickly become comfortable working with PageMaker.

For example, as illustrated in Fig. 4-4, all commands having to do with opening and saving files, or with placing previously-prepared word processing or graphics files are grouped under the "File" menu. Similarly, all commands relating to modifying your work on the screen are grouped under the "Edit" menu. The "Page" menu allows you to insert or delete pages, to jump to different pages in a publication, or to change your view of the publication you're working on.

77

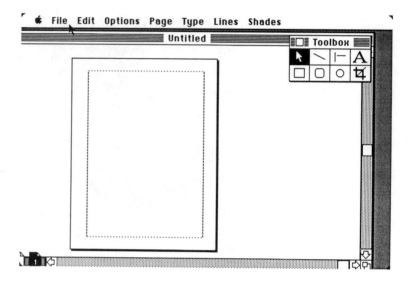

Figure 4-3

A great deal of your work will be done from the "Type" menu, which permits you to change typeface, type size, type style, and to adjust letter, paragraph, and word spacing.

In most cases, when you open a command, a dialog box (Fig. 4-5) appears, which offers you further options. For example, clicking on the "Type Specs" command permits you to choose or change typeface, type size, and leading (which refers to the vertical spacing between lines). You can also choose boldface, italics and boldface italics, among other options.

The commands grouped under "Lines" permit you to control the width and style of new and existing lines, as well as the width of lines outlining shapes such as boxes and circles. The "Shades" menu permits you to fill boxes and circles with a variety of shades and patterns.

Direct Keyboard Access

It is important to note that most of the PageMaker commands appearing under the various menu headings can be accessed in two separate

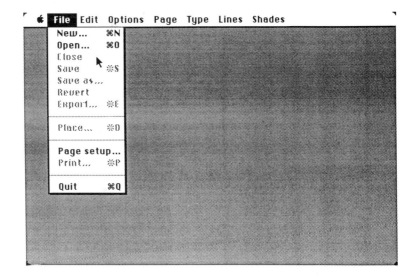

Figure 4-4

Figure 4-5

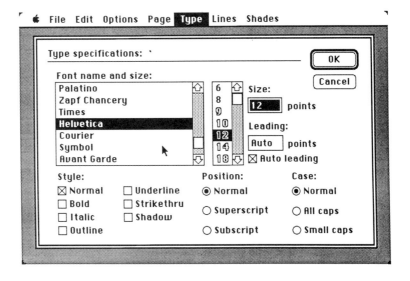

ways. The first is by dragging down the heading and releasing the mouse button at the command you desire. Alternatively, you can use keyboard shortcuts. Direct keyboard access saves time by eliminating the need to switch between the keyboard and mouse and back again.

You will quickly grow to appreciate PageMaker's dual-mode operation. While you'll probably start out using the menu bar, as your familiarity with PageMaker increases you'll find yourself accessing PageMaker commands directly through the keyboard shortcuts more and more. In PageMaker for the PC, these keyboard shortcuts make frequent use of the function keys. In the Macintosh version of PageMaker, these keyboard shortcuts use various keys pressed along with the Command or Option keys.

Both PageMaker for the PC and PageMaker's Macintosh Version 2.0 use the computer's numeric keypad to move around in stories you have placed in PageMaker documents.

THE PAGEMAKER TOOLBOX

The PageMaker toolbox (Fig. 4-6) appears initially at the upper right of both versions of the PageMaker screen. You can, however, grab it and move it to a different location on the PageMaker screen if it's blocking part of your publication. Or, you can temporarily remove it completely from the screen.

The commands found in the Toolbox are used in conjunction with those found in the menu bar. Most of your work will be done with the "Select" and "Text" tools. Other tools permit you to draw lines, boxes and circles, and to crop illustrations.

Selecting Graphics

The Pointer icon in the upper left of the PageMaker Toolbox is used to select text and graphics for deletion, copying, movement or resizing.

When you select a graphic, such as a vertical line, for example, you

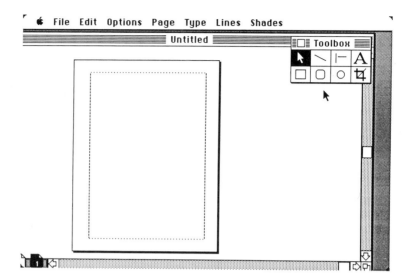

Figure 4-6

Figure 4-7

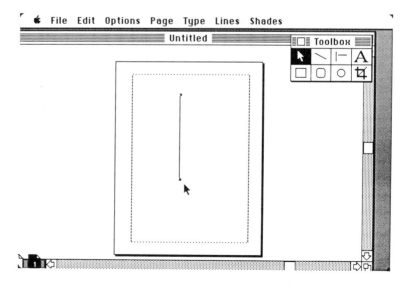

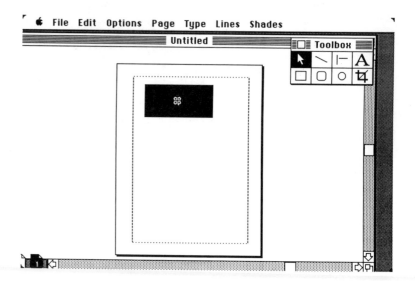

Figure 4--8

can move it from side to side or up and down (Fig. 4-7). Or, if you select the line at its end, you can stretch it or shorten it.

Similarly, if you select the middle of a rectangle, you can move it from place to place within the PageMaker publication (Fig. 4-8).

If you select a handle on the middle of one of the sides, you can enlarge or reduce the figure to fit the space available for it (Fig.4-9). Selecting one of the corner handles stretches or compresses the rectangle in two ways at once.Hold the Shift key down as you move the handles, however, and although the size of the rectangle changes, its proportions do not.

The Select tool is also used to change the appearance of lines (Fig. 4-10). To make a thin line thicker, for example, you first select the line, and then pull down the "Line" menu and click on the thickness of the line you desire.

Selecting Text

The Select tool is used when placing, moving, and deleting text, as well as to change column widths.

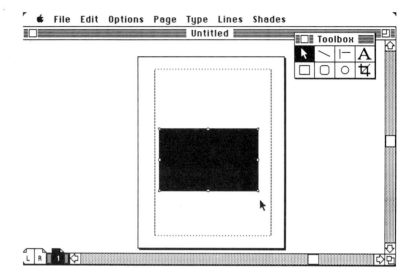

Figure 4-9

Figure 4-10

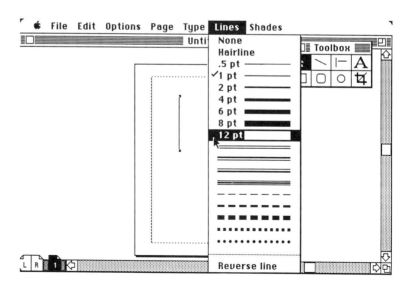

Figure 4-11

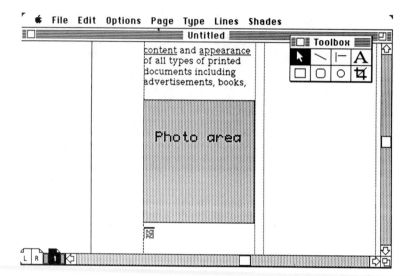

Figure 4-12

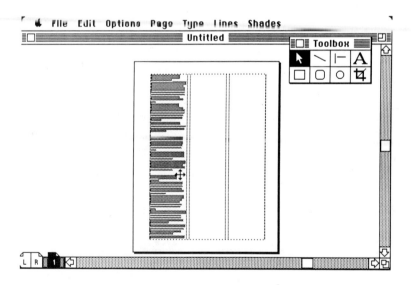

For example, when you are placing text, the text stops flowing when it hits the bottom of the PageMaker screen, or an existing text or graphics element. To continue placing text in the next column, you must reload the "text gun" by clicking on the "+" sign at the bottom of the text block. You can then continue in the next column, or below the text or graphics that interrupted the flow of text (Fig. 4-11).

Using the Select tool and clicking in the middle of a text block, you can move the block around as if it were a graphics element (Fig. 4-12). The text block can be moved up or down, or to the left or right.

The movement of a text block can be limited to the horizontal or vertical direction by holding down the Shift key when clicking on the text or graphic you want to move.

A "+" at the bottom of a text block indicates that there is more text to be placed (Fig. 4-13). A "#" indicates the end of a text block. By clicking on one of these symbols and dragging, you can roll up the text block like a window shade. This allows you to shorten a column to add a photograph, or to align the bottoms of a series of columns.

The Select tool can also be used to adjust the width of a text block

Figure 4-13

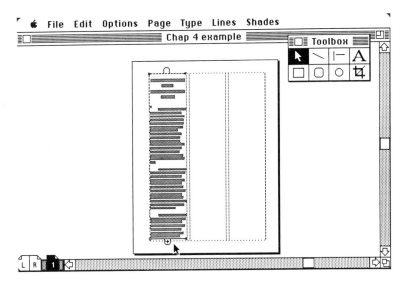

(Fig. 4-14). By clicking and dragging the ends of the window shade bar at the top or bottom of a text block, you can make that block wider or narrower than the column guides on the page.

This is an easy way to create run-arounds—where text is placed adjacent to an illustration or large letter used as a graphic element.

Diagonal Line

The Diagonal icon is used to draw lines at any angle. If the Shift key is held down, however, the lines are automatically drawn horizontally or vertically. The width of the lines is determined by the line size and shape you have chosen in the dialog box.

Perpendicular Lines

This tool is used for drawing vertical or horizontal rules, or lines, to separate adjacent columns or to separate topics within a column.

The Perpendicular drawing tool is also used to create page borders, as

Figure 4-14

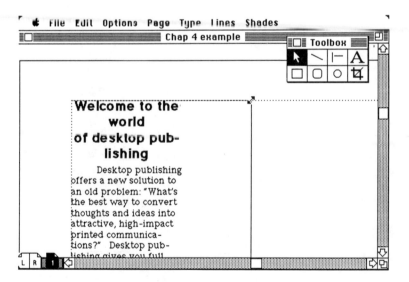

shown in Fig. 4-15). Note that borders of different thicknesses can appear at the top and sides of a page.

The Perpendicular Lines tool draws lines at a 45-degree angle when used in conjunction with the Shift key.

Once again, the thickness of the lines drawn using the Diagonal or Perpendicular tool is determined by the "Line Thickness" setting you have selected in the "Lines" pull-down menu.

Text

Click on the "A" in the PageMaker Toolbox to select the Type function. This tool is used to add, delete, or modify text. For example, to enter new text—such as a headline or caption—select the Text tool by clicking on the "A," and move your cursor to the point where you want to add the text (Fig. 4-16). Click once to select the insertion point, and start typing. Text will immediately appear.

Highlighting Text

To change typeface, type size, type style, leading, or paragraph spacing, select the Type tool by clicking on the "A" in the Toolbox,

Figure 4-15

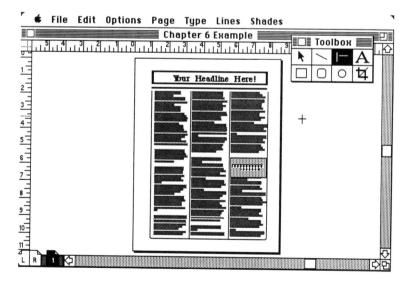

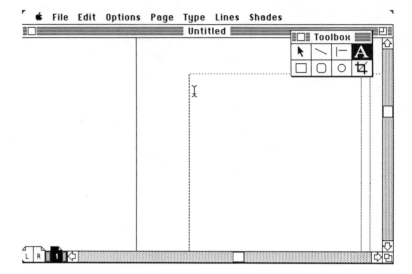

Figure 4-16

and then highlight the text you want to modify (Fig. 4-17). Click on the first letter whose characteristics you want to change, and drag the I-beam pointer through the word, sentence, paragraph, or story to the end of the portion you want to modify.

Highlighted text appears in reverse; that is, white words against a black background (or black type against a white background).

After the text has been highlighted, pull down the Type menu and click on the Type Specifications, Paragraph, Indents/tabs or Spacing commands. This will open the dialog boxes necessary to change the appearance of the text. You can then change typeface, type size, type style, leading, indents, and paragraph, word and letter spacing.

Or, you can go to the "Cut" or "Clear" choices in the "Edit" menu (Fig. 4-18) and remove the highlighted section from the page either temporarily or permanently.

Rectangle

Click on the Rectangle tool at the lower left of the Pagemaker

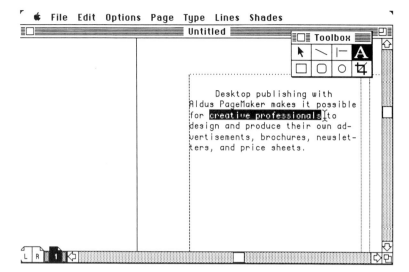

Figure 4-17

Figure 4-18

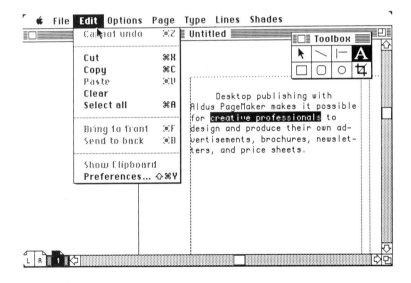

Toolbox when you want to draw boxes or squares. The box will be drawn with the lines and shading you have previously chosen.

Create an insertion point by clicking at the place where you want a corner of the box to to start (Fig. 4-19). Hold down the mouse button as you move toward the opposite corner of the box. Your box will be completed, and filled in with the shade you have previously chosen, when you release the mouse button.

You can create a perfect square by holding down the Shift key as you move the mouse (Fig. 4-20).

Rounded-Corner Box

This tool is similar to the one above, except that the corners of the box drawn do not meet at right angles, but rather are curves drawn to the radius you have previously selected in the "Rounded Corner" dialog box under the "Options" menu. The radius of the corner decreases as the size of the box decreases.

Circle

The Circle tool lets you draw ovals and circles as you drag the mouse. Like graphics created with the Box tool, ovals and circles are drawn with the line thickness and interior shading previously selected in the "Lines" and "Shades" menus.

You can draw perfect circles if you hold down the Shift key as you drag the mouse.

Cropping Tool

The Cropping tool is used to remove unwanted portions of an illustration or scanned photograph. You can remove material from the top, bottom, or sides of an illustration or photograph to meet space or esthetic requirements.

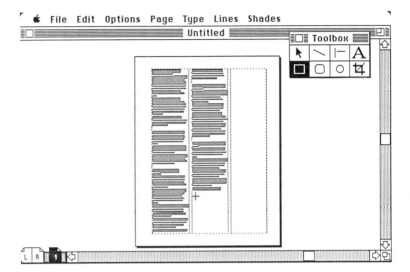

Figure 4-19

Figure 4-20

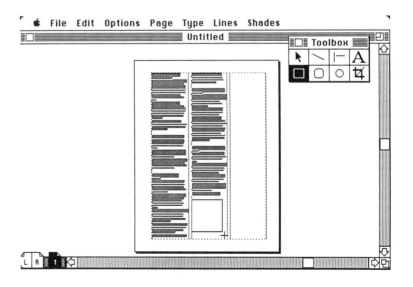

To crop a drawing, for example, select the Cropping tool by clicking on the overlapping "L"s in the lower right of the PageMaker toolbox. Then move the tool to one of the corners or sides of a piece of artwork (Fig. 4-21). As you move it into the area of the figure it removes the portion "behind" it. The proportions and size of the artwork remain the same while unwanted details are eliminated from its perimeter.

PUBLICATION AREA

This part of the screen shows your work in progress. PageMaker permits you to see your publication at a variety of sizes. You can see an entire page reduced to screen size, or you can choose half-size, three-quarter-size, actual size, or twice actual size, views. Typically you will see only a portion of the page when you are working at anything other than "fit in window" size.

Pagemaker permits you to work on either one page at a time or on two-page spreads. A single-page view presents your publication slightly larger than it appears when you select "Fit in Window."

The single and two-page "Fit in Window" views permit you to observe the overall appearance of a page or spread. Although large headlines will be readable, you will not be able to make out words and sentences. Body copy in the "Fit in Window" page views is replaced by *greeking* (Fig. 4-22)—small "x"s that represent individual letters and the spaces between words.

Greeking permits you to concentrate with the overall appearance of your publication, without being distracted by content. It also speeds up PageMaker's operation by making it unnecessary for each character to be redrawn when you change view sizes."Greeked" words usually become legible when your publication is shown at actual size (Fig. 4-23) or 50% or 75%. You can then make out individual words.

You'll find the 200 % enlargement (Fig. 4-24) useful in placing text and graphics accurately.

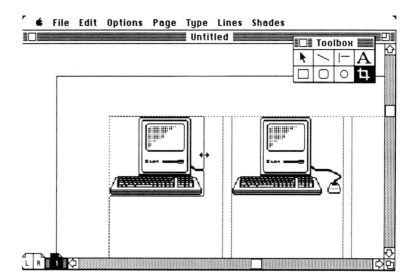

Figure 4-21

Figure 4-22

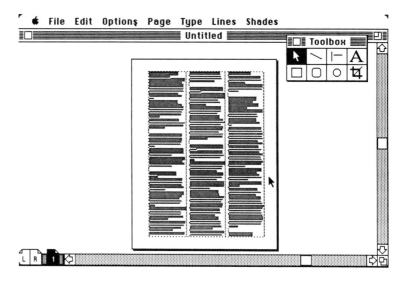

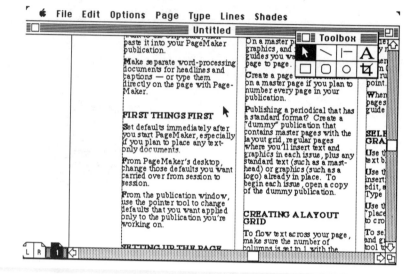

Figure 4-23

Figure 4-24

Scroll Bars

Scroll bars appear along the right-hand and bottom edges of the PageMaker screen (Fig. 4-25). Scroll bars permit you to move around the PageMaker screen quickly and easily.

Clicking on the "up" arrow moves the PageMaker publication downward (the equivalent of moving the screen window upward) so you can see the top portion of your document. Clicking on the "down" arrow moves the publication toward the top of the screen, exposing the bottom portion of the document.

Clicking on the "left-pointing" arrow moves you toward the left-hand side of the document, clicking on the "right" arrow brings you to the right-hand side.

Clicking on the arrows moves the publication a little at a time. For faster movement, click on the elevator boxes within the scroll bars and move the box up or down, or sideways. By grabbing the elevator box and dragging it, you can quickly change your view of the PageMaker page. A little practice will probably be necessary for you get an intuitive feel for translating box movement into screen movement at various levels of enlargement or reduction.

Master Pages

At the lower left of the PageMaker screen are two symbols, which resemble sheets of paper with their respective left and right hand top corners bent over (Fig. 4-26). Click on these to set up *master pages.* Master pages permit you to establish a format that will be maintained on all the pages in a publication.

You can add both printing and non-printing elements to your master pages, both of which will be repeated on every page.

Non-printing elements are represented by dotted lines. These elements include column and margin guides, as well as horizontal and vertical guides used to align text and graphics. Printing elements include page borders and column rules, design elements such as boxes, and infor-

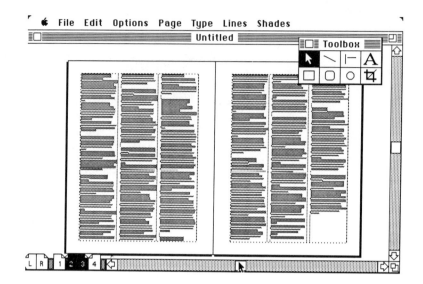

Figure 4-25

Figure 4-26

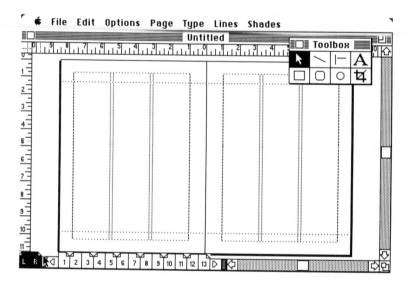

mation such as publication and chapter titles, and page numbers.

You can set up separate left- and right-hand master pages. This permits page numbers to appear at the outside edges of left and right hand pages and allows different left- and right-hand running heads.

Master page setups are saved when you click on one of the page numbers to the right of the left and right-hand page symbols.

Page Numbers

To the right of the Master Pages symbols is a series of numbers in little "houses"—actually page-pair icons (Fig. 4-27). These indicate which page or two-page spread you're working on. The currently active pages are highlighted in reverse.

To move to a different page (or spread), simply move the mouse pointer to the page (or spread) you want displayed on the PageMaker screen and "click."

Up to sixteen page numbers can be displayed at a time. When your publication includes more than sixteen pages, only the sixteen pages closest to the currently active numbers are shown. "Click" on the left-

Figure 4-27

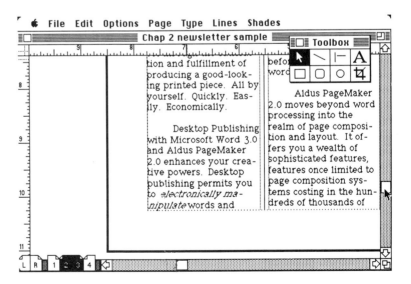

or right-hand arrows next to the page numbers to view a higher or lower range of numbers. The numbers will scroll in the direction you have pointed to. A PageMaker file can contain up to 128 pages.

Note, however, that you can create longer documents by using the "Begin Page Numbering At . . ." command when setting up your publication. (For example, you can begin numbering the pages of your second file at page 129, your third file at page 257, etc.) You can create documents with as many as 9,999 pages by stringing together various PageMaker files.

Helpful Hint

The page number icons make it convenient to back up your Page-Maker publication frequently while you're working on it. Every time you click on a page number your file will be updated with your most recent changes.

ICON AREA

The bottom of the Windows screen of the PC version of PageMaker, shown in Fig. 4-28, contains a rectangular area displaying icons representing other Windows-compatible programs that have been loaded and are available for use. This area can be eliminated, permitting a larger view of your PageMaker publication. To do this, use the "Zoom" command found under the Windows symbol at the upper left of the PageMaker screen.

To switch to a different Windows-compatible program, simply pick up the icon representing the program you want to use and move it into the active area of the PageMaker screen. Instantly, that program will take over the screen, and the PageMaker program will be represented at the bottom of the screen by its own icon.

The same function can be accomplished on the Macintosh version of PageMaker using the "Switcher" command. It permits you to substitute one program for another instantly, making it simple for you to move from a word processor to a graphics program to PageMaker.

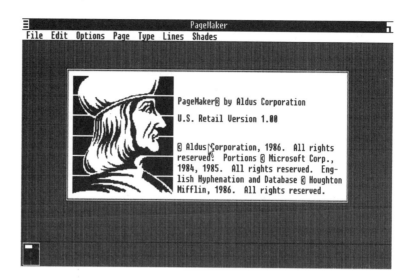

Figure 4-28

5

Basic PageMaker Commands

Powerful Simplicity

Now that you've had a brief introduction to the Page-
Maker screen, it's time to become acquainted with the
commands that appear when you pull down one of the
menus in PageMaker's menu bar.

Note that keyboard shortcuts are often listed following a
command name. In most—although not all—cases, similar shortcuts are available in both the Macintosh and PC
versions of PageMaker. In many cases, where the
Macintosh version uses the Command key, the PC version uses the Control key. Similarly, where the Macintosh version uses the Option key, the PC version often
uses the Alt key.

The only area where this scheme breaks down concerns the function keys found on the PC. The Macintosh has no function keys. However, as we'll see, there are Macintosh equivalents to the PC function-key commands.

As you investigate the various PageMaker menus you'll notice that some commands are displayed on the screen in a lighter shade than others. This means that they cannot be accessed at that time. For example, you cannot "Revert" unless a file has been both saved as well as changed since it was last saved. Similarly, you cannot "Undo" a command until you have executed one.

FILE COMMANDS

The File menu shown in Fig. 5-1 includes the commands necessary to open and save publication files, to place text and graphics files created with other programs, and to print PageMaker publications.

New

Use the "New" command when you are starting work on a new Page-Maker publication. When you access the "New" command, you are immediately presented with PageMaker's "Page Setup" dialog box shown in Fig. 5-2.

The Page Setup dialog box permits you to define the physical size of your PageMaker publication, establish the number of pages you expect it to contain, and indicate whether pages will be printed horizontally or vertically.

You can use several standard paper sizes for your PageMaker publication. The most common ones automatically present themselves for selection. Or, you can use PageMaker's "custom" feature to create publications as small as business cards or as large as 17-by-22-inch newspaper pages. Printers' crop marks—which indicate where a page is to be trimmed to size—can be added automatically if they are desired.

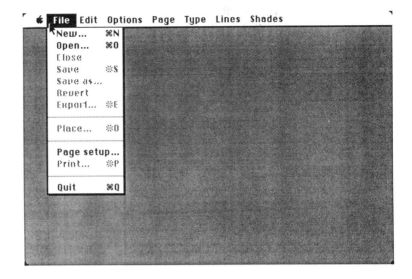

Figure 5-1

Figure 5-2

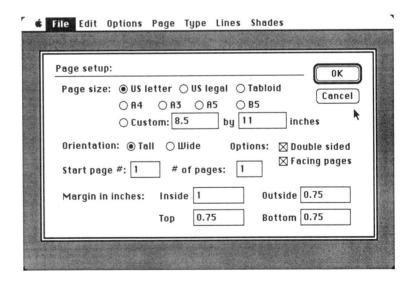

Very large documents can be printed by overlapping a series of 8 1/2-by-11-inch pages—or larger ones if your printer can handle them.

The Page Setup dialog box is used to define the top, bottom and side margins of your page, and also permits you to accept the "double-sided printing" option. This option is normally used when you are preparing publications that are to be bound. The inside margins of two-sided publications require more space, depending on right or left-hand page placement.

You are also given the opportunity to work on single pages, instead of accepting the double-sided "facing pages" default.

On PageMaker for the PC, you are also reminded which printer is currently targeted. This is important because the selection of typefaces and type sizes you can use is limited to those available on the printer you have selected.

When you have indicated the specifications of your project, click "OK" or press your computer's "Return" (or "Enter") key.

Helpful Hint

You'll find that pressing the Return or Enter key is a timesaver compared to moving the mouse and clicking on "OK." It's available for most PageMaker commands and using it will soon become second nature to you.

Open

The Open command is used to resume working on a previously-saved PageMaker publication. This command immediately presents you with the "Select Publication" dialog box.

The "Select Publication" dialog box (Fig. 5-3) permits you to scroll through the PageMaker publications stored on your disks and choose the one you want to open. Use the up and down arrow keys to locate

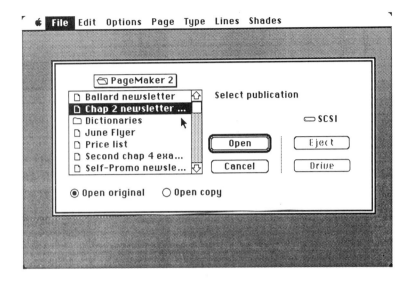

Figure 5-3

your previously saved publication quickly. The name of the publication selected is highlighted in the "Publication Name" box.

You can open a publication in three ways: by double-clicking on its title in the scroll box, by highlighting its name and then clicking on the OK box, or simply by pressing "Enter" when the publication you want to open is highlighted.

Use "Open Original" when you are resuming work on a project. Use the "Open Copy" option if you have saved an "empty" format for your publication—perhaps master pages for a newsletter. When you save it, you can title this publication with the specific month or date of issue. Saving the copy will preserve the "empty" template, so you can use it over and over again.

Save

The "Save" command is used during work on a publication to commit your work to a file. It is used after a publication has already been named.

The first time you save a new publication, you will be presented with PageMaker's "Save As" dialog box (Fig. 5-4). This prompts you to provide your publication with a title.

Note that after a publication has been saved the first time, PageMaker automatically makes a mini-save of your publication every time you turn a page. This provides an extra measure of protection for your work, although you should still plan on making frequent saves as you work on your publication.

Remember, as you are working on your document, changes you make on the screen (i.e., drawing borders, adding or editing text, resizing graphics), are preserved only in your computer's memory. *These changes are not made permanent until you save them!* Thus, if you accidentally unplug your computer by crossing your legs and pulling the line cord out of the wall, your work will be lost. Frequent saves prevent these problems from happening.

Helpful Hint

You do not have to use the "Save" command to save your PageMaker publication as you're working. Simply click the pointer on the cur-

Figure 5-4

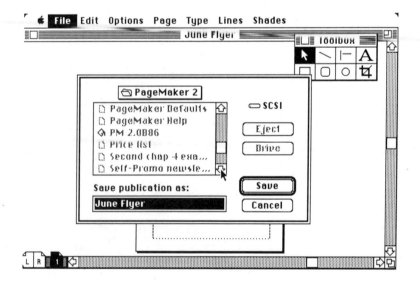

rent, highlighted, page number at the bottom of the PageMaker screen (Fig. 5-5). This will immediately update your files with your latest changes.

Save As

The "Save As" command is used when you want to save more than one version of your document. For example, you might want to try out two widely-differing design approaches. You could do this by saving the first version under its original title, and the second under a slightly different one. That way, if the second version didn't work out you could return to the original.

The "Save As" command can also be used to make a second, or backup, copy of your work. In the Macintosh version of PageMaker the "Save As" dialog box permits you to change folders and eject disks. The "Save As" dialog box in the PC version permits you to access different sub-directories and disk drives to store and retrieve files. For example, although you might be working from the hard disk, you might want to make a backup copy of your work on a floppy in case your hard disk crashed.

Figure 5-5

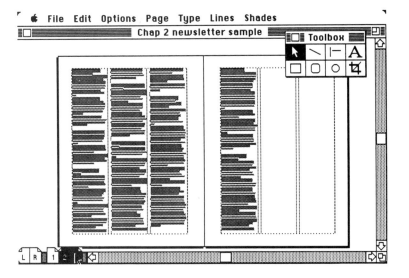

You can also use the "Save as" command to make an additional copy of your work to be taken to an outside laser printer or typesetting service.

Revert

The Revert command is one of PageMaker's most useful ones. Revert might be considered a "multiple Undo." *Revert returns you to the last saved copy of your work.* Suppose, for example, you had been working on a page that just didn't come together. You liked the page the way it looked before you made your changes. Revert makes it possible to return to your starting point.

Close Publication

Use "Close Publication" when you want to stop working on one PageMaker publication and begin working on another.

If you have made changes since the last time you saved your work, Close Publication presents you with a dialog box that asks you whether or not you want to save your work (Fig. 5-6). If you choose

Figure 5-6

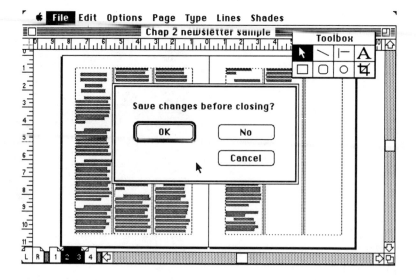

not to save it, any changes made since your last "save" will be lost. If you have never saved your publication—not the best of ideas—and you indicate that you want to save your work, you will automatically be taken to the "Save As" dialog box where you can name your file.

Place

The Place command is one of PageMaker's most powerful and frequently-used commands. It is used to integrate previously prepared text and graphic files into your PageMaker publication.

The Place dialog box illustrated in Fig. 5-7 permits you to scroll through your file folders and subdirectories to locate the file you need. Use the up and down arrows on the scroll bar to view more files.

In the PC version of PageMaker, you can select whichever disk drive you need. And, by moving the down arrow to the ellipsis, or row of dots, at the bottom of the list you can get to the root directory of your hard disk. This presents you with a list of subdirectories. From there, you can access any of them by double-clicking on the appropriate one as it becomes highlighted. When you're in the proper subdirectory,

Figure 5-7

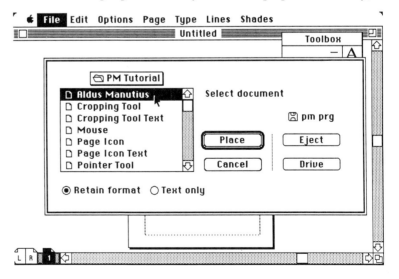

click on "Place" and scroll until you've located the specific file you want to place.

On the Apple Macintosh, you can use the "Place" command to choose between a hard disk or various floppy-disk drives. Use "Eject" to remove one disk and insert another.

When placing text, the pointer on the PageMaker screen turns into a miniature page.

When placing graphics created with paint-type applications, i.e., PC Paint or Apple's MacPaint, the pointer turns into a paintbrush.

And the PageMaker pointer turns into a drawing pen when placing draw-type graphics.

In Version 2.0 of PageMaker for the Macintosh, the pointer is loaded with the "EPS" symbol when placing files containing encapsulated Postcript images.

Place the "loaded" pointer at the upper left hand corner of the area where you want the text or graphics to be placed (Fig. 5-8). You can place text and graphics either on the PageMaker drawing board—next

Figure 5--8

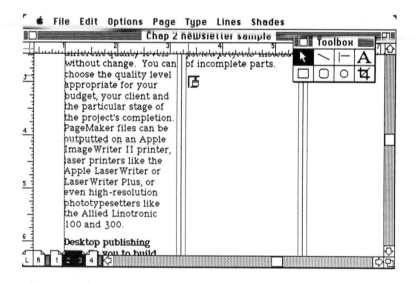

110

to the publication you're working on—and move it as needed into your document using PageMaker's "Select" command. Or, you can immediately place the text or graphics right into the publication.

Page Setup

The Page Setup command lets you change certain options while working on a project. It duplicates the Page Setup box with which you're presented when you open a new file. Page Setup permits you to change the size of your publication, for example, by changing margins or adding pages.

Print

The Print command presents you with a dialog box that lets you control all aspects of printing.

From the Print dialog box (Fig. 5-9), you can specify whether your project will be printed in collated or reverse order, and can define which pages and how many copies are to be printed. You can scroll

Figure 5--9

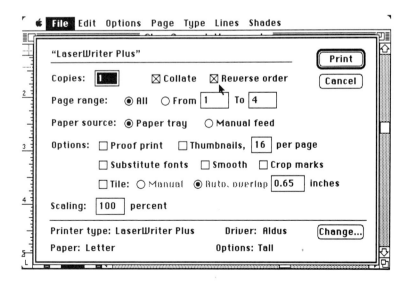

through a list of the various printers that may be attached to your computer and, if you are using a dot matrix printer, choose either "Draft" or "Final" quality.

The "Thumbnails" option permits you to print miniature versions of each of your pages, as shown in Fig. 5-10. With a PostScript printer such as the Apple LaserWriter or LaserWriter Plus you can print miniature versions of up to 16 pages on a single 8 1/2-by-11 sheet of paper.

When instructed to, PageMaker will add printers' cropping marks (Fig. 5-11) to documents smaller than the paper they're to be printed on. Commercial printers will appreciate this. These crop marks are also useful when preparing publications for printing in more than one color to assist in getting the proper registration.

Tiling permits you to create large publications—such as posters and full-size newspaper pages—by printing portions of a page on separate sheets of paper. These individual sheets are joined together to make a complete page as depicted in Fig. 5-12. You can determine the placement of each tile manually, or you can have PageMaker can do it

Figure 5-10

PM.Chapter 1

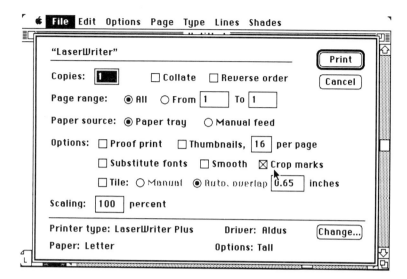

Figure 5-11

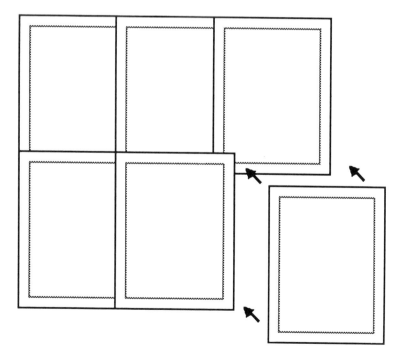

Figure 5-12

automatically. When manual tiling is being used, you can specify the amount of paper overlap.

PageMaker has a scaling feature that permits you to print enlarged or reduced versions of each page (Fig. 5-13). This is useful when you want to see working copies of large-size publications (such as posters) or when you're making signs.

Scaling is also useful when you find that your page layout is approaching the maximum image area your laser printer can print. (Phototypesetters such as the Linotronic 100 and 300 can cover a full 8 ½ by 11-inch area. Most laser printers have quarter-inch non-printing margins.) Scaling your page to approximately 95% actual size permits you to proof it accurately before it's sent to the typesetter.

Target Printer

"Target Printer" on the PC version of PageMaker presents you with a dialog box permitting you to choose among several printers connected to your computer. This highly important command determines the

Figure 5-13

```
 ⌂ File  Edit  Options  Page  Type  Lines  Shades

 "LaserWriter"                                        [ Print ]

 Copies: 1          ☐ Collate   ☐ Reverse order       [ Cancel ]

 Page range:  ◉ All   ○ From 1    To 1

 Paper source:  ◉ Paper tray    ○ Manual feed

 Options:  ☐ Proof print   ☐ Thumbnails, 16 per page

           ☐ Substitute fonts  ☐ Smooth  ☐ Crop marks

           ☐ Tile:  ○ Manual  ◉ Auto. overlap 0.65  inches

 Scaling: 66  percent

 Printer type: LaserWriter Plus      Driver: Aldus    [ Change... ]
 Paper: Letter                       Options: Tall
```

typefaces, type sizes, and type styles available to you.

The "Target Printer" command allows you to specify whether you're using an Apple LaserWriter or Apple LaserWriter Plus (which offers you a greater variety of type choices). If you select the Hewlett-Packard LaserJet you are taken to a second-level dialog box where you can specify which font cartridges or downloadable fonts you have installed. Your choices will be reflected in the "Type Specs" dialog box you will encounter later.

EDIT COMMANDS

The Edit commands help you as you revise your PageMaker publication. Many of them involve the use of the Clipboard—a temporary holding area that permits you to exchange information easily between programs.

Undo

Undo permits you to reverse your last action and returns the Page-Maker screen, and the publication, to the way it looked before that action was undertaken.

For example, if you had deleted text but decided you wanted it back, Undo would put it back in place (Fig. 5-14).

It is important to note that you can "undo" your "Undo." This permits you to toggle back and forth, comparing your "original" version with your "revised" version.

Just about any PageMaker operation can be undone. You can return type to its original size after it has been enlarged or reduced, change the shading pattern of boxes or circles and change the thickness of the lines used for boxes or page borders. You can return objects that have been moved, including margins and columns, to their original locations.

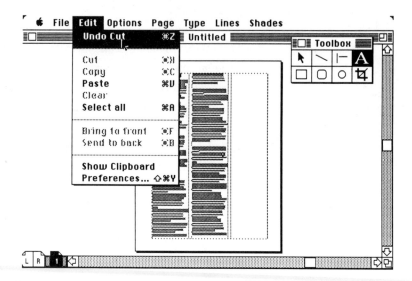

Figure 5-14

It is easy to select the wrong thing when using the "Select" tool. For instance, you may inadvertently select and move a page border instead of the block of text you wanted. Undo instantly rectifies your error. Simple mistakes such as this can cause large headaches in page-layout programs without an Undo function.

Cut

PageMaker's Cut, Copy, and Paste commands are used in conjunction with the Select and Type commands found in the toolbox. Cut removes the type or graphic you have selected from the screen, and places it in the clipboard.

Text or graphics on the Clipboard can be replicated on different pages of your PageMaker publication, or exchanged with other programs currently active.

Bear in mind that only one selection can be on the Clipboard at a time. When you cut text or a graphic and place it on the Clipboard, it replaces what was already there!

Copy

Copy is similar to cut, *except that the original text or graphics remain on the PageMaker screen.* Copy permits you to use the same words or graphic images in more than one place in your publication.

Paste

Use Paste when you want to return text or graphics to the PageMaker screen from the Clipboard. Text is pasted where you have the Page-Maker pointer. Graphics are pasted into the center of the PageMaker screen. You can then use PageMaker's Select command to move the graphic to its final location.

Clear

Use Clear when you want to delete text or graphics without sending them to the Clipboard. Clear is useful when you want to preserve text or graphics previously placed in the Clipboard.

Important!

It is extremely important that you recognize the difference between "Cut" and "Clear." "Cut" removes material from your PageMaker publication and places it on the Clipboard so it can be moved to another location. "Clear," however, deletes the material from your computer's memory. It cannot be placed elsewhere, because it no longer exists.

Select All

"Select All" has several important applications.

When you are in the Text mode, and your pointer is within a story, you can use this function to select all of the type included in the story

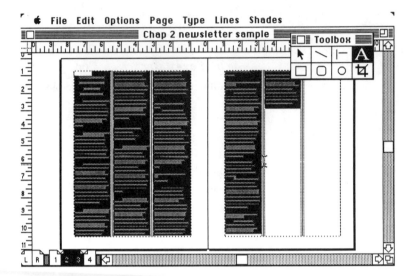

Figure 5-15

(Fig. 5-15). This makes it easy to change the specifications of text that has already been placed, *as well as of text in the file that has yet to be placed.* This is a great timesaver. Without it you would have to place the entire file before you could change its typeface, type size, line spacing, or type style.

Use Select All to find the "handles" that define the edges of all the text and graphic elements on the page (Fig. 5-16). This makes it easy to erase an entire page. Simply hit "Backspace" after Select All, and you're presented with a clean working environment.

Select All also makes it easy to change one or more graphic or text elements.

Helpful Hint

Select All is especially useful if you are trying to find "hidden" copy—for example reversed type that no longer shows against a black background, or white-on-white, or a text or graphics element you have temporarily "lost."

118

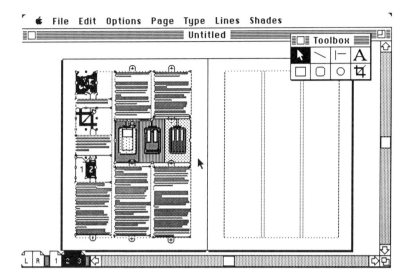

Figure 5-16

Bring to Front

Bring to Front changes the stacking order of text and graphics on the page. PageMaker documents are created in layers. For example, layers of type can be placed on top of graphic elements such as reversed boxes, or one layer of text may overlay another. Only the top layer can be modified. Bring to Front permits you to access a background layer for deletion or revision. This command is frequently used when creating reversed headlines, adding a shaded background to type, or adding shadow boxes behind photos or illustrations.

Send to Back

Send to Back is the opposite of Bring to Front. It brings to the front text or graphics hidden on the bottom layer of your PageMaker publication. For example, you may have decided to highlight a paragraph by placing it within a screened box. If you create the screened box after you placed the text, the box will obscure it. By selecting the screened box and using the "Send To Back" command, the text will again be visible (Figs. 5-17 and 5-18).

119

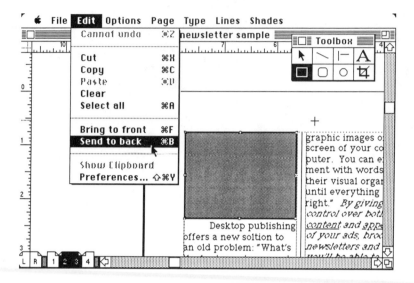

Figure 5-17

Figure 5-18

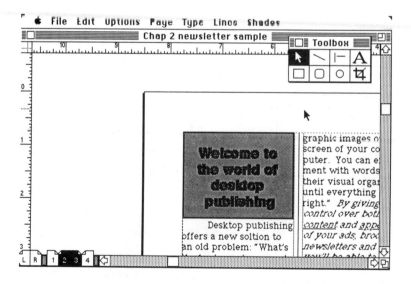

Preferences

Preferences changes the unit of measure used for on-screen measuring, as well as those that appear in dialog boxes. This includes the units of measurement found on the PageMaker rulers.

You thus enjoy the option of working with inches, decimal inches, millimeters, picas and points, or ciceros—a unit of measurement popular in Europe—depending on which measurement you're familiar with from previous work.

OPTIONS

These commands help you specify or modify the tools used to lay out your publication. These commands are typically of the ''set and forget'' sort. They relate to measurements, alignment guides, and columns.

Several of these commands can be set to be activated automatically as default settings when you start PageMaker. The commands are always available, however, so you can turn features on or off as you need to.

Rulers

PageMaker's horizontal and vertical rulers permit precise placement of text and graphic elements. These rulers automatically change their scaling according to the current page view. Spacing is shown in smaller increments as you increase page view.

Rulers (Fig. 5-19) can be turned on with the Rulers command. A check-mark appears next to the command to show that the rulers are active. Clicking again on the command removes the rulers.

You can easily adjust the zero position of your rulers by moving the PageMaker pointer to the little box formed at the intersection of the horizontal and vertical rulers, and moving it to the spot where you want to make your measurements (Figs. 5-20 and 5-21). You can make

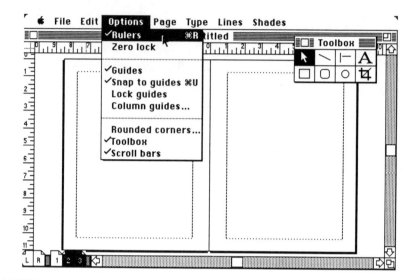

Figure 5--19

Figure 5-20

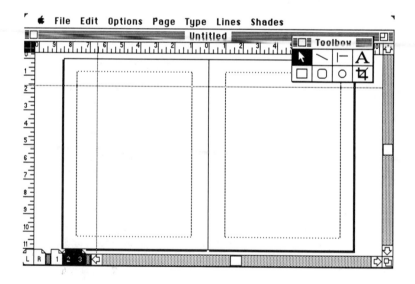

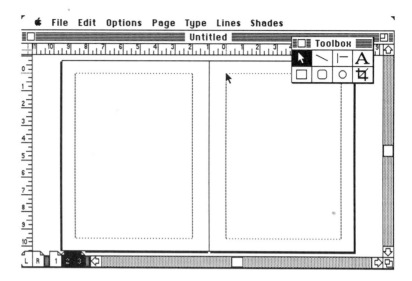

Figure 5-21

your measurements from the upper left-hand corner of the page, the upper left hand margins, or—when using facing pages—the intersection of the two pages.

Zero Lock

This locks the ruler's zero point and eliminates the possibility of moving it inadvertently.

Guides

PageMaker is easy to work with because it presents you with a variety of non-printing margin, column, and ruler guides. You can have up to 40 vertical and horizontal guides for aligning text and graphics.

Non-printing guides are shown as dotted lines (Fig. 5-22). As can be seen in Fig. 5-23, these sometimes interfere with your ability to visualize what a printed page will look like. The "Guides" command permits you to turn off these non-printing visual elements, so you can better visualize how your page will turn out.

123

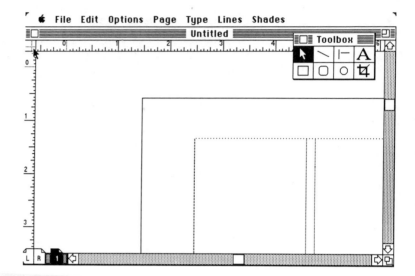

Figure 5-22

Figure 5-23

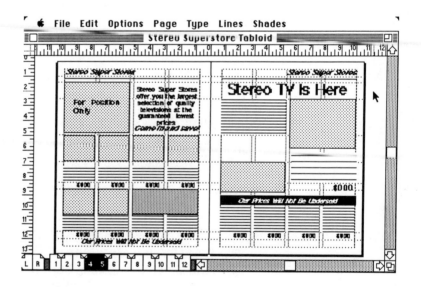

To hide all non-printing guides temporarily, click on the "Guides" command. You'll see just the text and graphics that will appear when you print your publication (Fig. 5-24).

Snap-To Guides

A lot of PageMaker's power comes from its Snap-To Guides. Margins, columns, and ruler guides exert a magnetic "pull" that makes it easy to align text and graphics accurately. Simply position the pointer in the general area of the margins, columns, or alignment guides, and PageMaker will do the rest.

It's occasionally necessary to turn this magnetic power off, however—for example, when you want to align text and graphics next to, but not necessarily right on, a margin or column guide. This might be the case when you wanted to add a vertical column rule between two column guides.

With Snap-To Guides active, the rule would tend to snap between the left or right hand columns. When Snap-To Guides is turned off, you can position it exactly where you want it.

Figure 5-24

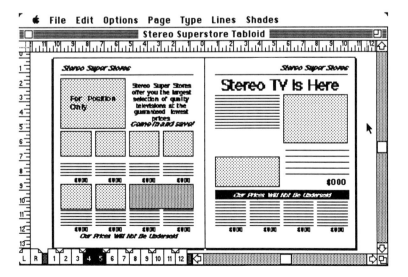

Column Guides

You can create up to 20 columns on a page. Columns define the width of the text you place within them.

When you choose "column guides" and you're working with single pages, you're presented with a dialog box (Fig. 5-25) that allows you to specify the number of columns you want on the page, plus the space you want between them.

There are two Column Guides dialog boxes. When working with double-sided facing pages (Fig. 5-26), you are given the choice of using different column setups for the left and right-hand pages.

You can use the Column Guides feature either while setting-up master pages, or to define columns for individual pages. This permits you to deviate from your publication's master design for non-standard pages, such as worksheets and indexes.

Unless you specify otherwise, columns are spaced equally on a page (Fig. 5-27).

Figure 5-25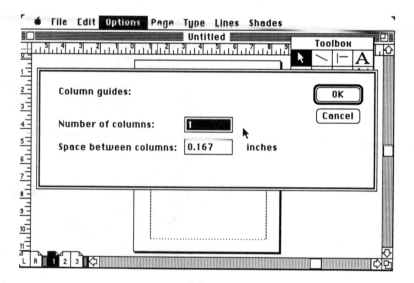

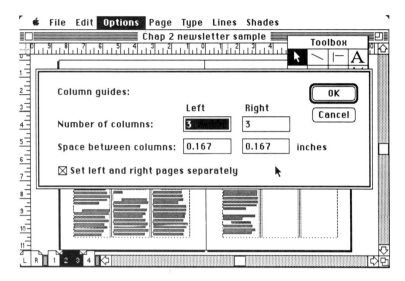

Figure 5-26

By using the Select tool in the PageMaker toolbox, however, you can create custom columns—or columns of unequal widths (Fig. 5-28)— by dragging a pair of column guides to the left or right.

Lock Guides

With Lock Guides turned off, it's possible to change your column settings accidentally when selecting adjacent text or graphics. This can create three columns of slightly irregular width, for example, instead of the three equal-width columns you had originally created.

The Lock Guides command permits you to lock column and ruler guides into place so you don't accidentally move them. This protects your master page setups from accidental change.

Rounded Corners

The "Rounded Corners" command presents you with a dialog box (Fig. 5-29) that permits you to change the appearance of the corners of the boxes you use as graphics elements. You can have right angles, or choose from a selection of curves.

127

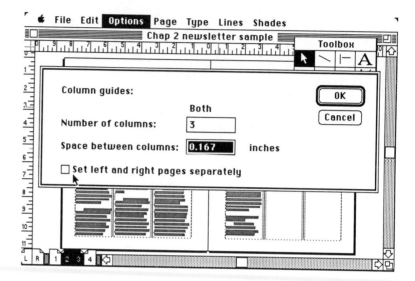

Figure 5-27

Figure 5-28

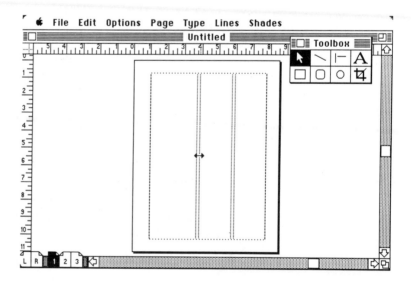

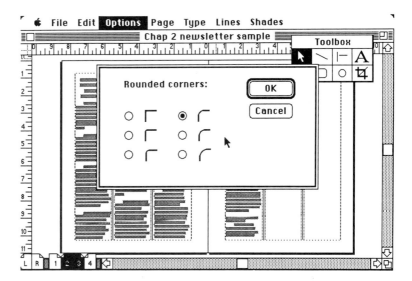

Figure 5-29

Toolbox

Clicking on the Toolbox command removes the Toolbox from the PageMaker screen. This prevents it from covering part of your publication when facing pages are shown, as well as making available more pasteboard area for storing text and graphics prior to their placement in your PageMaker publication.

Scroll Bars

The scroll bars can be removed from the PageMaker screen (Figs. 5-30 and 5-31), providing more working space on the PageMaker pasteboard.

PAGE MENU

The commands in the Page menu are used primarily to change your view of the PageMaker publication you are working on. You can view the overall appearance of a complete page or two-page spread displayed at the largest size it will fit on the screen or you can view your

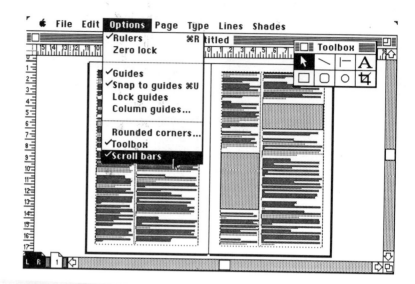

Figure 5-30

Figure 5-31

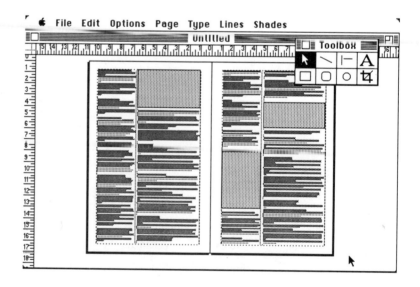

work at various degrees of enlargement or reduction.

Both the PC and Macintosh versions of PageMaker permit you to access these commands directly with keyboard and mouse shortcuts. Unless you are working with a full-page monitor, you are likely to use the Page commands quite frequently.

The Page commands also make it possible for you to move quickly from page to page in your publication, as well as to add and delete pages from it.

Actual Size

This displays your publication at approximately its actual size—depending, of course, on the size of the screen of your monitor. With a Microsoft Mouse on the PC version of PageMaker, you can go directly to Actual Size by clicking the secondary mouse button. Alternatively, you can use the keyboard shortcut and press Control-1. The "1" stands for 100%.

With the Macintosh version, you can go to 100 % size with Command-1.

75% Size

This size permits a large-scale view of your publication showing more of its page than the Actual Size one. The keyboard shortcut is Control-7 (Command-7 on the Macintosh).

50% Size

At this size, PageMaker shows slightly more of the page than it does at 75% size. On most monitors, you will still be able to make out individual words. Control-5 in the PC version of Pagemaker brings you to this half-size image; Command-5 is the Macintosh-version equivalent.

131

Fit in Window

Fit in Window shows a complete page or two-page spread on your monitor. The keyboard shortcut is Control-W for the PC version or Command-W for the Macintosh version.

200% Size

This shows the page at approximately twice its actual size, and is frequently used for accuracy in aligning text and graphics precisely. The PC keyboard shortcut is Control-2; on the Macintosh it's Command-2.

Go to Page

This command presents a dialog box that lets you move directly to the page number you specify. It also allows you to move directly to either the left or right-hand master pages.

Go to Page is especially useful when working on large documents. It makes it unnecessary for you to scroll through the numbers to get to the point you want.

Insert Pages

This command presents you with the dialog box shown in Fig. 5-32. The Insert Pages command permits you to specify how many pages you want to add, and whether you want to add them before or after the page currently selected. Page numbers of the pages following the insertion are automatically adjusted to reflect the pages you have inserted.

Remove Pages

You can remove one or more pages from your PageMaker publication, along with everything on them. The page numbering on the re-

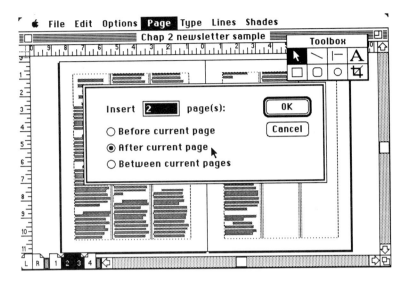

Figure 5-32

maining pages is automatically changed to reflect the pages that have been removed.

Caution! Remove Pages" is one of the few PageMaker commands that cannot be undone. You can't change your mind after pages have been removed and restore them to your publication--once they're gone, they're gone.

Display Master Items

This command permits you to remove or restore text and graphics brought over to the page you are working on from your publication's master pages.

Copy Master Guides

This displays (or hides) non-printing guides, such as columns and alignment rules, brought from a master page to the page you are working on.

TYPE MENU

The Type menu permits you to change the appearance of type selected with the Text tool, accessed by highlighting the large letter "A" in the PageMaker Toolbox. You will probably work frequently with the Type commands' dialog boxes. No other group of commands has such a profound influence on the appearance of your publication, and much of PageMaker's sophisticated power comes from the commands in this section.

You can set type specifications *before* you enter text from the keyboard or place it from word processed files. You can also change the specifications of text that has already been placed. To do this, you first highlight it with the Text tool found in the PageMaker Toolbox and then indicate the new specifications.

Helpful Hint

It is important to remember that you must set the type specifications **before** you highlight the "A" in the PageMaker Toolbox. If you first select "A" in the Toolbox, and then change a type specification, text will still appear in the form that was in effect when the "A" was selected.

Normal

This command permits you to replace boldface, italic, underlined, or strike-through type with plain type.

Bold

Permits you to convert text to boldface.

Italics

Permits you to convert existing text to italics.

134

Underline

You can underline new or existing text.

Strikethru

Strikethru is used in legal documents to "cross out" text.

Type Specs

The dialog box that appears when you select the Type Specs command gives you total control over both typeface and type size. You can also adjust leading, or vertical spacing between lines.

The dialog box (Fig. 5-33) shows the various typefaces available with the printer you have chosen. Use the up and down arrows to scroll through the possibilities. Double-clicking when the typeface you want has been highlighted selects it.

Figure 5-33

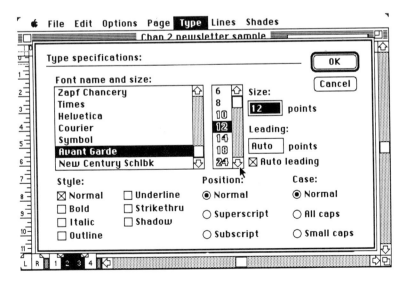

Similarly, the dialog box shows you the range of type sizes available to you. You can scroll up and down through the list, or simply type in the point size you want.

You are immediately informed if the type size you have chosen is not available on the printer you have targeted. (For example, with Hewlett-Packard LaserJet printers, you can choose only those type sizes that are available on the font cartridges or downloadable fonts you selected during the "Target Printer" or "Page Setup" operations.)

You can also adjust type position--normal, superscript or subscript (the latter two also adjust the type size)--and can specify whether you want type that is both upper and lower case (i.e., normal), all capitals, or small capitals.

Important Shortcuts

Because the ability to change type specifications is so intrinsic to PageMaker's power, PageMaker has made many of these commands especially easy to use. PageMaker for the PC, for example, uses the ten function keys to permit you to change the appearance of type without having to access the Type Specs menu. These functions are:

- ■ **Function Key 5** chooses normal type.

- ■ **Function Key 6** chooses boldface type.

- ■ **Function Key 7** chooses italic type.

- ■ **Function Key 8** underlines highlighted type.

- ■ **Function Key 9** chooses the next smaller type size.

- ■ **Function Key 10** chooses the next larger type size.

In the Macintosh environment, PageMaker 2.0 permits you to increase or decrease type size by pressing the Option, Command, and Greater Than (for increasing type size) or Less Than (for reducing type size) keys simultaneously. The Shift and Option keys are used together by themselves to restore normal type, or are used with B (for bold), I (for italics) or slash (for strike-through) type.

Paragraph

The Paragraph dialog box (Fig. 5-34) offers you even more control over the appearance of your publication. You can specify the spacing between paragraphs, paragraph alignment and indents, and letter spacing and hyphenation.

Hyphenation can be performed automatically—the mode you will normally use—or you can choose to be prompted at each line-ending where a word is to be split.

Indents/tabs

This dialog box presents you with a ruler. On it, you can change the position and alignment of up to 20 tab stops. You also specify the leader, or pattern, that fills the space between tab stops. You can choose a series of dots or dashes, a solid line, or a sequence of any two characters.

Figure 5-34

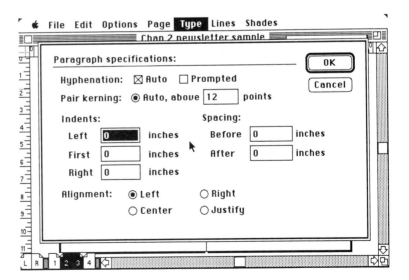

Spacing

Another sophisticated PageMaker typesetting tool, Spacing (Fig. 5-35) controls the amount of horizontal space PageMaker inserts between words and characters. It also varies the spacing between words in justified type, (explained below), and the hyphenation zone that determines how and where words in unjustified text will be hyphenated.

Align Left, Align Center, Align Right, Justify

These commands permit you to define how words and paragraphs will relate to the column guides that contain them. Most of your type will probably be set "Align Left." "Align Center" is used to center text such as headlines. "Align right" is often used for captions.

The Justify option is used to create paragraphs containing lines of equal length. Justification adds tiny spaces between words so the last characters in each line extend to the right hand margins. Examples of justified and non-justified type are shown in Fig. 5-36. Justification increases word density, meaning more words can fit in a given column of type.

Figure 5-35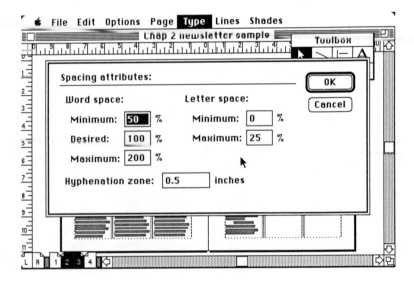

Right-Aligned Text	Justified Text	Centered Text	Left-Aligned Text
Get your text and graphics documents ready before you start PageMaker.	Get your text and graphics documents ready before you start PageMaker.	Get your text and graphics documents ready before you start PageMaker.	Get your text and graphics documents ready before you start PageMaker.
Set up project-oriented folders: one for all the documents for a particular publication, one for "boiler-plate" or standard documents of text and graphics, and one for your applications.	Set up project-oriented folders: one for all the documents for a particular publication, one for "boilerplate" or standard documents of text and graphics, and one for your applications.	Set up project-oriented folders: one for all the documents for a particular publication, one for "boiler-plate" or standard documents of text and graphics, and one for your applications.	Set up project-oriented folders: one for all the documents for a particular publication, one for "boiler-plate" or standard documents of text and graphics, and one for your applications.
Want to use just part of a long document? Save just that part as a new document. Or, if the document is from a Macintosh application, cut the part you want to the Clipboard, then paste it into your PageMaker publication.	Want to use just part of a long document? Save just that part as a new document. Or, if the document is from a Macintosh application, cut the part you want to the Clipboard, then paste it into your PageMaker publication.	Want to use just part of a long document? Save just that part as a new document. Or, if the document is from a Macintosh application, cut the part you want to the Clipboard, then paste it into your PageMaker publication.	Want to use just part of a long document? Save just that part as a new document. Or, if the document is from a Macintosh application, cut the part you want to the Clipboard, then paste it into your PageMaker publication.
Make separate word-processing documents for headlines and captions — or type them directly on the page with PageMaker.	Make separate word-processing documents for headlines and captions — or type them directly on the page with PageMaker.	Make separate word-processing documents for headlines and captions — or type them directly on the page with PageMaker.	Make separate word-processing documents for headlines and captions — or type them directly on the page with PageMaker.

Figure 5-36

The opposite of justified type is "flush left/ragged right." Paragraphs set ragged-right are characterized by equal word spacing and white spaces at the ends of most lines. Few words are hyphenated—only those that would leave an unnaturally large gap at the end of a line.

Reverse Type

Reverse type (Fig. 5-37) is white type appearing against a black background. Reverse type is frequently used for headlines to add emphasis to them.

LINES MENU

The various options offered by the Lines menu shown in Fig. 5-38 are self-explanatory. They permit you to control the width and pattern of new and existing lines.

Your width and pattern choices will be reflected in the lines you draw with the PageMaker drawing tools selected from the Toolbox. Lines, boxes and circles will be affected.

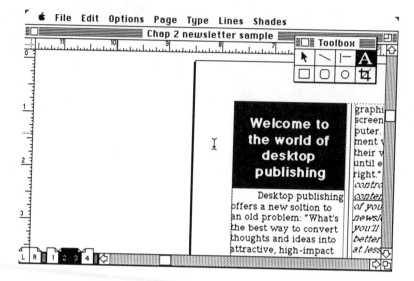

Figure 5-37

Figure 5-38

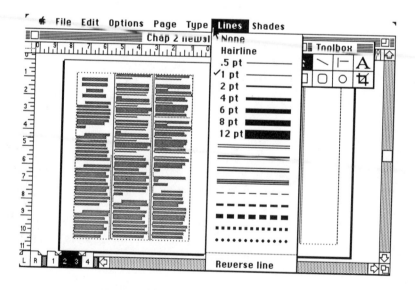

Helpful Hints

The "None" choice permits you to draw a box that will appear simply as a filled-in area without a border. For example, use "None" if you are drawing squares and want to have grey squares without a black border.

Similarly, choose "None" if you want to indicate the placement of lines of copy or a graphic in a layout without a border (Fig. 5-39).

Reverse Lines lets you draw white lines on a dark background.

Use double lines, and combinations of thick and thin lines, for page borders or to call attention to headlines and subheads. These can be used to draw boxes, or to create rules above and below the text.

SHADES MENU

Boxes and circles can be filled with a variety of shades and patterns accessible from the Shades Menu shown in Fig. 5-40. Box and circle shading can be black, or 10%, 20%, 30%, 40%, 60% and 80% tints (shades of gray).

Figure 5-39

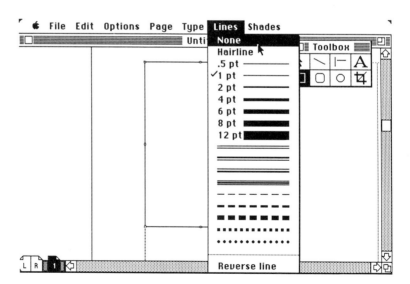

"None" is transparent, allowing what is behind it to be seen. Use "None" when drawing a box around a headline.

"White" covers text and graphics behind it. Use "white boxes," for example, when you want to hide repeating master page elements on an individual basis.

Menu Summary

This concludes our examination of the basic PageMaker commands. As you can see, there are a lot of them, but they are logically organized and, in many cases, self-explanatory. Regardless of whether you're using PageMaker Version 2.0 for the Macintosh or PageMaker for the PC, you will soon become familiar with them, as well as with the keyboard shortcuts that make them easy to use.

Figure 5-40

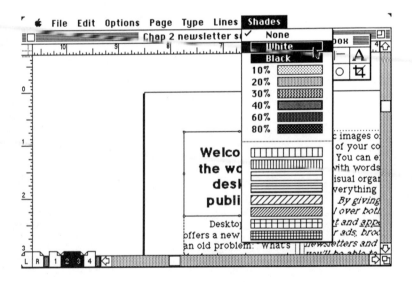

Putting PageMaker to Work

Watching Your First Project Take Shape

Now that you have familiarized yourself with the basic PageMaker commands, it's time to begin your first project. Like learning how to ride a bicycle, there is no substitute for direct hands-on experience.

The example that follows is designed to complement, not replace, the excellent PageMaker tutorial that accompanies both PageMaker for the PC and PageMaker Version 2.0 for the Macintosh. This tutorial is highly recommended. It provides an excellent introduction to the basic PageMaker commands for placing text and resizing graphic images.

143

Instead of repeating the material contained in the PageMaker tutorial, this chapter is intended to present the major steps involved in creating a typical PageMaker publication from scratch, as well as to review the major PageMaker commands and show how they interact with each other. It's also intended to make you aware of some possible problem areas and show you how to avoid them.

The following sequence assumes that you have already set up your computer and printer and are familiar with their basic operation. To help you relate the information to something you're familiar with, we'll use the book you're reading as an example.

Page Setup

The starting point for any PageMaker publication, regardless of whether you're preparing overhead transparencies, newspaper ads, or newsletters, is to open a new file by pulling down the File menu and releasing the mouse button on "New." You are immediately presented with the Page Setup dialog box shown in Fig. 6-1.

Immediately, one of the major differences between PageMaker and other desktop publishing programs becomes obvious. With Page-

Figure 6-1

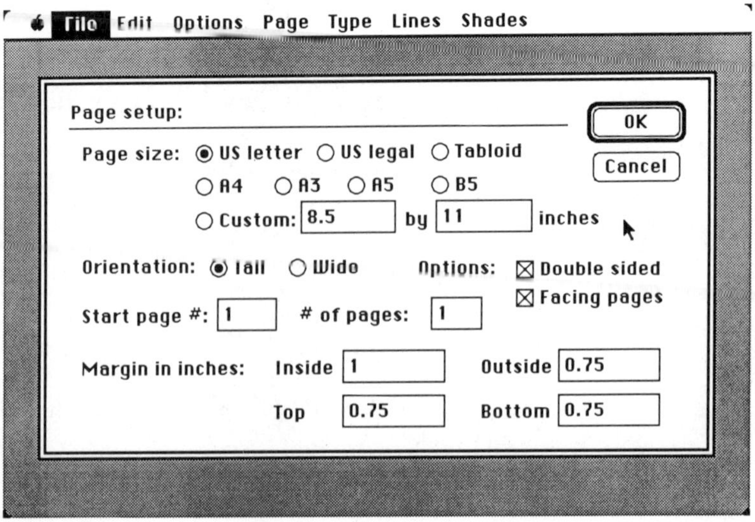

Maker, you can specify any size publication, from business card size up to 17 by 22 inches. Other desktop publishing programs limit you to the basic European and American paper sizes, or present you with a standard 11-by-17-inch tabloid. To select a nonstandard page size, click on the first box, (which will turn black), and type in the horizontal width of your publication. Then, tab over to the second box, which will also turn black, and type in the desired vertical dimension.

At this point, you can also define whether you want your publication to be vertically or horizontally oriented.

The Page Setup box opens with two frequently selected options already selected for you, "double-sided" and "facing pages."

"Double-Sided" appears as a default because PageMaker is often used to prepare brochures or newsletters. Double-sided publications frequently have a deeper inside margin, needed for binding or stapling. Click on "Single-Sided" only if you are going to work on single-sided publications, for example a series of transparencies for overhead projection.

Note that when you click on "Double-Sided," the "X" in the box disappears, and the Facing Pages option turns grey. This is because when you are printing on only one side of a sheet of paper, you do not see both pages side by side.

Note that "Facing Pages" can be defeated separately. This is useful if you are working with a big-screen monitor such as the Radius FPD. Defeating the Facing Pages option permits you to to concentrate on a single page at one time.

The Start Page # option is normally "1." However, if you are preparing each chapter of a book as a separate PageMaker file—a recommended procedure—you would replace "1" with the correct page number.

Next, you can define the number of pages you expect to have in your PageMaker publication. This is not critical, as you can add or subtract pages at any point, using the Insert or Remove commands found under the Page menu.

The final step in page setup is to define the margins, or image area, of your publication. This is the starting point for creating a distinct "look" for your publication. By choosing deep margins, you create visually inviting, "open" publications. Narrow margins fill a page more completely.

Note that the inside margin default of one inch is larger than the top, bottom, and outside margin defaults. The extra inside margin space is sufficient for most double-sided publications. This space is needed to provide room for binding or stapling your publication.

When setting up margins, be aware of the limitations of most laser printers. The image area of most laser printers, and many typesetters, is smaller than the paper size. For example, the Apple LaserWriter's image area is approximately 8 by 10.9 inches. If you create a larger publication than your printer can handle, the outside edges will not be printed.

If necessary, you can get around this limitation by reducing page size during printing—for example, specifying "97%" instead of the accepting the scaling default of "100%" in the printer dialog box (Fig. 6-2) if you are using a PostScript-based printer such as an Apple Laser-Writer or QMS PS-800. (Scaling is not possible with Hewlett-Packard LaserJets, unless you are using Hewlett-Packard's Desktop Publishing Kit based on the HP Document Description Language.)

Your reduced-size printed page can later be enlarged by 3% on an office copier. This type of scaling is useful if you are using your Laser-Writer for proofing your document, but intend to have it typeset on an Allied Linotronic 101P.

The only difference between the page setup for PageMaker for the PC and Version 2.0 for the Macintosh is that PageMaker for the PC reminds you of which printer has been targeted. This is presumably because PCs are more likely to be used with multiple printers.

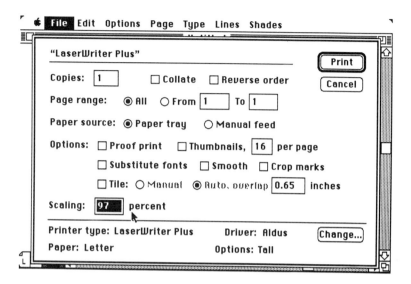

Figure 6-2

Note that you can, if you like, return to the Page Setup box at any time. This permits you to defeat—or activate—the Facing Pages option, for example.

Master Pages

A great deal of PageMaker's power comes from its Master Pages feature. The Master Pages option permits you to establish and maintain a distinct graphic identity for your publication. Master Pages permits you to establish borders, columns, page numbers, and text alignments that will be automatically repeated on each page.

Helpful Hints

There are two potential problem areas associated with Master Pages. One arises from neglecting the Master Page option, and immediately beginning work on the first page of a publication. Avoid this temptation, unless you are sure you are preparing just a single-page document. If you neglect to establish master pages, you will be forced to start each page from scratch. At best, this will waste a lot of your time. At worst, each page of your document will look slightly different.

Another pitfall to be avoided is setting up your master pages, and then forgetting to leave Master Pages before beginning work on your publication. Instead, you begin placing text and graphic images in the Master Pages area. You will soon realize your mistake when you turn to the next PageMaker page, and find that everything you placed on the last one is also there! Using "Select All" and "Cut," it is possible to salvage some of your work, but only with time and frustration.

Columns

One of the first steps you are likely to take in setting up your master pages is to define the size and placement of columns. Go to the Options menu, drag it down, and click on "Column Guides." The dialog box shown if Fig. 6-3 presents itself. Notice that you are able to define both the number of columns and the space between them.

By clicking on the "Set Left and Right Pages Separately" option, you can establish columns for both pages at once.

Figure 6-3

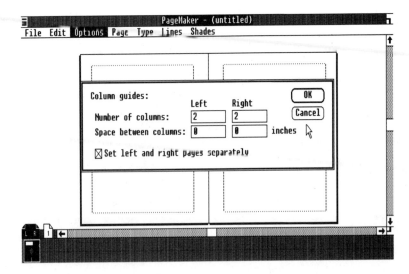

The "Number of Columns" option box is already highlighted. If you want a different column spacing, tab to the "Space Between Columns" option box and enter a new figure. When you are satisfied with the number of columns and spacing, click on "OK" or use your Enter or Return key.

Note that columns appear evenly spaced, but you can change this. You can grab any pair of columns and move them to the left or right.

This book, for example, uses a two-column format, with a narrow left-hand column for subheads and a wider right-hand column for body copy (Fig. 6-4).

Note that when you change column widths, you change only one page at a time. To make sure that both pages are identical, use PageMaker's rulers to measure the width of the narrow column accurately. To do this, choose Rulers from the Options menu and place the pointer in the small box where the horizontal and vertical rulers intersect. Drag the box to the intersection of the left- and right-hand margins. To make a 1½-inch left-hand margin, use the select tool from the PageMaker toolbox to grab the column guide and move it until the left-hand ver-

Figure 6-4

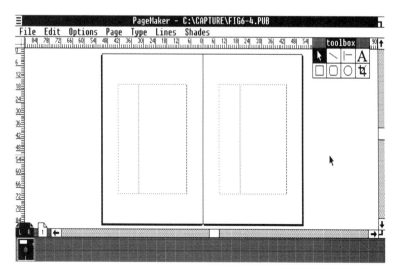

tical line is one and three-quarter inches from the intersection of the margins.

For accuracy, you might want to go to a larger screen magnification. To go to an "Actual Size" view using PageMaker for the PC, press Control-1 or move the pointer to the intersection of the column guides and top margin of the paper and click on the right hand mouse button. To go to "Actual Size" with the Macintosh Version 2.0, move the pointer to the intersection of the column guides and top margin, press the Command and Option keys, and click the mouse button.

To return to normal page view on the PC version of PageMaker, click the right hand button. Similarly, Option-Command-Click will return you to Fit in Screen in the Macintosh version of PageMaker.

Next, place your pointer once again in the small box where the left- and right-hand margins intersect, increase to Actual Size view, and drag the ruler to the top-left corner of the right hand page. Once again, select and move the column guides to the one-and-three-quarter-inch point.

Design Elements

The next step is to include any design elements that will be repeated on all the pages of your publication. These elements frequently include borders. Borders can be created easily using PageMaker's line-drawing tool or box-drawing tools.

Perhaps the simplest page border is a plain box around the entire page. Once it is drawn, you can vary the thickness of the lines forming the box. Or, you can create borders using a combination of thick and thin lines. Borders do not have to extend the full width of a page.

The default line thickness is one point, or $1/72$-inch. To make a rule thicker, select it using the PageMaker's Select tool. You do this by placing the pointer on the rule and clicking the mouse button. Two round dots appear, one at each end of the line. These two dots indicate that the rule has been selected. Next, go to the "Lines" menu, and click on the "6 Point" option. The line immediately becomes thicker than it was when you created it.

The rules above the page numbers on each page of this book, and those alongside the running heads at the top of each page, were created in this way.

Alignment Guides

It is important that each column of body copy begin the same distance from the top of the page. It is equally important that the bottoms of all the columns line up. PageMaker makes it easy to do this with its *alignment guides.*

To align the tops of all copy areas, pull down a non-printing alignment guide from the horizontal ruler at the top of the PageMaker screen. Pull down a second horizontal rule and use it to indicate the bottom of the copy area (Fig. 6-5). These guides will be used when placing text.

Figure 6-5

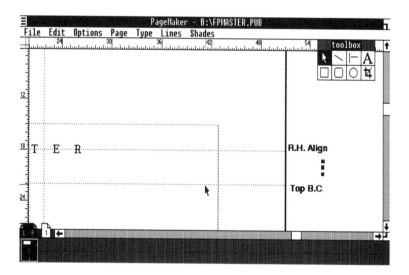

Headers and Footers

In addition to allowing you to place graphics elements automatically on each page, PageMaker's Master Page function permits you to have words appear automatically on each page. In the case of this book, the book title appears on the upper-left-hand corner of each page, and the chapter title on each right-hand page.

Adding Type

To add repeating information to your sample, select the Text tool from the PageMaker toolbox by clicking on the large letter "A." Notice how the pointer turns into an "I-beam." Place this I-beam where you want to begin typing and click. Type the words, "Using Aldus PageMaker."

Then, highlight the text by moving the I-beam to the left hand edge of the words, dragging the pointer through them. Then, click on "Type Specs . . ." from the Type menu. The Type Specs dialog box will appear similar to the way it did in Chapter One. You can now choose the typeface and type size you feel is most appropriate. (Note that, in the case of this book, the repeating title is set in small caps with extra spacing between the letters.)

Follow the same procedure to add the chapter title to each right-hand page. Note that the chapter title is set in upper and lower case italics, to providing a visual contrast to the book title.

Page Numbering

Besides allowing you to automatically add graphics elements and alignment guides, PageMaker's Master Page feature can number your pages for you, as well.

Select the Text tool, and place the I-beam at the position on the page where you want page numbers to appear, and click. To add page numbers using the PC version of PageMaker, enter the key sequence Control-Shift-#. On the Macintosh Version 2.0 version of PageMaker, the correct key sequence in Command-Option-P.

Pages will be automatically numbered from then on. As a refinement, you can also created composite page numbers, where words are added to the numbers. Examples of composite numbers are "Page 2" and "Section 3, Page 2."

An example of preliminary-layout master pages used for this book is shown in Fig. 6-6.

With this, your master pages are complete. You can click on the "Page One" icon and begin to place type and assemble your publication.

TEXT OPERATIONS

Placing Text with PageMaker for the PC

Once you have defined your master pages, it's time to begin placing text. The text of this book was written with Microsoft Word 3.1.

Figure 6-6

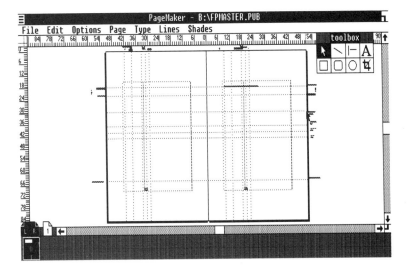

PageMaker for the PC and PageMaker Version 2.0 for the Macintosh make it easy to locate specific word-processed files. With PageMaker for the PC, when you select "Place" from the File menu, you are presented with a list of disk drives. If a coworker has prepared the files on a floppy drive inserted in drive A: or B:, clicking on drive A: or B: will get you a list of the files on the disk in that drive.

In most cases, however, your text will probably have been saved in your word-processing subdirectory, or in a subdirectory contained inside that one. PageMaker for the PC makes it easy to locate the specific directory or subdirectory in which the files are located. Simply click on the series of dots, or ellipses, at the bottom of the screen. This will cause a list of subdirectories to appear. Double-click—press the mouse button quickly twice in a row—on the subdirectory you need, and its files will be displayed.

Alternatively, you can scroll through the list of subdirectories using the "up" and "down" arrows. When the subdirectory you want to access is highlighted, click on "it to see its contents.

When you have located the specific file you want to place, click on Place.

Note that you are offered the option of "Retain Format" or "Text Only." Use the Retain Format option if you already set up typefaces, type sizes and line spacings when you wrote the copy. Choose Text Only if you want to accept PageMaker's default specifications and lose whatever formatting may be contained in the document.

After pressing Return or clicking on Place, you will be returned to the PageMaker screen showing your publication. Now, however, the pointer has been changed to resemble the upper left-hand corner of a book or page. Place the pointer in the upper left hand corner of the column in which you want the text to appear, and click. The type will flow down the column, stopping when it hits the bottom of the page, a graphic object, or text already in place.

Note that the top of the text block is indicated by a line with a loop at the top, as well as with small circles at the right- and left-hand sides. A similar line appears at the bottom of the text block. The loop in the center of the bottom line contains either a plus sign (+) or a number sign (#). The plus sign indicates that the word processed file contains more text waiting to be placed. The number sign indicates that the entire file has been placed.

A "+" sign is also used at the top of each column to show that the text in the column is continued from a preceding column (or page).

Depending on the screen view you are using, type may or may not be readable. In most cases, if you are using the Fit in Window default, type will be indicated by small x's. If you go to an actual-size screen view, however, you will be able to read the words you have placed.

To continue placing text (Fig. 6-7), simply click on the plus sign at the bottom of the first column. Move the loaded pointer to the top of the second column and click again. Type will now flow down this column. You can continue this process until the entire word-processed file has been placed—as indicated by the appearance of the "#" symbol following the last line of type.

If your file is too long to fit on a single PageMaker page, or on facing

Figure 6-7

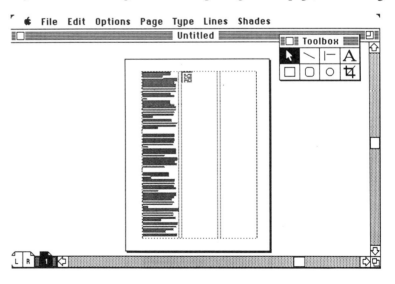

pages shown on your screen, simply move the pointer down to the page number icons, and click on the next page—or pair of facing pages. While your text pointer is "loaded" with type, you can also use the Insert Pages feature to add additional pages to your PageMaker document.

Placing Text with PageMaker Version 2.0 for the Macintosh

Placing text with PageMaker Version 2.0 on the Macintosh is very similar to doing so on the PC. After executing the Place command, you are first offered a list of files contained within the PageMaker folder. To view other files—if, for example, your word processed files are on another drive such as a second hard disk or an 800K floppy disk—click on Drive.

In most cases, though, you'll click on the icon representing your hard disk. This will present you with a list of all of the file folders contained there. Click on the folder that contains the file you want to place in your PageMaker publication. Again, you have the choice of deciding whether you want to import a formatted file or have Page-Maker reformat the file.

Scroll through the choices presented and double-click, or click on Place, when the appropriate file is highlighted. When you do, text will flow down the column the same way it did with PageMaker for the PC.

Placing Text with TOPS

If you are using Centram's TOPS networking system with the Macintosh, when you click on Drive the name of other computers currently active in the network as file servers will appear on the Macintosh's screen. This allows you to place text prepared on any of those other computers, regardless of whether they're Apple Macintosh or MS-DOS systems.

Changing Column Width

Once type has been placed in a PageMaker publication, it can be modified in a variety of ways.

One of the first things you might want to experiment with is changing column width. To change the width of a column of type, choose the Select tool from the PageMaker toolbox, and click on one of the two small circles on the line at the top of the text block.

For example, drag the right hand dot to the left. Notice how the entire column of text becomes narrower (Fig. 6-8).

Or, drag the right-hand dot further to the right. Notice how the entire column becomes wider (Fig. 6-9).

You can also shorten the length of columns. For example, as illustrated in Fig. 6-10, the text now extends below the alignment guide indicating the lower boundary of text area. To cure this, simply click on the bottom "+" sign, move the bottom line up to the alignment guide, and release the mouse button.

Remember, however, that the text is all joined together. Thus, as you shorten column one, the type removed from column one is moved to column two . . . and type that originally appeared at the bottom of column two is pushed to the top of column three.

Similarly, if you delete words, sentences or paragraphs from column one, text from column two will be moved back to fill in the empty space.

Reformatting Text

The Select All command in PageMaker for the PC and Version 2.0 for the Macintosh makes it easy to reformat entire word processed files. With this command, you can change the typeface, type size, line spacing, paragraph spacing, and word spacing of the text that has been placed in your PageMaker publication, as well as of text not yet

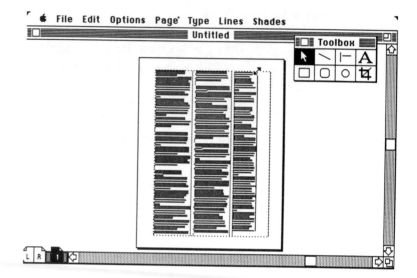

Figure 6-8

Figure 6-9

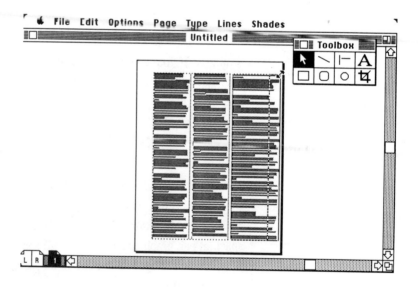

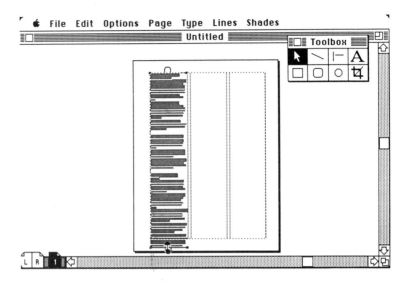

Figure 6-10

placed. You can also remove an entire word-processed file from your PageMaker publication.

Start by choosing the Text tool from the PageMaker toolbox and select (highlight) a portion of the text already placed. Do this by placing the I-beam pointer anywhere in the story, holding down the mouse button, and dragging the I-beam through a few sentences before releasing the button.

This section of text is now highlighted (Fig. 6-11). Now move to the Edit menu and click on the Select All command. Or, use the keyboard shortcut: Control-A if you're using PageMaker for the PC or Command-A with Macintosh Version 2.0 version of PageMaker.

Any editing or formatting you do at this point will affect the entire file. In most cases you will use one of the commands found under the Type menu to change the appearance of the file. You can change the typeface, type size, line spacing, alignment, letter spacing, word spacing or paragraph spacing of the entire story, using the commands described earlier. You can also adjust the hyphenation zone if you want to tighten-up or add more white space to your columns.

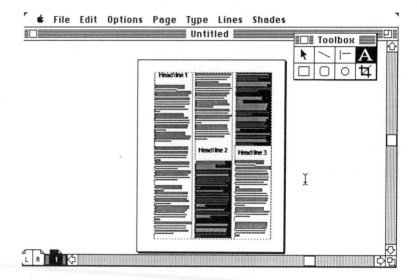

Figure 6-11

Using Select All you can also place the entire story on the Clipboard if you want to move it to another section of your PageMaker publication. (Be aware, however, that the clipboard memory is limited, and that your computer may not have enough memory to permit the clipboard to hold all of the story.)

You can, with Select All, even cut, or eliminate, the file completely.

Headlines

You can add headlines to your PageMaker publication in a variety of ways. Headlines require special treatment, as they often span one or more columns of your PageMaker publication.

Using PageMaker's Text tool, you can type in headlines at the spot where they're going to appear in your publication, or you can type them on the work area on the screen surrounding the publication and drag them to their final destination. This is often the easiest method.

Let's say you want to add a headline centered over the three columns of type shown in Fig. 6-12. Your first step is to make room for the headline by lowering the text that will be below it.

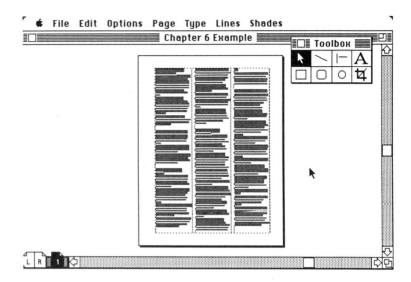

Figure 6-12

Start by pulling down a horizontal alignment guide from the ruler so your three columns of text will begin at the same point (Fig. 6-13).

You want to align each column of text to this guide. Click on the loop of the text block in the first column and move it down until it is aligned with the guide (Fig. 6-14).

Next, click on the "+" sign at the top of the second column, and pull it down until it, too, is aligned with the horizontal alignment guide. Do the same with the "+" sign at the top of the third column. The page will now look like the one in Fig. 6-15).

Now you can type in the headline you want. However, if you type it on the PageMaker publication where you intend it to appear, its length will be restricted by the column guides. Instead, drag the entire publication lower on the screen, creating a work area at the top in which to prepare the headline, which can then be moved into position.

If you're using the PC version of PageMaker, hold down the Alt key as you click on the left mouse button and drag the publication lower on the screen. With the Macintosh version, hold down the Option key as you click on the mouse button and drag.

161

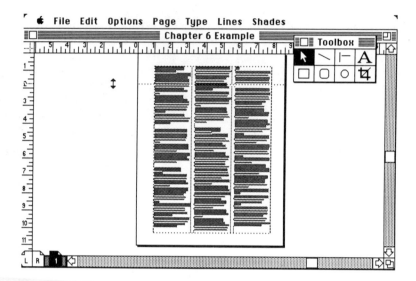

Figure 6-13

Figure 6-14

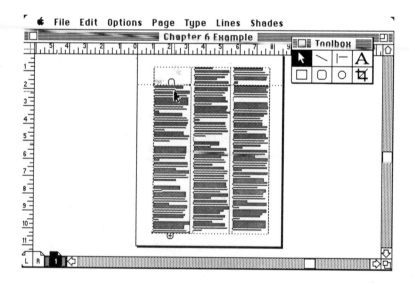

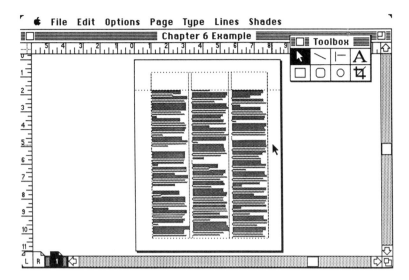

Figure 6-15

When there's sufficient space outside the publication to prepare your headline (Fig. 6-16), click on the Select tool in the PageMaker toolbox. Open the Type Specs dialog box (Fig. 6-17) and choose the typeface and type size you want for your headline.

Typically, if your body copy has been set in Times Roman, use a contrasting Helvetica Bold typeface. Choose a type size sufficiently larger than the body copy to make your headline stand out. Click on Centered.

With the types specifications set, you can select the Type tool in the PageMaker toolbox and type in your headline.

Then, choose the Select tool from the toolbox, place the pointer on the headline, and click the mouse button. You can then drag the headline into position in your publication.

The lines indicating the top and bottom of the newly created text block often will not be the same length as those delineating your columns. With the Select tool, grab a dot at the end of one of the lines and drag it until the headline margins equal the page margins (Fig. 6-18). This will ensure that your headline will be properly centered.

163

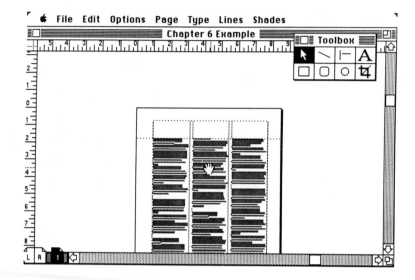

Figure 6-16

Figure 6-17

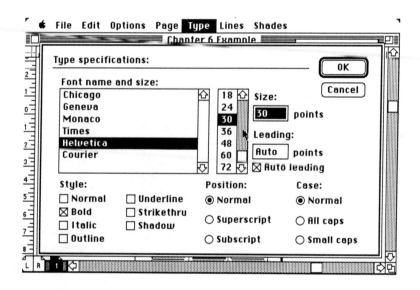

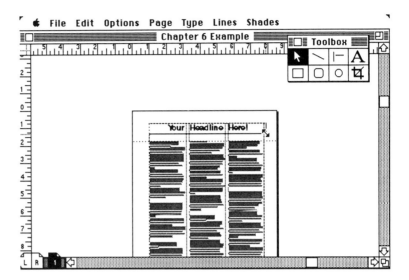

Figure 6-18

Modifying the Headline

Once the headline has been moved into place, it can be manipulated until it is in correct proportion to the rest of the page. By using the Text tool and selecting, or highlighting, the headline, you can return to the Type Specs dialog box and try out different type styles and sizes.

Leading

You can also tighten up line spacing, if too much white space appears between the lines. PageMaker's automatic line spacing default often results in too much white space between lines. Figure 6-19 shows what a difference line spacing can make in appearance. Note, too, that this book was set with extra line spacing, for a clean, easy-to-read look.

The effects of letter spacing, too, are often noticeable, especially in headlines. Awkward situations can occur between certain pairs of letters, as with the like small "o"s following large "T"s in Fig. 6-20.

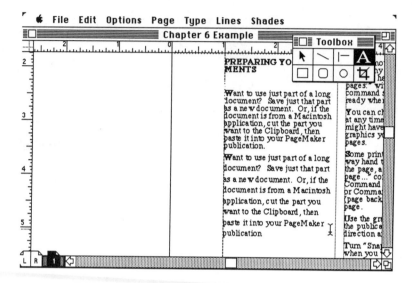

Figure 6-19

Kerning is the process of tightening up letter spacing for the best appearance. PageMaker permits you to specify kerning if you are unsatisfied with that which it has chosen for you. Compare the kerning in Fig. 6-20 with that in Fig. 6-21.

Interrupting Text

Sometimes, after text has been placed, you may want to interrupt it temporarily—perhaps to insert a photograph, or callout or pull quote (a quotation that summarizes the material around it).

To do this, choose the Select tool from the toolbox and click on the bottom window shade (the "+" sign on the line at the bottom of the text block). Drag the text upward to the point where you want to insert the photograph or callout and release the mouse button (Fig. 6-22).

Next, click on the "+" sign at the bottom of the text block. This will "load" the pointer with text. Move the pointer down to where you want to resume the text, and click. Your page should look like the one in Fig. 6-23.

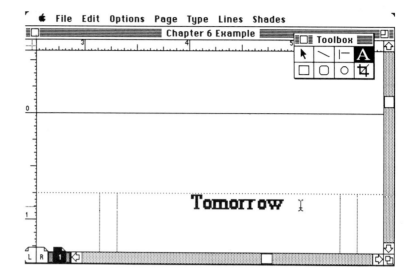

Figure 6-20

Figure 6-21

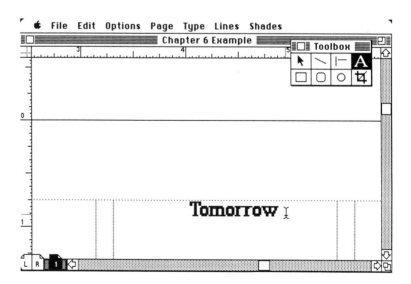

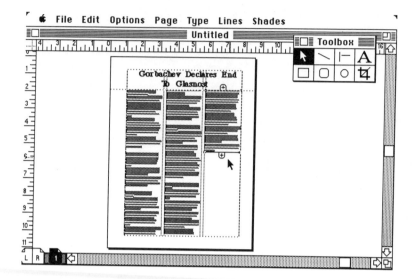

Figure 6-22

Figure 6-23

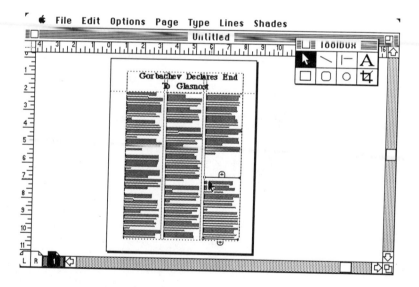

Remember that the text in the following blocks will have moved to accommodate the extra space. The story you have placed will be extended by the length of the "hole" you have just added.

Adding Graphics for Emphasis

With the "hole" in place, there are several things you can do. One is to use PageMaker's Rectangular drawing tool to make a shaded box within it (Fig. 6-24). To do this, select the Rectangle drawing tool and, starting at any corner of the area, drag the box until it fills the space you want. This box can be used to indicate the placement of a photograph or illustration that will be inserted later.

Or, if you are going to insert a callout, move to the Shades menu and choose an appropriate level of grey to fill in the box. From the "Shades" menu, choose the percentage of black that you feel is appropriate.

If you are going to use reversed type (white type against a black background), choose "Black." If you are going to use black type, choose a 20% or 30% shade to set it off (Fig. 6-25).

Figure 6-24

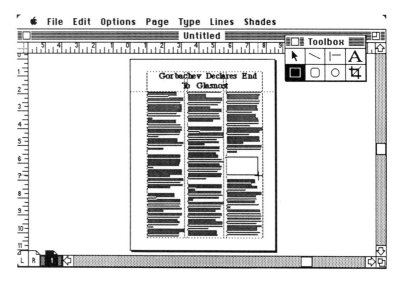

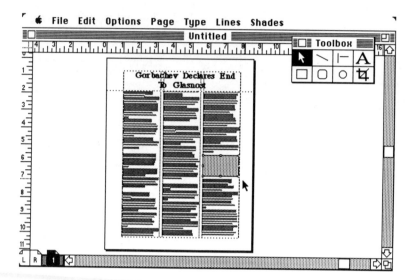

Figure 6-25

Finally, type in the quotation that summarizes the material you want to emphasize. Choose the Text tool and enter the text from your keyboard. After you have entered it, select the text and use the options presented by the "Text Specs" dialog box to change it to an appropriate typeface and type size.

Notice that something in Fig. 6-26 doesn't look quite right. This is because the type extends to the original column borders, and has no space around it. To cure this, choose the Select tool from the toolbox and expose the bars at the top and bottom of the quotation.

Drag the circle on the left-hand side of the top bar to the right, and the right-hand circle to the left. This will provide sufficient "air" to set off the quotation (Fig. 6-27).

Column Rules

To add a bit of character to the page, you might want to add thin rules between the columns. This exercise will illustrate the importance of being able to switch between various views of the PageMaker page.

170

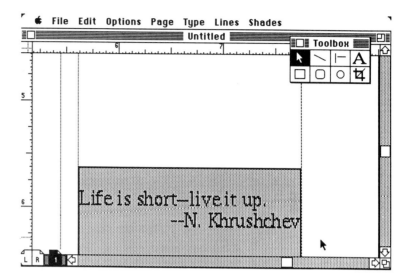

Figure 6-26

Figure 6-27

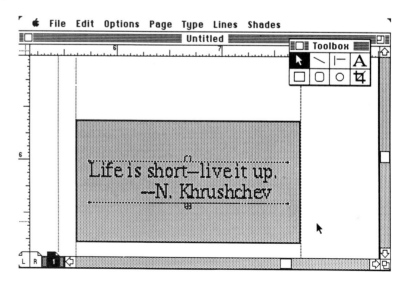

Select the Perpendicular Lines drawing tool and try to draw a line between columns one and two. Note how the line jumps back and forth between the two column guides. This is because of PageMaker's snap-to feature that assures properly lined-up type. To override the snap-to guides, start by going to an actual size page view.

With PageMaker for the PC, click the right-hand mouse button when the pointer is positioned in the area of the publication you want to view at actual size. With the Macintosh version, use Option-Command, and click when the pointer is at the point you want centered on the screen.

Next, from the Options menu, defeat the snap-to guides by releasing the mouse button when the pointer has this command highlighted. Now you will be able to draw vertical column rules between the column guides without the rules being attracted to one or the other of the columns (Fig. 6-28).

After you have drawn the vertical rules, return to the Options menu and reactivate the snap-to guides. This will ensure accuracy in further type placement.

Figure 6-28

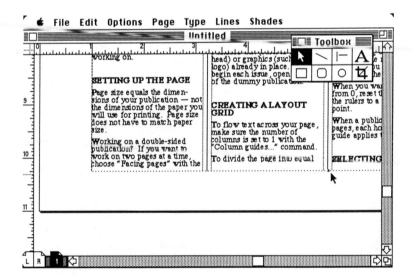

Saving Your Work

By now you have invested considerable time on this particular project, and it is important that you save your work. PageMaker automatically makes a "mini-save" of your work every time you change a page. However, it's strongly recommended that you get in the habit of saving your work periodically as you go along.

Let's face it, executing Control-S (on PageMaker for the PC) or Command-S (on the Macintosh version) is a lot easier than going back and reconstructing a page if something should happen—perhaps a brief power interruption that erases your work, or (as has happened to the author) crossing your legs and inadvertently unplugging the computer!

Printing

Printing is the final—and most rewarding—part of working with PageMaker. It is the time when your concepts and ideas become actualized.

It's advisable to print often, so that you can monitor continually how well your publication is turning out.

The Print command, found under the File menu, opens a dialog box (Fig. 6-29) that offers you several choices. You can print your entire publication, or simply the page you're currently working on. The Print dialog box allows you the option of enlarging or reducing page size, and of printing thumbnails—reduced-sized versions of each page. Up to 16 thumbnail pages can printed on a single sheet of paper.

The primary difference between PageMaker for the PC and the Macintosh Version 2.0 at this stage is that PageMaker for the PC allows you to select the printer you're going to be using. This is presumably because MS-DOS computers are more likely to be connected with local area networks containing more than one printer

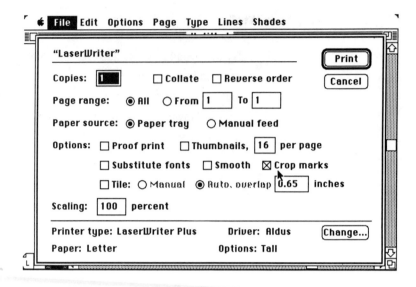

Figure 6-29

and printer type, while most Macintosh computers will be used with LaserWriter printers.

PROJECT MANAGEMENT

Regardless of the size of the project you're working on, the same three steps are involved:

1. Decide on the concept of the project.

2. Organize all the necessary parts.

3. Develop a firm mental picture of what the finished project should look like when completed.

This should be done *before* you turn on your computer and begin to design and produce your project.

Defining the Concept

The starting point is to ask yourself a number of questions about your project. In answering them, you'll find it will begin to take shape quickly.

Hint: You may want to use your word processor to enter the following Project Management Worksheet into your computer so you can print out copies as you need them. That way, you can create separate Project Management WorkSheets for each project easily.

The worksheet includes five types of questions, dealing with: schedule, purpose, environment, content and resources.

PROJECT PLANNING WORKSHEET

Description: _____ (What kind of project is it: newsletter, brochure, proposal, annual report, visuals, etc.?

Today's date: _____

Street date: _____ (When does this project have to be in the hands of customers or business associates?)

Print date: _____ (When does the project have to be ready for printing or duplication to meet the street date?)

Who is the audience? _____

What is the purpose of the project? _____

What action do you want the audience to take? _____

How does this project relate to other communications your firm has sent this audience? _____

How does it relate to competing messages? _____

What artwork is needed? _____

How many photographs, illustrations or charts will be included? _____

Has the copy already been written, or will it be written as you prepare your project? _____

How much copy is there? _____

Does the copy consist of one long section or many short ones? _____

Who is going to proofread the project? _____

How is the success of the project going to be measured? _____

Functionality

When using PageMaker, remember that graphic design is a tool, not an end in itself. Graphic design succeeds only to the point that it helps the reader better understand the message you're sending.

"Who is your audience," and "What is the message you're trying to communicate?" are basic questions that must be answered before you begin to design your publication.

The more detailed your answers, the more effective communication will be.

Appropriateness

Graphic design works to the extent that it is appropriate to the target audience and the message being communicated. A whimsical invitation to an informal kite-flying festival requires a totally different graphic approach than a financial prospectus involving hundreds of thousands of dollars.

Environment

Similarly, the environment in which your message must also be considered before you begin work. Few ads, brochures, or newsletters appear in a vacuum. Most print communications appear in the context of previous publications from your firm and your competitors.

Thus, before you begin working on an ad, newsletter or brochure, you have to consider the appearance of your existing corporate communications. Your current project must fit into your firm's existing corporate identity.

As a starting point, ask yourself: "What typefaces, colors and publication sizes do I use in current publications?"

Also, you have to design your publication in the context of the print communications your competition is sending your audience. Your newsletter or brochure must stand apart from those of your competitors. Otherwise, you might inadvertently end up generating business for them!

Getting Started

Next, you'll want to take an inventory of currently available materials that can be included in your publication: For example, does your firm's logo already exist as a graphics file ready to be placed into your PageMaker publication?

Have all the photographs and illustrations required been prepared? Has copy been planned or written? How much is there? How is it divided up?

The amount of artwork and copy you use will determine the number, size and placement of columns, as well as the type size you use. The number and size of the text files that will be incorporated in your publication will influence its design.

A newsletter consisting of numerous two and three paragraph stories will be designed differently than a publication built around one or two major sections or topics (Figs. 6-30 and 6-31).

Conceiving the Final Project

What do you want the final project to look like? By this time, you

Figure 6-30

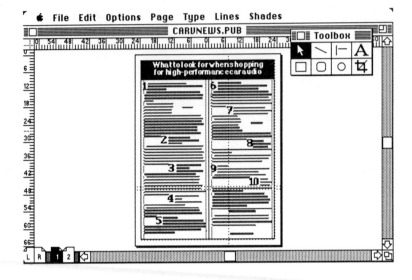

Figure 6-31

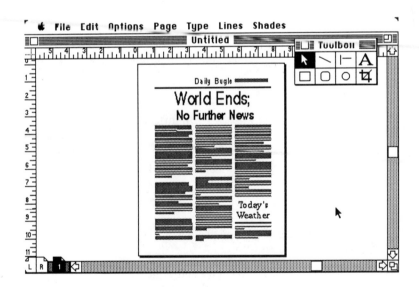

should have begun to develop some firm ideas concerning the appearance of the final project.

An excellent starting point for developing your design skills is to maintain a scrapbook or file folder of graphics ideas that you like . . . or dislike. Every time you run across an advertisement, annual report, brochure, newsletter or other printed communication that appeals to you, put it in this file.

Try to analyze what it is that you like about those pieces. Ask yourself questions such as:

- What do you like about each?

- What were the designer's goals?

- How did the designer achieve them?

- What margins were used (wide, narrow)?

- How many columns were used?

- How wide were the columns, and how were they spaced?

- What is it about the type that you like?

- How could the publication be improved?

- What would you do differently?

The point of maintaining a sample file is not to *copy* the work of others, but to *build upon* it. The goal is to use what others have already done as a starting point for your own publication designs. That makes it unnecessary for you to reinvent the wheel each time you sit down to work.

Your personal creativity will grow as you become more sensitive to the work of others. Ideas will come more easily and more frequently as you learn to take advantage of the experience of those who have gone before you.

C H A P T E R

Typical PageMaker Projects

PageMaker Case Studies

One of the best ways to understand PageMaker's power is to observe how quickly it can be put to work in typical business applications.

PRESENTATIONS

Visual presentations are an excellent place to start. At one time or another, just about everybody—corporate executives as well as self-employed professionals—have to address a meeting. Strong visuals and handout materials can greatly enhance the communicating power of even the best-prepared presentations.

181

PageMaker makes it possible to prepare your own good-looking visuals and handout materials, even under last-minute conditions.

Imagine, for example, that you're a department head. It's late Wednesday afternoon, and you suddenly find out that the head office is making an unscheduled visit tomorrow. This is your chance to present your ideas for reorganizing your department, or for developing an alternative marketing plan.

Or, imagine you're a consultant who has just one day to prepare a new business presentation. Or, perhaps you've just found out that tomorrow you have to present your ideas for reorganizing your client's advertising department.

The PageMaker Difference

In most cases, you would not have time to prepare visuals to accompany your presentation. With PageMaker, however, you can prepare visuals as well as powerful and convincing handout materials. These handouts will reinforce your ideas in the days and weeks that follow your presentation.

PageMaker Features

PageMaker's capacity to assist you in preparing strong visual-presentation materials quickly and easily for meetings and seminars comes from several of its features, notably Master Pages and its ability to print thumbnails (reduced-size copies of a publication).

PageMaker gives you immediate feedback as you work on your project. Because you can see what you're doing as you do it, you'll be able to improve your project as you work, instead of having to wait until it's finished to make corrections that should have been obvious earlier.

Page Setup

Start by opening a new file. This will automatically open the Page Setup dialog box.

There, turn off the Double-Sided feature. (Since you are not preparing a newsletter or book, you do not need extra space for binding on the inside margins.) Notice that the "Facing Pages" option is automatically disabled when you deselect the double-sided option.

Since extra space is not needed on the inside margins, tab over to the "Inside Margin" specification box. Type in ".75" to change it from the 1-inch default, and to match the .75-inch default that automatically appears in the top, bottom, and outside margin specification boxes.

Estimate the number of visuals you will be preparing. As a rule of thumb, plan to use one visual for every two-and-a-half minutes of your presentation.

Unless you are delivering a lengthy and complex speech, try to keep the number of visuals under 16. This is the maximum number of thumbnails that can be printed on a single sheet of 8½-by-11-inch paper (which allows for easy duplication on an office copier).

Click "OK" or hit the Return or Enter key when you have set up your page (Fig. 7-1).

Figure 7-1

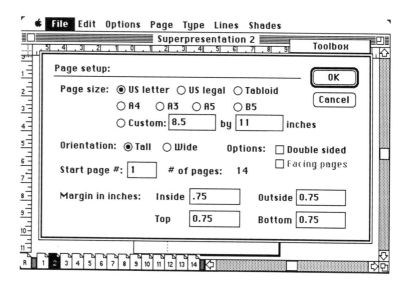

Master Pages

Click on the "Master Pages" icon at the bottom of the page, then open the "Options" menu and click on "Rulers."

When the rulers appear, click the pointer on the small box at the intersection of the left and right rulers. Drag the box to the point to where the left- and right-hand margins of the PageMaker page intersect. Notice how vertical and horizontal dimensions are now measured from this point.

Pull down the "Shades" menu bar, and click on "Black."

Then, go to the PageMaker toolbox and click on the Box drawing tool. Starting at upper-left-hand corner, (where the top and left-hand margins intersect), draw a large rectangle by holding down the mouse button and extending the box over to the right hand margin and down $3\frac{1}{2}$ inches. Release the mouse button. Notice how the rectangle turns black when you do.

Pull down a horizontal ruler from the top ruler and create a horizontal guide $1\frac{3}{4}$ inches from the top margin. This horizontal guide indicates the center line of the reversed (black-rectangle) headline area.

From the left hand ruler, pull over a vertical ruler and create a vertical guide at the 1-inch mark.

Pull-down additional horizontal rulers to indicate "4 inches" and "9 inches." These guides indicate the maximum copy area for your presentations. Copy that appears above or below these guides will make your visuals appear too crowded for easy reading.

Pull down an additional horizontal guide and place it $6\frac{1}{2}$-inches from the top margin. This will be the center line of the "copy" area of your presentations.

Finally, at the extreme bottom of the presentation area, use PageMaker's Place command to personalize your presentation and handout materials by adding your firm's logo (if it has been already been scanned and stored as a graphic image.) Or, personalize your presentation by typing in the title and date of your presentation. Choose an appropriate type size and typeface. Be sure to center your logo or presentation title. (Do not allow the material at the bottom of your visuals to dominate them, however.)

Open the "Options" menu and click on the "Lock Guides" command. This will prevent you from changing your Master Page setup inadvertently by grabbing and moving a guide instead of a block of text.

So far, your page should look like the one in Fig. 7-2.

Creating Your Presentation's Headline

Begin work on the headline by clicking on the Page One icon at the bottom of the PageMaker screen.

Pull down the Type menu, and click on "Reversed Type." This creates white words against a black background. Pull down the menu again, and click on "Align Center." Pull down the menu again, and open the Type Specs dialog box. (Remember, you can also go directly to that

Figure 7-2

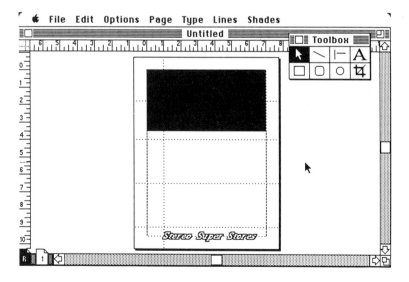

dialog box by using Command-T on the Macintosh, or Control-T on PageMaker for the PC.)

Change the type size to 38 points, and adjust the leading to 42 points. Click on "Bold" (Fig. 7-3).

Click on the Text icon in the PageMaker Toolbox, and choose an insertion point in the reversed area. Enter the headline of the first visual that will appear in your presentation.

Take a close look at your headline. It should contain between four and seven words, and all the lines should be about the same length. If the lines are not breaking to your satisfaction, and one line is much longer or shorter than another, use the "Enter" or "Return" key to force a line-break where you want it.

As you are typing in your headlines, do not hyphenate any words. Remember that short headlines are easier to read than long ones. Ideally, your headlines should contain just two, three, or—at most—four lines of type.

After you have entered your headline and all lines are about the same

Figure 7-3

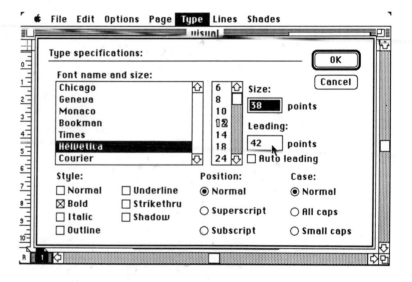

length, hold down the Shift key and click on the "Select" arrow in the toolbox. This restricts the text block to only horizontal or vertical movement. Holding down the Shift key with your left hand, adjust the vertical placement of the text so that it is in the center of the reversed area. There should be equal amounts of space above and below it. Use the $1^3/4$ inch ruler as a guide.

Don't worry if your first attempt is off-center (Fig. 7-4). Simply open the Edit menu and click on "Undo Move." This will restore the text block to its original position, and you can try again (Fig. 7-5).

Supporting Points

After you are satisfied with the appearance of your first headline, open the Options menu and click on "Column Guides." Make sure the guides are unlocked and when the dialog box appears, indicate that you want two columns. Click on "OK," or use the Enter or Return key.

Click the Select arrow in the PageMaker toolbox and move the column guide until the right hand line overlaps the one-inch vertical

Figure 7-4

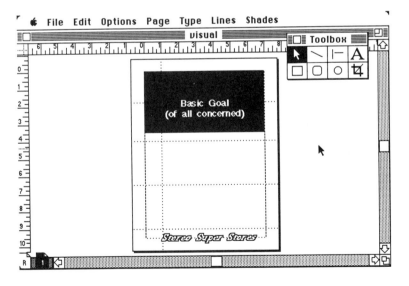

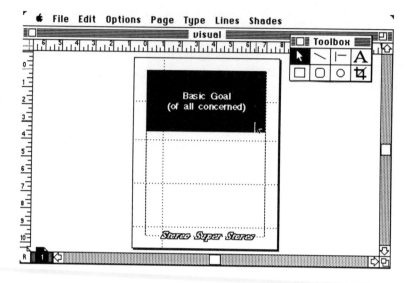

Figure 7-5

line. You will know that the guide is correctly placed when the vertical guide appears lighter than the vertical guide to the left.

Pull down the Type menu and click on "Align Left."

Then pull down the Type menu again, and open the Paragraph dialog box (Fig. 7-6). Enter ".4" in the right-hand "Space After" column. This automatically adds extra space between each of the points you want to make, to set the ideas apart and create a more "open" and visually-appealing page.

Turn off PageMaker's automatic hyphenation feature by clicking the "Automatic" box. (Hyphenated words are difficult to read from a distance. If hyphenation is absolutely essential, words can be hyphenated manually using "discretionary" hyphens.)

Pull down the Type menu and open the Indents/Tabs dialog box (Fig. 7-7). Grab the first tab on the ruler and drag it to the one-inch point.

Pull down the Type menu and click on the Reverse Type option. This will return type to normal black on white appearance.

Pull down the Type menu again and open the Type Specs dialog box.

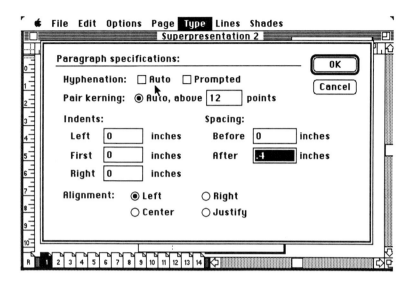

Figure 7-6

Figure 7-7

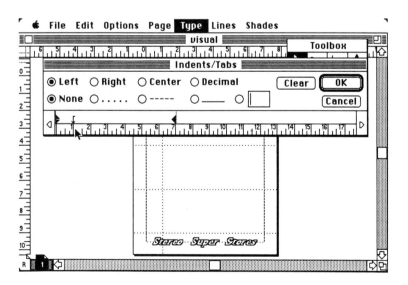

Change the type specifications to "36 Points." Click on "Automatic Leading."

Click on the Type symbol in the PageMaker Toolbox, and choose an insertion point in the right hand column on the one-inch vertical line.

Start by typing an asterisk and entering a single tab. Summarize your first idea in two to four words. Press Enter when you have finished. Alternatively, you can number each of your supporting points rather than using asterisks.

Insert a second asterisk or number, enter a second tab, and type in your second supporting point. Continue until you have covered the points that summarize and support your first headline. Your screen will probably look something like the one in Fig. 7-8.

When you have finished, click on the Select arrow in the toolbox and, while holding down the left-hand Shift key, adjust the vertical placement of the text block so that equal amounts of text appear above and below the 6½-inch horizontal center line (Fig. 7-9).

Save your work. Check and recheck it for typographical errors. Make

Figure 7-8

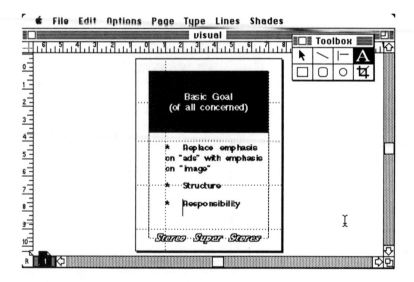

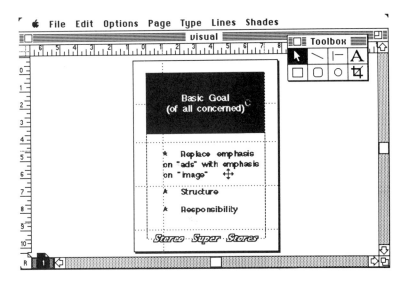

Figure 7-9

whatever changes in line endings are required for visual balance. At this point, you may want to go back and underline or italicize certain key words. To do this, highlight the words after first selecting the Text command in PageMaker's toolBox.

Turn the page and begin work on the second page of your presentation. Repeat the same steps. It's a good idea to print each page as you go along. That way, you'll be able to create each page as a natural continuation from the preceding one.

Note that the two-column format is not a part of the master page setup, but is established on each page after the reversed headline has been inserted. This is so the headline will be centered across the full page instead of being restricted to the right-hand column.

Adding Visuals

Up to this point, all your headlines and supporting text have been typed in, but you are not limited to this method.

For example, you can easily use PageMaker's powerful Place command to add a diagram, chart, or graph to your presentation. You might want to include a graph prepared using a spreadsheet such as Lotus 1-2-3 or Microsoft Excel. Or you might want to include a tree chart prepared using Decision Resources's ChartMaster or Living VideoText's More.

To do this, open the File menu and select the Place command. Insert the disk containing the appropriate graph or search through the various subdirectories contained on your hard disk (Fig. 7-10). When you find the file you want to add, double-click its title, click the "OK" box, or use the Enter or Return key.

Your pointer will now become "loaded" with the proper file. Move the pointer to the place where you want the graph inserted and click (Fig. 7-11).

Then, adjust the size of the inclusion using the Select tool. If you want to include the entire chart or graphic, simply grab the lower-right-hand dot and you will be able to adjust the graph to fit the space you have available (Fig. 7-12).

Remember that you do not have to use the entire chart or graphic.

Figure 7-10

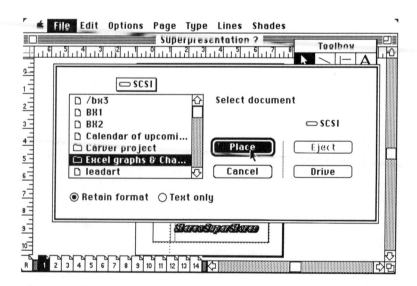

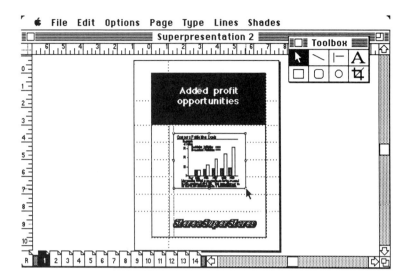

Figure 7-11

Figure 7-12

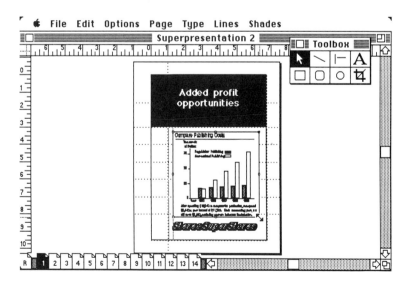

You can crop it, eliminating unnecessarily details. This will concentrate your audience's attention on just the important details. To do this, use the "resizing" tool found in the PageMaker Toolbox. After cropping, you can again resize your graph to the proper proportions using PageMaker's Select command.

Adding, Moving and Deleting Pages

If you need more pages than you originally anticipated, open the Page menu and click on the "Add Page" dialog box. In most cases, simply click on the "Add After Current Page" option.

Several PageMaker features make your work easier. For example, if one of your pages isn't turning out right, simply open the Options menu, click on "Select All" (Fig. 7-13), and hit the Backspace key. This will erase everything on the page, leaving you with a blank master page to start all over with.

If you are developing your presentation as you write it, you might find that you would like to add a page between two previously created

Figure 7-13

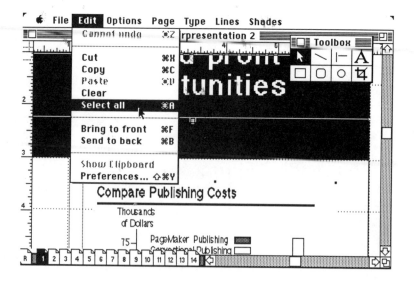

pages. PageMaker 2.0 for the Macintosh and PageMaker for the PC permit you to define where your pages will be inserted.

Print out your visuals. Have a colleague or family member check them for correctness and typographical errors—it's very easy for you to overlook your own mistakes!

When you have finished preparing the visuals for your presentation, there are several ways you can print and enlarge them.

a) The easiest approach is to use your laser printer to print out $8^1/_2$-by-11-inch copies of your visuals, then enlarge them to 11-by-17 inches on an office copier with an "enlargement" feature. After they have been printed out and enlarged, simply mount them on heavy cardboard of a contrasting color. Rubber cement, or a spray can of adhesive cement, makes this a quick and easy process.

b) If your presentation is to be given in a large darkened room equipped with a screen and overhead transparency projector, use your laser printer to print your visuals on special 3-M transparency acetate sheets. This will permit your presentations to be read easily by a large audience.

If you're in a large city, a commercial copying service may be able to make even larger copies—up to 17-by-22 inches. Above this size, however, you will probably find that the type begins to break up and that the the reversed black area behind the headline begins to lose impact.

c) A third method is to take your PageMaker data disk to a commercial typesetter with a Linotronic 100 or 300, and have him professionally typeset your visuals. This higher-resolution printing will permit better-looking presentations that can be enlarged photographically to 17-by-22 inches, or even larger. Again, the visuals should be mounted on heavy cardboard having a contrasting color.

Thumbnails

Finally, if you are using a PostScript printer such as an Apple Laser-Writer or QMS PS-800, you can use PageMaker's Thumbnail feature to prepare handout copies of your visuals for everyone who attends your presentation. Up to 16 visuals can be accommodated on a single 8½-by-11-inch sheet of paper.

To print out thumbnails, pull-down the File menu and open the Print dialog box. Click on "Thumbnails." Start printing by clicking on "OK" or using the Enter or Return key. PageMaker will automatically reduce each page and print it sequentially on an 8½-by-11-inch page. Those attending your presentation will have no trouble following the logical development of your ideas.

Options

No two PageMaker users use PageMaker in exactly the same way. PageMaker's flexibility, of course, is one of its many virtues. You can, for example, use PageMaker's automatic page numbering feature to number your visuals.

Another option is to use PageMaker's tiling feature to create larger visuals. PageMaker permits you to create large, poster-size publications by "tiling," or overlapping, laser-printed pages. The Automatic Tiling feature found under the Print command automatically provides a ¾-inch overlap. Tiling permits you to create a larger visual, which can be then copied and enlarged even further.

Once the visuals for a presentation have been produced and saved, they can be easily modified. For example, if you have customized your presentation by adding the prospective client's name to the bottom of each page, by opening a second copy of the file and going to the Master Page setup, you can customize the visuals for presentation to another client by replacing the first client's name with a different one.

Visuals that do not relate to the new client's needs can be removed using PageMaker's Remove Pages option. After you have modified the master page and removed inappropriate pages, press "Print," and your laser printer will create an entirely new set of visuals and handout materials.

Other Presentation Choices

Transparency paper for overhead projectors is available. This is loaded into your laser printer just like conventional paper. The finished transparencies are mounted in sturdy carriers.

Or, you can take laser-printed originals to a slide preparation company and have color slides made from laser printed output. As many colors as desired can be added. Different-colored type and backgrounds can be used.

As you become more familiar with PageMaker, you will begin to experiment with type sizes and typefaces. Feel free to experiment with type sizes and line spacings until you have created the presentation format that works best for you.

Always remember that "less is more," and that large type and a few, well-chosen, short words always work better than small type and long sentences.

NEWSPAPER ADS

If you are a retailer, PageMaker can save you money and help you prepare better ads in less time. In retail applications, PageMaker can be used quickly and profitably as either a design tool or to produce camera-ready ads. PageMaker will prove of great value to you, regardless of whether you present your newspaper with camera-ready ads, or have the newspaper set the type as well as enlarge and reduce artwork.

PageMaker's strength as a retail advertising tool comes from its ability to help you establish a consistent format that can be maintained easily from ad to ad. The essence of successful retail advertising is to be found in presenting a consistent image to the public. There should be a strong family resemblance in all of your ads, but should appear distinctly different from those of your competition. If each of your own ads looks different from the others, however, you're wasting time and money . . . and confusing the public. You're reinventing the wheel each week.

In addition to increasing the power of your advertising by making it easy to achieve ad-to-ad consistency, PageMaker makes it easy to prepare tight layouts for the newspaper's composing room to follow. PageMaker can also be the catalyst to help you develop a more efficient process for producing your ads.

How PageMaker Can Help

PageMaker's strength as a retail advertising tool comes from its ability to establish a series of master ad templates in a variety of sizes. You can create templates for:

- Full-size, 17-by-22 newspaper pages

- Junior pages (14 by 17 inches). These dominate a page, and can be almost as effective as full-size pages, but cost approximately twenty percent less. Space is left for one column of editorial along one side of the page, plus room for five inches of editorial above the ad.

- Tabloid pages, 11 by 17 inches

- Three-columns-by-10 inches

Here are the steps you should follow to create effective ads with PageMaker:

Step One: Create templates and establish standards for the major ad sizes you will be using.

198

Step Two: Create an inventory of scanned images representative of the artwork you'll be using in each week's ads.

Step Three: Create an inventory of generic product captions.

Step Four: Assemble the above into ads by opening a copy of the template you're going to be working with. This preserves the integrity of the original template.

Step One: Create Standardized Ad Formats

The first step in improving the quality and production efficiency of your advertising is to create a series of templates that define:

■ The borders and margins that will surround your ad

■ The amount of space that will be devoted to headlines and subheads

■ The number and spacing of columns

■ The size and placement of artwork

■ Identity areas—address, phone number, and other consistent information

These templates should be accompanied by written instructions in a notebook. This notebook will formalize standards. It could contain information such as:

Headlines for full-page ads will be in set in upper- and lower-case 60-point Helvetica Bold on 62-point leading.

Headlines for tabloid pages will be set in upper- and lower-case 48-point Helvetica bold on 50-point leading.

Helvetica Narrow will be used for long headlines.

The first line of product descriptions will be set in Times Roman bold, set 12 points over 14.

Product captions will be set in 11-point Times Roman, using 11.5-point leading.

Step Two: Create Generic Illustration Files

The starting point to making the best possible use of PageMaker's power is to realize that most of your ads are usually assembled around similar-appearing products.

If you are an audio/video retailer, for instance, most of your ads will include videocassette recorders, speakers, compact-disc players, TVs, and car stereos. With very few exceptions, the shapes of most brands and models are very much alike.

In a similar fashion, if you own a Volvo automobile dealership, the shapes of the cars you are advertising will be similar, regardless of whether you're advertising the basic 740-series model or a top-of-the-line turbo-charged 760 with leather upholstery. And, if you are an appliance dealer, the shapes of all washing machines and driers you sell are similar—regardless of the brand names you're promoting.

Thus, the starting point for using PageMaker as a retail advertising tool is to create a set of scanned images that describe the generic shape of the products you're going to advertise each week.

You'll probably want to include three different views of each basic product category and shape: Views facing to the right, views facing to the left, and straight-on views. The following, for example, is a "needs" list for a typical audio/video retailer:

- Audio receiver: left, right, straight-on views

- Home compact disc player: left, right, straight-on views

- Speakers: left, right, straight-on views

- Videocassette recorders: left, right, straight-on views

- ■ "Walkman-type" portable cassette players: left, right, straight-on

- ■ Portable AM/FM radios: left, right, straight-on

- ■ Table model TV's, left, right, straight-on

- ■ Console TV's, left, right, straight-on

- ■ Big-screen projection TV's, left, right, straight-on

Each of these scanned images would be stored as a separate paint-type graphics file. Files might be identified as:

RECLEFT

RECRGHT

RECSTRT

CDLEFT

VCRSTRT

CONTVRT

PROTVLFT

The words "for position only" should be included prominently somewhere in each of these images. This is to emphasize that, at this point, you are not using them in your ads, simply to help you design and produce better looking ads. Later in the production cycle, your "FPO" graphics will be replaced by photographs or illustrations supplied by the manufacturer whose products you're advertising.

For this reason, image quality is not as important as image shape and size. Your goal is simply to provide your newspaper or printer with "for-position-only" guidance.

There are two corollaries to this. One is that since your goal is simply to show generic shapes, rather than high-quality reproduction-quality images, you do not have to invest in an elaborate scanner. An inexpensive scanner will serve just fine.

Equally important, since you are simply building up a set of layout tools that will be used over and over again, you you do not have to purchase a scanner at all. You can simply bring samples of your "generic shapes" artwork to a commercial desktop publishing service and have them scan the images for you. Or, you might be able to locate a friend with a scanner and enlist his assistance in helping you out.

Hint

It's important that all scanned images be created from artwork of approximately the same size. Generic, or "no-name" artwork can be created using an office copier with enlarging and reducing capability. Or, if you have one available to you, you can use a photostat camera. When scanned images are placed into your PageMaker advertisement, they should appear at the most frequently-used size.

Step Three: Create Standard Product Captions

The final step in preparing to make the best possible use of PageMaker's power to produce better advertising in less time is to create word-processed files for your most-frequently-advertised products. Two- or three-sentence captions should be created for each of the products you regularly advertise. These should be stored together in a separate subdirectory or file folder, from which they can be retrieved whenever needed.

You should assign file names to make use of the alphabetizing power of PageMaker's Place command box. Setting up your files this way should make it possible to scroll through the Place dialogue box to locate the specific model number you're interested in. For example: Zenith TVs could be stored as ZEN1022, ZEN2205, ZEN3509. As your files grew in size, you might create separate subdirectories or file folders for major manufacturers or categories of products.

Step Four: Putting It All Together: Producing Your Newspaper Ads

Start by opening a template (Fig. 7-14) for the particular ad you're working on. Using PageMaker's Text commands, insert a headline that supports the particular theme or campaign you're currently using.

Place the graphic which will represent the ad's dominant visual element (Fig. 7-15).

Using PageMaker's Select command, resize the graphic to the dimensions required (Fig. 7-16). Do this by grabbing one of the corner handles. **Remember to hold down the Shift key as you resize the graphic, to maintain the proportions of the original artwork.**

Place the first product caption for the dominant visual (Fig. 7-17).

By enlarging the window shade handles with the Select command, increase the caption area to that it is proportional to the size of the artwork (Fig. 7-18).

Add text if necessary to fill-out the caption, and enlarge the type size to suit the illustration size (Fig. 7-19). Then, use the Text command to enter a large price.

Figure 7-14

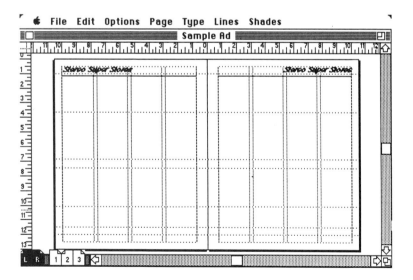

203

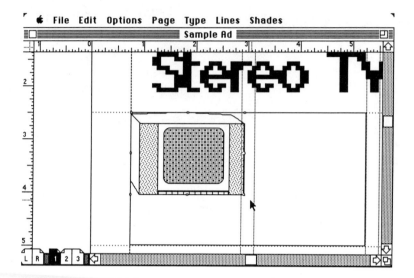

Figure 7-15

Figure 7-16

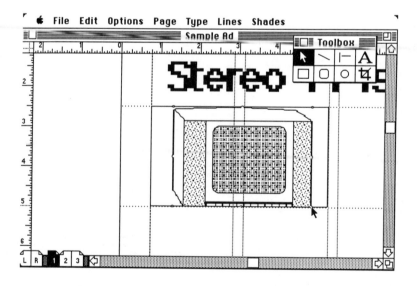

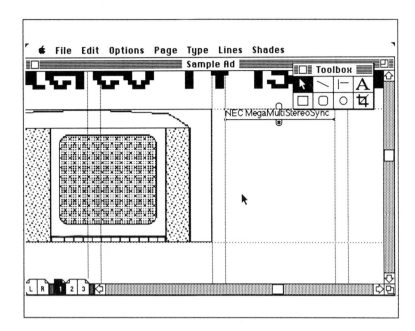

Figure 7-17

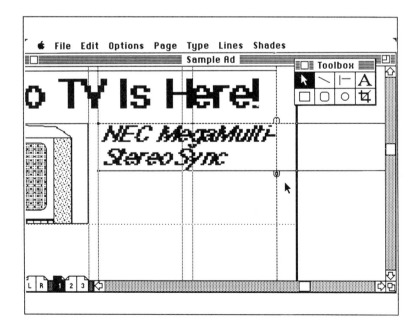

Figure 7-18

Figure 7-19

Complete the ad by placing additional position-only artwork and captions. Use the text commands to enter prices, as illustrated in Fig. 7-20.

When you're through, you can give your ad to your newspaper for typesetting. Or, you can take your PageMaker files to a professional typesetter for high-resolution typesetting. In many cases, however, you will find that laser-quality output will be suitable for newspaper use. Standard newsprint is so porous that ink-spread lessens the impact of quality typesetting.

Hint

If you're a heavy and frequent advertiser, produce your ads as pages in a publication, printing out just the ad you need each week. But at planning time, once a quarter, print-out thumbnails of all of your ads. That way, you can see at a glance how they all fit together. This will make it easy to see at a glance how successful you were maintaining consistency.

206

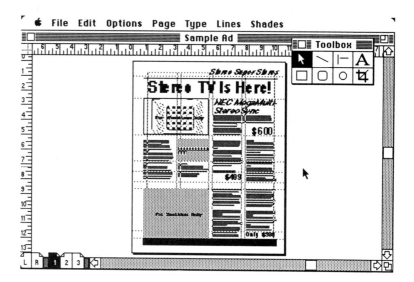

Figure 7-20

NEWSLETTERS

The essence of a successful direct-mail program is sending the right message to the right people at the right time—at the lowest possible cost. Here's a simple way of creating a visually strong, yet simple-to-produce, four-page newsletter.

The format has been chosen for maximum flexibility. It permits you to include a variety of articles, both long and short.

Creating a Newsletter

Consistency is the essence of a successful direct-mail program. A successful newsletter program consists of sending the right message to the right people at the right time—at the lowest possible cost. Page-Maker makes it easy to achieve this goal.

Many of the techniques used to create successful newspaper ads are used in creating a newsletter. These include:

- Establishing templates to ensure page-to-page and issue-to-issue consistency

- Preparing written standards sheets describing the styles to be used throughout the book

- Creating a library of "position-only" graphics files representing frequently used illustrations and photographs.

You will probably need to create two additional graphics files. One will contain your newsletter's masthead. The masthead can be created either from scratch with a graphics program or it can be a scanned image. In either case, storing the masthead as a graphics element permits it to be used full-size on the front cover of your newsletter, or reduced for use on inside pages.

Similarly, you will also want to save a scanned image of your firm's logo for easy placement.

Newsletter-Design Considerations

Several issues influence the design of your newsletter. One of the most important is the number and length of the topics that will be included in each issue.

Newsletters built around a few major topics should be designed differently than newsletters focused around several shorter topics.

Another important factor is flexibility. Will each issue be similar in terms of article balance or are there likely to be major issue-to-issue differences?

Finally, your newsletter should also be designed in the context of your firm's existing corporate identity. Type choices and colors should reinforce your firm's "look" as it appears on existing letterheads, brochures, and literature sheets.

Your newsletter should also be designed with an eye to your competition. Your newsletter should look distinctly different from theirs.

Sample Newsletter

The newsletter sample in Fig. 7-21 was designed to be used as an easy-to-produce self-mailer that would permit maximum flexibility in article length. It was also designed for easy production using a minimum of different typefaces and type sizes. This makes this newsletter format an excellent choice for use with Hewlett-Packard LaserJet printers.

A three-column format was chosen, with headlines clustered in the narrow left-hand column on each page. This permits the reader to scan the headlines rapidly, picking out the articles of interest to him. Headlines are easy to read because they are surrounded by plenty of white space. The flush-right alignment of the headlines provides a distinctive look for the newsletter and makes it easy for the reader to relate each headline visually to the article it describes.

Body copy for each topic is contained in two columns to the right of the headline. White space and horizontal rules separate one topic from another.

Each newsletter topic or article should be placed from a separate

Figure 7-21

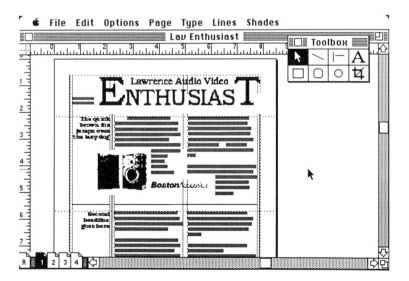

word-processed file. This will simplify their placement, and prevent editorial changes in the first article from disrupting the layouts of those that follow.

Note the flexibility this format provides. Articles and topics can be as short as two paragraphs, or as long as a full page. You can either "tease" readers or tell the whole story.

This format makes maximum use of artwork to provide the greatest issue-to-issue differentiation. Notice how sometimes the photographs overlap the vertical line between the headline and body copy, how sometimes the artwork is contained within the first body-copy column, and how sometimes the artwork is placed in the middle of the two body-copy columns with even fuller wrap-arounds.

Placing Articles

Start by placing the first article in the first body-copy column. Then, isolate the headline. There are two different ways in which you can do this.

The first is by rolling up the window shade to the bottom of the headline, and then grabbing the headline and moving it to the left-hand headline column (Fig. 7-22). Highlight the text. Then open the Type menu and select "Right Alignment." Open the Type menu once again, and select "Type Specifications." Change the specifications to 14-point Times Roman bold on 15 point leading.

Go back to the Select tool, and select the headline. Click the plus sign in the bottom window shade and load the pointer with the remaining text (Fig. 7-23). Place the first column of body copy. When the text stops, click on the "pound" sign at the bottom of the text block, and roll up the window shade to approximately the halfway point. Click on the "plus" sign that appears at the bottom of the shortened first column and load the pointer with the text. Place this text in the second body copy column.

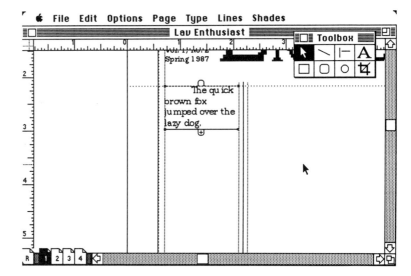

Figure 7-22

Figure 7-23

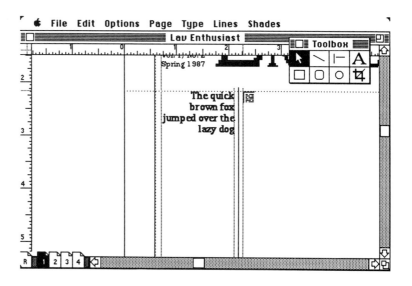

Alternatives

Here's another way you can isolate the headline from your body copy and place it in the headline column.

Place the first column of body copy. Click on the Text tool, and highlight the headline by pulling the pointer through the sentence. Pull down the Edit menu and click on "cut." Move the cursor to the headline column and click to create an insertion point (Fig. 7-24).

Pull down the Edit menu and click on "Paste." The headline will be restored (Fig. 7-25).

Once again, highlight the text and change the specifications to 14-point Times Roman bold on 15-point leading, aligned right.

Finishing Touches

After you have placed both columns of body copy, adjust their bottoms until they are of approximately equal length. Adjust the body copy to accommodate artwork. Notice how you can indent type to run

Figure 7-24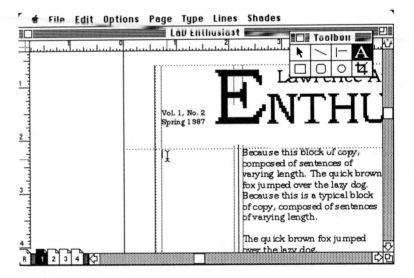

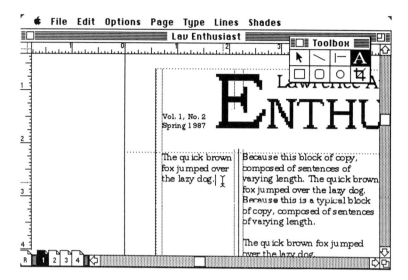

Figure 7-25

around artwork, as in the speaker illustration at the top of the first page of the sample. Or, you can make one column of type shorter than the other if you like.

To create a run-around like the speaker illustration, roll up the body copy to a point just above the illustration.

Click on the "plus" sign, and reflow the type as a separate text block (Fig. 7-26).

Select the new type you have just placed. Grab the left-hand handle on the top window shade and pull it to the right, far enough to accommodate your photograph. The text block will follow the shape you have just indicated (Fig. 7-27).

Hint

As it is being placed, type flows until it hits a line or graphic image. As you become familiar with placing type and estimating the length of text blocks, you may want to add horizontal lines to separate one article from another. This will speed up newsletter production.

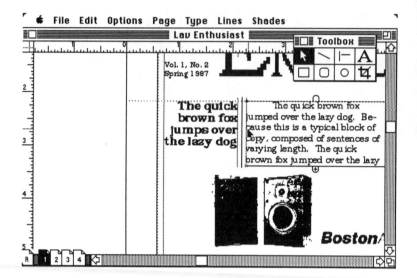

Figure 7-26

Figure 7-27

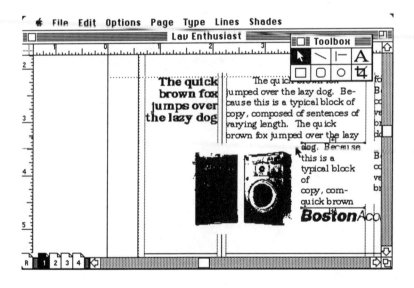

Next, you want to insert the horizontal lines that separate article topics from each other. Notice how these horizontal lines break where they intersect the vertical line separating the headline column from the body copy columns. It is imperative that these lines be precisely the right length.

Details

One of the keys to good-looking newsletters is consistent spacing. It is essential that headlines and body copy begin the same distance down from the horizontal and vertical lines that organize each article.

It is also important that articles end the same distance above the horizontal line separating one topic from the next.

There are two ways you can make such accurate measurements.

One way is to make frequent use of PageMaker's rulers, resetting the zero point to whatever you want to measure. For example, when placing the text for the second article, you could reset the horizontal zero point to the rule you have created to separate the first article from the second (Fig. 7-28). Then, all you have to do is pull down an alignment guide one pica down from the horizontal rule.

An alternative way is to create a one-pica measuring tool, or place-holder, which can be stored on the pasteboard along with your master page template (Fig. 7-29). Measuring tools can be created easily using PageMaker's Rectangle drawing tool. As many measuring tools as you need can be created, and they'll will appear automatically each time the template master is called up.

Enlarge the page to 200% and reset the ruler's zero point to an arbitrary point on the pasteboard.

To create a one-pica measuring tool, make a one-pica square (Fig. 7-30). Remember: Squares are created by holding down the Shift key when using the Rectangle drawing tool.

___

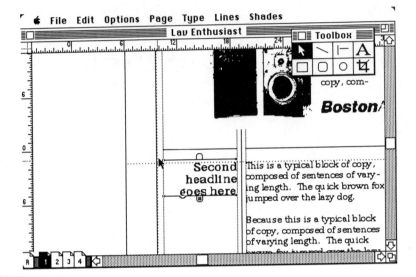

Figure 7-28

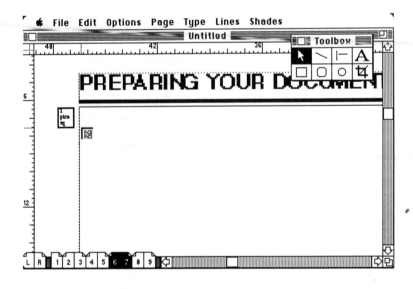

Figure 7-29

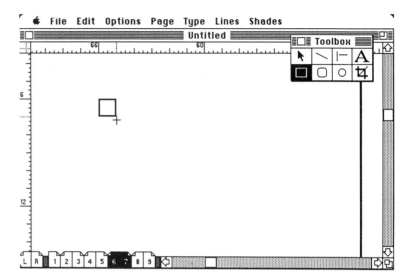

Figure 7-30

To make it easier to locate the one-column marker, you may want to add a label next to it.

If your newsletter design will include frequent two-pica measurements, you might also create a two-pica measuring device, and so on. Each should be clearly identified by a label next to it (Fig. 7-31).

To set them apart, you might consider using different fill shades for each, as shown in Fig. 7-32.

Putting Placeholders to Use

Use the placeholders with PageMaker's Copy feature.

1) Select the placeholder using PageMaker's Select tool.

2) Copy the placeholder to the Clipboard.

3) Use the Place command to bring a copy of the placeholder into your publication.

4) Select the placeholder and move it to where it's needed. Add an alignment rule next to, or beneath, it as needed.

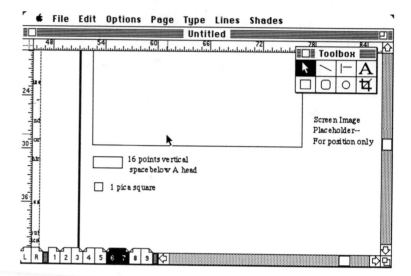

Figure 7-31

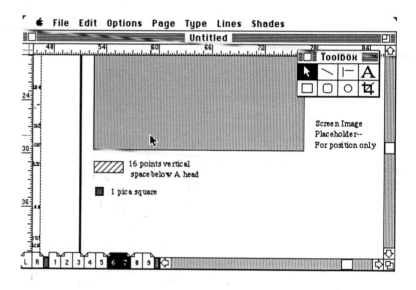

Figure 7-32

5) Select and Clear (or backspace) the placeholder after it has served its purpose.

Hint

You may want to keep your measuring devices in a separate graphics file, and import them as needed through the clipboard feature. This will permit them to be used in more than one PageMaker publication.

SALES TRAINING GUIDE

The Carver Sales Guide entitled "How to Increase Car Stereo Profits," which will be discussed in the following paragraphs,is an example of an application where PageMaker shines. It has a lot of lessons to teach.

One of the most important of them is simply that it exists. Sales guides such as this are often created under last-minute deadline pressure. The existence of the sales guide is a tribute to the speed with which good-looking publications can be created by people who know what they want to accomplish, even if they have had no extensive art training.

With the exception of the signature on the front page, the page-12 photographs, and the Carver logo appearing on each page, the entire piece was completed using PageMaker. The total time required was less than eight hours.

There is another lesson to be learned from this publication. Originally, the Sales Guide was designed in a "narrow column/wide column" format (Fig. 7-33). However, in this format, it occupied more than twenty pages. Budgetary considerations forced the decision to move to a 3-column format, permitting a reduction in the number of pages to 12.

If conventional typesetting and pasteup methods had been used in doing this, the reformatting would have costs hundreds—more likely

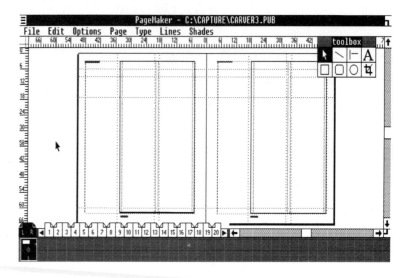

Figure 7-33

thousands—of dollars and occupied several days. With PageMaker, however, the job was done on a Sunday afternoon.

Elements of Success

The Carver Sales Guide illustrates how easy it is to design a good-looking publication if you establish a strong format and use a relatively small number of typefaces and type styles.

Note that all headlines use the same typeface and type size, and are centered on the page the same distance from the top. Similarly, all body copy is the same size, all subheads are the same, and all sidebars—or short subjects—are in italics. This consistency improves the appearance of a publication and speeds up production in several ways: It eliminates the need to make decisions constantly while producing the publication, makes it easy to estimate copy requirements, and it makes it easy to predict problems in advance—i.e., pages where there may be too much, or too little, copy.

The design and production of the Carver Sales Guide was simplified by PageMaker's Master Pages feature. The basic elements defining

220

each page were automatically placed on the page as work began (Fig. 7-34). These included:

1) Top and bottom borders

2) Side borders and vertical rules

3) Page numbers

4) Logo location

One of the reasons for the publication's clean overall appearance is consistent spacing throughout. All body copy begins the same distance down from the top of each page, and ends the same distance from the bottom of each page.

PageMaker's Paragraph and Spacing/Indent features were used to ensure consistent spacing between paragraphs, and consistent paragraph indents.

To ensure consistent headline placement, the headline area was divided in half by a horizontal center guideline. Two and three-line headlines were centered on this guideline (Fig. 7-35), ensuring equal

Figure 7-34

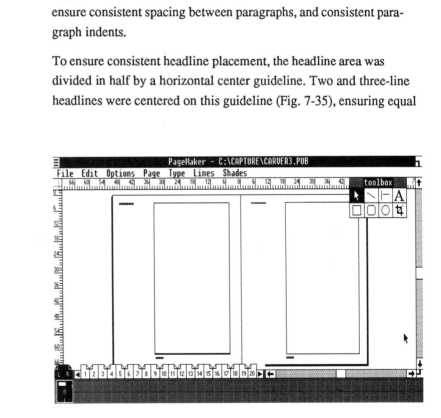

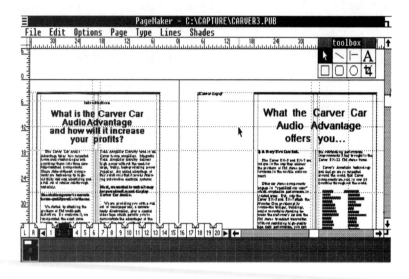

Figure 7-35

white space above and below them regardless of how many lines they occupied.

In this case, the Carver logo was indicated by the word "logo," which the printer replaced with the firm's actual logo. Another way of including the logo on each page would have been to use a scanner to create a graphic image of it. This graphic could then have been placed on the master pages, and enlarged or reduced to fit available space.

Production of the Carver Sales Guide was speeded up by dividing the master manuscript file into separate files for each topic and sidebar. This greatly reduced the time needed for their placement. Changing type and spacing specifications for the sidebars took just seconds using PageMaker's Select All command.

In the chapter "Looking Your Best In Print," we discuss the importance of consistency, and in "Working With Graphics," how type itself can become a graphic element. These points are illustrated by the way the consistent placement of page numbers in the sales guide's table of contents (Fig. 7-36) creates an attractive vertical line that repeats and reinforces the verticality of the vertical column guides (Fig. 7-37).

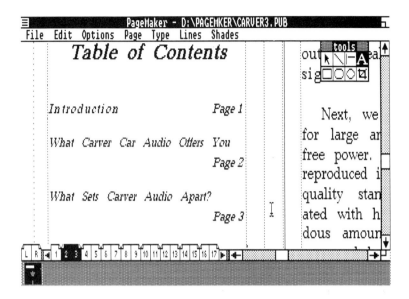

Figure 7-36

Figure 7-37

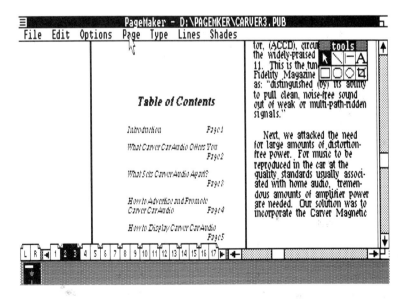

If the page numbers had been placed at random, at the end of the sections, the table of contents would not have looked as good.

Color

Although most laser-printer output is not in color, the Carver Sales Guide is printed in two colors. The artwork submitted to the printer had a tissue overlay that indicated which parts were to be in color. Since "less is always more," the use of a second color was limited to the page borders and the italicized sidebars.

FORMS

The "Carver Bonus Program" and "Carver Car Audio Accommodation Purchase Form" are typical examples of PageMaker's ability to produce good-looking communications under last-minute conditions.

The two forms illustrate how you can work intuitively with Page-Maker, starting with a mental image of what you want to end up with, and working toward that conception in a step-by-step, trial-and-error process.

Because of time constraints, there were no layouts or earlier designs to draw upon. The two forms evolved from scratch during a period of about four hours' worth of experimentation.

Of greatest interest is the fact that substantial changes were made in the forms only about an hour before the forms went to the printer.

Although most PageMaker publications are based on previously prepared files that are placed in position, with these forms PageMaker's word processing features were used to write the text. Since only a few words were needed, it was easy to edit to fit as the forms were created.

The starting point for the forms (Fig. 7-38) was to define their size. Since the goal was to create a form that could comfortably fit into a number ten business envelope, an envelope was measured. One-

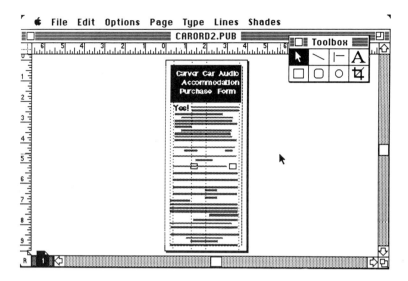

Figure 7-38

quarter-inch top, bottom, and side margins were used. The Double-Sided and Facing Pages defaults were switched off.

The first step was to create a reversed box to make the headlines stand out. This was done by choosing the "100%" command found under the Shades menu. Then, following a click on the Box Drawing symbol in the toolbox, a box was drawn to approximate dimensions.

Without abandoning the Box Drawing tool, the Type Specifications dialog box was opened and defaults set for:

- 36-point Helvetica type

- Boldface

- Centered

- Reversed

The Type tool was then clicked on, and "Carver Car Audio Accommodation Purchase Form" was written.

The Select was then used to select the reversed box. When selected, the Send to Rear command was chosen from the Edit menu. This

225

immediately brought the reversed type to the forefront. It became immediately obvious that 36-point type was too large (Fig. 7-39).

Two things could have been done. The reversed box could have been made larger, by grabbing one of the bottom handles and stretching the box, or the headline type could have been made smaller. Since a lot of information had to be included on the form, and the original box proportions appeared pleasing, the decision was made to reduce the type size. This was simply a matter of engaging the Text tool by clicking on the "A," highlighting the text, and—once again—pulling down the Type menu bar to reveal the Type Specifications dialog box.

The 36-point type size was changed to 30 points, and, to conserve space, "automatic" leading was replaced by 32-point leading.

The result (Fig. 7-40) was much more pleasing.

Next, another insertion point was chosen, and "Yes!" was prepared. This, too, appeared too large for its surroundings. The "Yes!" was highlighted by dragging the pointer through the word, and the Type Specifications dialog box opened, permitting a smaller, italicized type to be chosen.

Body copy was written next. An insertion point was chosen outside the order form, on the PageMaker drawing board. Copy was typed as if a conventional word processor were being used (Fig. 7-41). Note that PageMaker's Text tools make it easy to move around in copy being written. You can edit and delete using the mouse, or advance or retreat through the copy a word at a time using the numeric keypad along with the Command or Control keys.

When the copy was completed, the Select tool was engaged, and the copy "rolled-up" until only a single line remained between the two "+" signs. Clicking on he bottom sign "loaded" the PageMaker pointer with the text.

An insertion point was then chosen to the right of the exclamation point in "Yes!", and text was allowed to flow (Fig. 7-42).

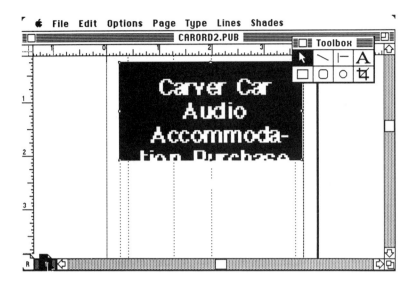

Figure 7-39

Figure 7-40

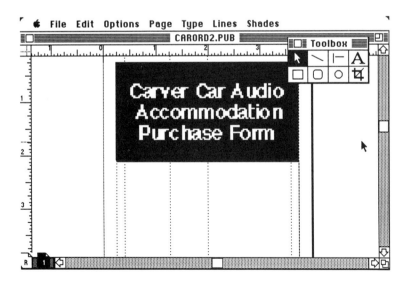

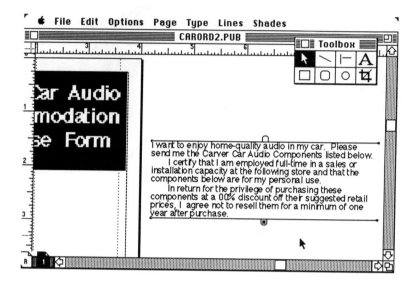

Figure 7-41

Figure 7-42

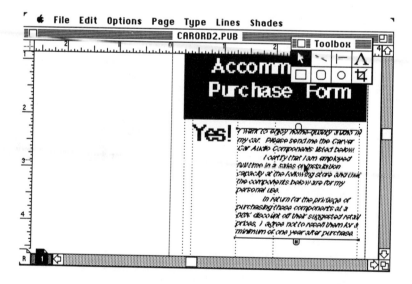

This didn't appear right, as the entire column was too narrow. Accordingly, the text block was again "rolled-up" from the "#" sign on the bottom to a point below the "Yes!" When the mouse button was released, a "+" sign appeared. Clicking on that sign once again "loaded" the pointer with text. An insertion point was chosen flush with the left-hand margin, under the "Y" in "Yes!" The text was reflowed, resulting in the form shown in Fig. 7-43.

One problem that became obvious at this point concerned the overly large indent of the first sentence of each paragraph. The two bottom paragraphs were highlighted by dragging the cursor through them after the Text tool had been chosen. The Tabs/indents dialog box under the Type menu was opened and the tab marker grabbed and moved to the left. Clicking "OK" created a form with a far more pleasing appearance.

Next, the remainder of the copy was written. Extra space was inserted after each "staff" to permit the later insertion of check-mark boxes to indicate the type of purchase. After the copy was typed, it was highlighted, and the Type Specifications dialog box opened, permitting a return to boldface type.

Figure 7-43

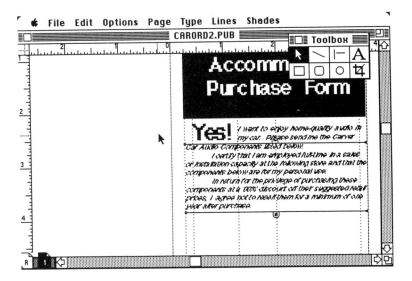

Three separate text blocks were created by creating a new insertion point for the sections beginning "Units desired," "Please make checks payable to," "Street," and "Send to." This was to provide the flexibility necessary to make it easier to move these text blocks around as separate units to achieve an attractive appearance for the form.

While the text tool was still engaged, the Shades menu was opened, and "None" chosen. A small box was then drawn to go next to "Sales Staff" (Fig. 7-44). The Select tool was then clicked, and the newly drawn box was selected. The Edit menu was then opened to Copy, and "Copy" selected by clicking.

The Edit menu was reopened, and Paste was selected. Instantly, a second box, of exactly the same dimensions as the original, appeared on the screen (Fig. 7-45). Copying the first box was easier than creating two different,but identical, ones.

A horizontal guideline was then pulled down from the top ruler, and the two boxes accurately aligned on it.

The are two ways the horizontal lines used for filling out the form could have been created. Horizontal 1-point lines could have been drawn following the words, using the Perpendicular Lines drawing tool. This method has the disadvantage that the lines are not part of the text blocks. Thus, if the text blocks had been raised or lowered, the lines would have had to be separately adjusted. Therefore, the lines were created using the Underline key.

To ensure that the lines would be the right length, a space was inserted after the semicolon in each category. Then, the underline key was pressed enough times to stretch the line across the width of the page. When the line broke, and the underline appeared on a second line, the Backspace key was hit until the underline returned to the same line as the word it followed (Fig. 7-46).

The "Name" text block was then highlighted, and justified. This ensured that the horizontal line would all stretch across the length of the page. Created in this way, the lines were always the right length

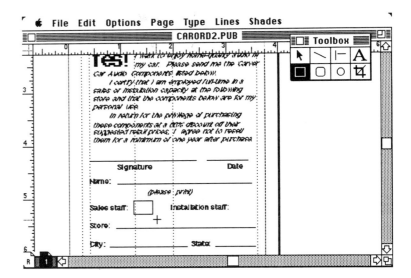

Figure 7-44

Figure 7-45

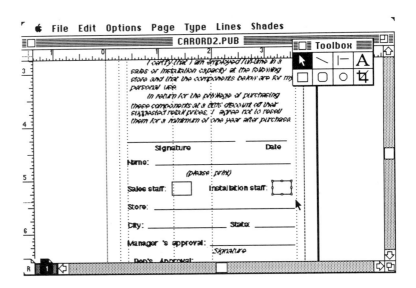

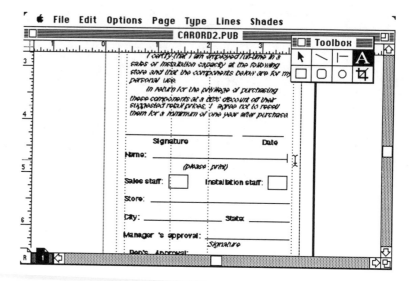

Figure 7-46

and, when the text blocks were raised or lowered, the lines followed.

Raising or lowering the "Name" text block was more difficult than with the others because the two "check mark" boxes were not attached to the text. Each time the text block was moved, the Send to Rear command had to be used, allowing the two check boxes to be selected and moved separately (Fig. 7-47). And each time the text block was moved, the horizontal guideline had to be adjusted to ensure that both boxes remained properly aligned.

A great deal of trial and error goes into the creation of a "design it as you produce it" form like this. Type specifications are changed, and text blocks raised or lowered on a purely subjective basis. But this is made relatively painless by PageMaker's "What You See Is What You Get" nature. You can experiment to your heart's content.

For example, before the piece was finally completed, the size of the reversed box at the top of the form had been enlarged and reduced several times. These changes went on until the hour before the presses began to roll. This normally would have required a great deal of time to accommodate, but took less than ten minutes with PageMaker.

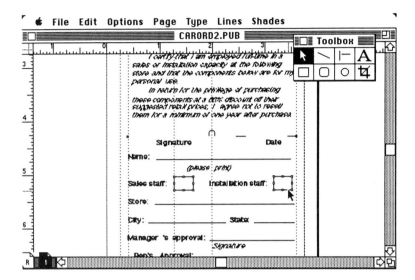

Figure 7-47

Carver Bonus Program Form

The PageMaker Bonus Program Form was similar in several ways to the Carver Order Form, except that its production could have been simplified by use of a second drawing program. In addition, more extensive use was made of PageMaker's Cut and Paste commands.

A more sophisticated page setup was used, based on the two-column format shown in Fig. 7-48. This simplified placement of the "Customer Order" information.

In the Bonus Program Form, a single vertical box was created, selected, and copied. Three copies were then pasted onto the Page-Maker publication, selected, and moved into position. ("Pasted" graphics always appear in the center of the screen and have to be moved into position.)

A mistake was made when the numbers "1," "2," "3," and "4" were added as reversed type. Created in this way, the numbers were not part of the boxes they were contained in. When the numbers were moved, the boxes stayed where they were (Fig. 7-49).

233

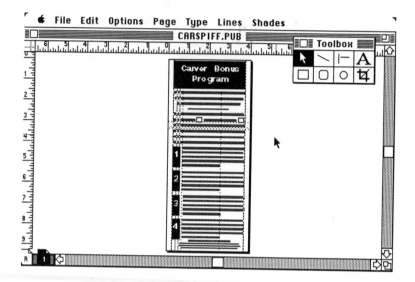

Figure 7-48

Figure 7-49

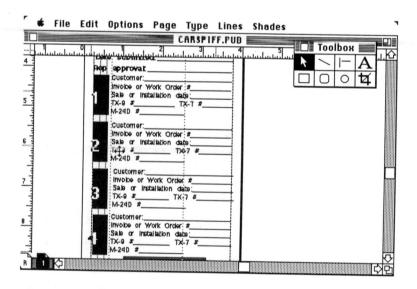

A much better alternative would have been to create the boxes using a graphics program such as Windows Draw, or SuperPaint, or Adobe Illustrator. The boxes and numbers would thus have been intrinsically related, and placed into the PageMaker publication together as single files. Numbers and boxes could thus have been moved around as units.

These are the type of "learn by doing" situations you will undoubtedly encounter yourself as you work with PageMaker.

The first "Customer" order text block was created, down to the "M-240" line. The Select tool was chosen, and a box created around the entire text block (Fig. 7-50). The Edit menu was opened and the Copy command invoked. The Edit menu was then reopened, and the Paste command chosen. Instantly, a second "Customer" text block appeared on the screen. The Select tool was chosen and the second "Customer" text block moved into position next to the "2" box (Fig. 7-51).

These steps were repeated twice more, until the form was complete.

The client subsequently requested several changes in the form. These changes were easy to make, as the each "customer information" text block could be grabbed and moved individually. The only problem

Figure 7-50

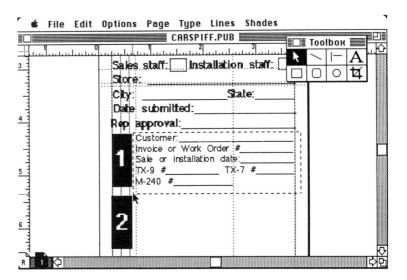

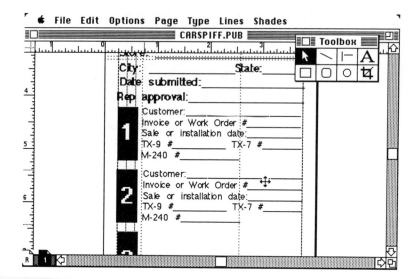

Figure 7-51

was that changing the location of the vertical boxes required special effort, since the numbers didn't follow the boxes. In each case, the box had to be selected and the Send to Back command invoked to cause the numbers to reappear. The numbers then had to be selected and moved to their new locations separately.

Hint: While manipulating these numbers, the importance of reducing selection handles to the smallest possible size became obvious. The numbers originally had large selection handles that extended to the right the full width of the original column (Fig. 7-52). These unnecessarily wide handles often interfered with selecting the "Customer" text blocks, and one would often be selected inadvertently and moved instead of the number.

This problem was solved by making the numbers' handles barely larger than the numbers themselves (Fig. 7-53).

SELF-MAILER

The Carver "How To Be An Informed Car Audio Buyer" is yet another example of PageMaker's capabilities.

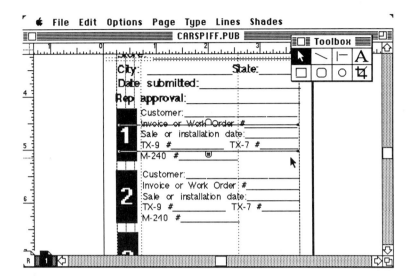

Figure 7-52

Figure 7-53

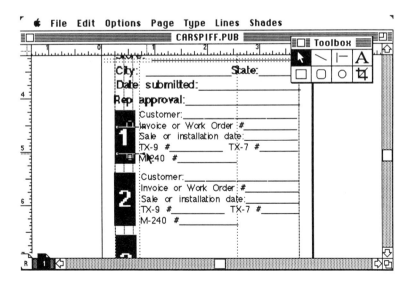

The newsletter was designed using a simple horizontal three-fold/six-panel format. It was intended to be provided to consumer electronics dealers, for customization with their own store logo and address.

By now, you can probably guess the basic steps of its production. Elements used before included the use of reversed headline panels, the consistent use of a few typefaces and type sizes, and strong organization based around boxes (Fig. 7-54).

New in this project was large numbers used as visual elements to organize the copy and guide the reader's eyes through the piece.

This would have been a difficult piece to create with early versions of PageMaker. The previous versions made it difficult to create columns of irregular length. Each time you wanted to change column length, you had to reset column guides.

With PageMaker 2.0 and PageMaker for the PC, however, changing column widths is as simple as grabbing the window shade handles at the top of each text block and moving them in or out to change column width. Text automatically flows to the newly selected width when you release the mouse button.

Figure 7-54

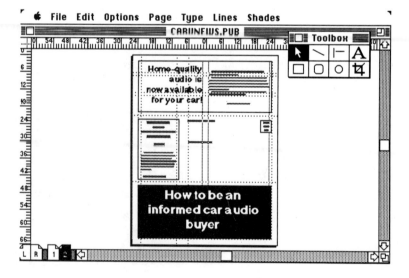

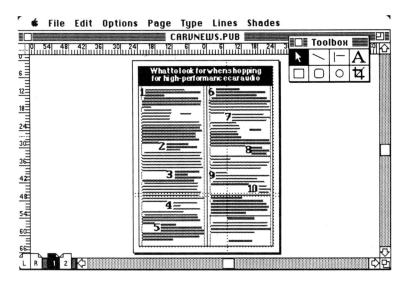

Figure 7-55

Notice the interest that's added by using flush-right copy for the "Home-Quality audio" headline. This could be heightened further by setting the column to the right of it flush-left (Fig. 7-55).

Working With Words

How to Organize Your Thoughts, Write Clear Copy, and Speed Up the Preparation of Your Publications

One of the most interesting byproducts of the growth of personal computing has been a return to basic writing techniques. Remember how you were taught in grammar school that the first step in writing a term paper was preparing an outline?

For many years, outlining fell out of favor. Now, however, outlining has been rediscovered. Most word-processing programs today incorporate outlining capability.

Outlining is of great importance to desktop publishing. It simplifies and speeds up your writing, plus making it easier to design and format your documents.

The first successful outlining program for personal computers was Living VideoText's ThinkTank. ThinkTank was available for both the Apple Macintosh and for MS-DOS computers. ThinkTank was followed in the MS-DOS environment by Ready!, a memory-resident program that could be invoked from within another program.

HOW TO USE AN OUTLINING PROGRAM

Outlining programs are wonderful writing tools; they free you from yourself. With an outlining program, you can let your mind roam free, and write down ideas and thoughts as they occur to you without the inhibitions arising from having to organize and evaluate them. After you've filled your page with ideas, you can go back and apply a "first things first" method of organization. You can also layer your arguments, making supporting facts subordinate to the arguments they support.

At any point, you can rearrange the sequence of your ideas until your points are made in as straightforward a manner as possible.

Once you've outlined your project, writing the copy becomes much easier. Chances are, the first-layer ideas will form your major headlines, and the second-level ideas become your subheads. At that point, all that will remain is to write the body copy from your outline.

WORKSHEET

How to Outline

Step One: What is the single most important idea you are trying to communicate?

_____

_____

_____

Virtually every project you work on should be reduced to a simple statement of intent. The more you can focus upon the primary purpose of your project—whether it's an advertisement or a newsletter or a book—and state its purpose as a single sentence, the easier it will be to write the copy for your project, and the more successful your project is likely to be.

Step Two: What arguments can be used to to support that important idea?

_____

_____

_____

Step Three: What other important ideas are you trying to communicate? What supporting facts are available to support them?

_____

_____

_____

Step Four: After you have exhausted all your ideas, and have filled several computer screens with thoughts and facts, go back and reorganize them. Arrange them in a logical sequence.

Outlining programs have "expand" and "collapse" capabilities, which permits you to hide the supporting facts and show just the major subject headings. This makes it easier to organize your ideas because, when you move a heading around, all the supporting facts that accompany it also move!

The success of outlining programs such as Living VideoText's ThinkTank, and of Ready!, has spilled over into the major word-processing programs in both the MS-DOS and Apple Macintosh arenas.

For example, both the MS-DOS and Macintosh versions of Microsoft Word incorporate built-in outlining capability.

Use your word processor's outlining capability in partnership with the worksheet above. Together, they will speed-up your writing and get your projects moving faster.

Headlines As an Expression of Intent

When writing your newsletter, brochure or book, start by organizing strong headlines. Headlines are one of the most important parts of a publication. Headlines attract or repel the reader. A strong headline will virtually ensure that a page will be read, even if the copy is less than perfect. Good copy under a poor headline, however, will rarely get read.

It pays to spend most of your time writing headlines.

Write from the Reader's Perspective

Remember that readers are very selfish. They care very little about you, your business, or your product. They are only interested in you, your business, and your product or service to the extent that it can help *them*.

Thus, try to see your business and prepare your headlines from the reader's point of view. When writing headlines, ask yourself these questions:

- "What do I want the reader to think of me?"

- "Why should he want to purchase my product or service?"

- "How can I make the reader want to buy what I have to sell?"

- "How can I relate my business to the reader's selfish needs?"

Subheads

Use frequent subheads throughout your newsletter, book or advertisement. Subheads help guide the reader through your publication. Subheads should summarize the important points contained in the body copy of your publication. They should maintain the reader's interest, constantly teasing him to read on.

How Much Copy Should You Write?

Stop writing when you have nothing left to say. Stop writing when you feel you have convinced the reader to purchase your product or adopt your point of view.

Remember that the purpose of desktop publishing is to help you communicate more effectively with others. Copy and content should come before graphic design. Graphic design is a tool that will strengthen your words and ideas, but it is no substitute for them.

Don't make the mistake of relying upon the tools of graphic design—discussed in the next chapter—to compensate for a lack of strong arguments and forcefully presented facts.

Writing Body Copy

Many people who are comfortable conversationalists have a great deal of difficulty writing. This is unfortunate, as writing is simply the act of having a "delayed conversation" with the reader. Your writing will gain in strength as you place increased emphasis upon the ideas you're trying to communicate, and avoid the temptation of writing in a specific style.

Editing

Remember that successful writing is often more a matter of what you leave out than of what you include. After you have written a first draft, simplify it as much as possible. Strive to communicate as many arguments and facts as simply as possible. Avoid unnecessary adjectives and adverbs. As Sergeant Joe Friday, of Dragnet fame, used to say: "Just the facts, ma'am!"

Eliminate unnecessary words. You may worry that your writing will be too short if you don't "fluff it up." Remember, though, that readers are always able to tell the difference between helpful information and useless fluff.

If you can make your points in a few words, set them in a larger type size! But don't include empty words for the sake of including them.

Preparing Word-Processed Files for Placement

The following simple techniques can speed your placement of word processed files in PageMaker documents.

1. Careful Proofreading

Editing and proofreading should take place before a word-processed file is placed in a PageMaker document. Although PageMaker makes it easy to select copy for revision, changes should be the exception rather than the rule.

It's important to remember that PageMaker does not contain a spell-checker. As a result, it is easy to make and overlook embarrassing errors when using it in its word-processing mode. Every time you add a headline or change a word in a PageMaker file, you're taking the chance of making a mistake that won't be caught until your publication is printed.

2. Avoid Wasted Space

Eliminate empty space between the top of the screen and the beginning of your text. This space causes problems when files are placed in PageMaker publications. Wasted space can cause PageMaker's window shade handles at the top and bottoms of text blocks to overlap adjacent text blocks or graphics (Fig. 8-1). This makes it difficult to se-

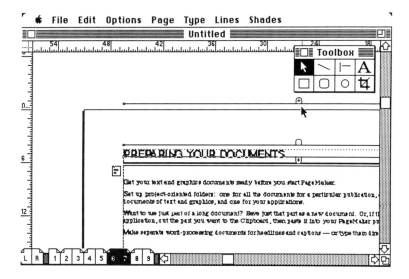

Figure 8-1

lect adjacent text or graphics for movement or editing. It slows you down by forcing you to:

a) Use Select All to show the selection handles on all the text blocks and graphics on a page

b) Use Send to Back to cause the text block you want to come to the surface

Space between paragraphs should be avoided. Avoid the temptation to insert an extra carriage return between paragraphs. Instead, use PageMaker's Paragraph Spacing command to add space uniformly between paragraphs as the text is placed. This approach allows extra design freedom.

Extra space between paragraphs in word-processed files also causes problems at the bottoms of columns, requiring an extra "detailing" step.

3. Eliminate Unnecessary Manuscript Information

Often, word-processed files contain identifying information that must be deleted during text placement (Fig. 8-2). This information might include client and project information, chapter and section identification, author's name, date, and version.

Rather than include such information in the body of the document where it will be placed in the PageMaker document, you can include it in your word-processed document as headers and footers (Fig. 8-3). Information in headers and footers, like page numbers, does not get placed in PageMaker files. This eliminates the need to delete this information after the files are placed in PageMaker documents.

4. Format as Much as Possible

There are several reasons you should do as much formatting as possible before text placement. First, formatting done during the word-processing stage does not have to be repeated during the document assembly phase. This is an especially strong argument for Microsoft Word 3.0 for the Macintosh and Microsoft Word 3.1 for the PC.

In it's Macintosh version, Microsoft Word's style sheets permit you to assign predetermined formats quickly and easily to entire paragraphs and sections of your document at a time. You can store and quickly retrieve:

- Typeface
- Type size
- Type style
- Alignment
- Line length
- Tabs and indents
- Paragraph spacing

This not only saves time, but maintains consistency. Any number of documents can be based on the same style sheet. This becomes even more important when several people collaborate on a project. Microsoft Word's style sheets will ensure that everyone's headlines, sub-

248

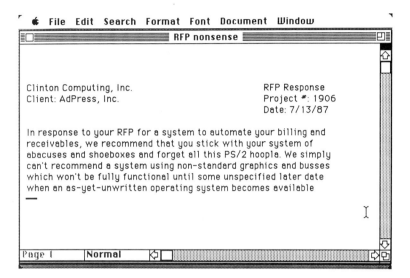

Figure 8-2

Figure 8-3

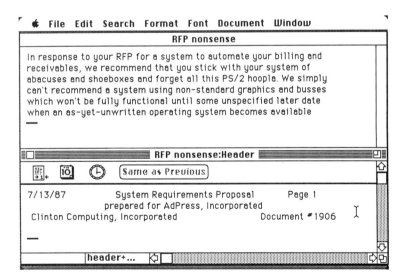

heads, body copy, and captions use the same typeface and type size, and are identically aligned. Microsoft Word's style sheets also assist copy fitting.

For example, Word's Repaginate command counts the number of lines a document contains. If each line in your word-processed document is as long as it will be when placed in a PageMaker document, it becomes relatively easy to decide whether or not an article will fit in the space you have available for it.

5. Break Long Documents into Smaller Files

It is important to remember that editing changes made at the start of a PageMaker text file "ripple through" the rest of the file. As file length grows, this "rippling" can take a lot of time. The longer the file, the longer it will take for these changes to be made.

In addition, in using PageMaker's window shades, and in highlighting text, it takes more time to grab and resize headlines, subheads, captions and callouts than it does to place new ones.

For this reason, even the simplest project should be broken into separate files for your various purposes. Each article in a multi-topic newsletter, for example, should be placed as a separate file.

BREAKING LONG FILES INTO SHORTER ONES

Most word processing programs make it very easy to "divide and conquer" your word-processed files. Here's how a 16-page sales training manual was subdivided for easy placement.

Step One: The Original Manuscript

The original document was created as a single manuscript. This contributed to easy stream-of-consciousness composition and made for easy revisions. The original version was printed out as a 40-page double-spaced document. Headlines, subheads, body copy and captions were all contained in one large word-processed file, accompanied by numerous sidebars and boxes.

It immediately became obvious that the "one big file" approach caused problems when the file was placed in the 16-page PageMaker document. Changes made on the first page caused drastic changes to the following pages. Adding or eliminating a sentence on page one caused headlines at the top of page fifteen to suddenly appear on the bottom of page fourteen, and so forth.

Step Two: Smaller Files

To get around this problem, WordPerfect's "block and save" feature, was used to break-up the original 40-page file into twenty-two smaller, more manageable files. Sidebars—short supporting articles designed to be placed in boxes alongside the body copy—were separated from the captions, charts, and body copy.

Each sidebar began with a "BX" designation, to indicate that it was to be placed in a box.

Remember that files being placed in PageMaker documents appear in the Place dialogue box in alphanumeric order. Accordingly, the first box was called "BX1," the second "BX2," the third "BX3," etc. This kept all the boxes together so they could be found rapidly at placement time.

Similarly, separate "section" files were created for each of the eight topics covered in the document. Originally, "shorthand" file names were used. However, this procedure rarely works out, as one person's shorthand is another person's confusion. Since PageMaker for the PC limits you to eight-letter file names, the end result was chaos at placement time. It was difficult to identify which topic went first.

Thus, a revised file-naming convention was used. The first topic was referred to as "Sect1," the second as "Sect2," and the third as "Sect3." This eliminated confusion, as it was now immediately obvious in which order the various files were to be placed. It didn't matter how long or short the topics were; what was important was that they

251

showed up in the Place box in the proper order. You, of course, will soon come up with your own convention for breaking up your files.

Consistency

The exact file-naming conventions you use is not as important as is your being consistent in your use of it. You must maintain consistency to make your own job easier, as well as the jobs of people who work with you. If you do not, you will cause confusion, and confusion results in wasted time.

Final Editing

You will probably make some editing changes in your text as you prepare your final PageMaker document. Remember to be consistent in these changes. Be sure to use the same typeface and type size for headlines, subheads, body copy, captions, and sidebars throughout. This, again, is another argument for Microsoft Word, as you can assign these formatting options as style sheets, eliminating the possibility of choosing 45-point type when you wanted 48, and so on.

If you edit text to make it fit available space, double-check to make sure that your work is totally error-free. Check and recheck your work—then give it to someone else to check again.

Make sure that you do not destroy consistency by changing line or paragraph spacing to squeeze in an otherwise too-long article. You will be better off editing your copy than destroying the continuity you have worked so hard to achieve in your publication.

HOW PAGEMAKER MAKES EDITING EASY

PageMaker for the PC and PageMaker Version 2.0 for the Macintosh make it extremely easy to edit text already placed in PageMaker documents. In addition, Macintosh version 2.0 of PageMaker includes an important "Export" feature.

Both versions of PageMaker permit one-step revisions. With most word processors, you have to go through a three-step process whenever you replace previously entered type. You must first highlight the text you want to delete, delete it, and then type in the new text.

Both the PC and Macintosh versions of PageMaker are similar to Microsoft Word, in that you simply highlight the text you want to replace and type in new text. The original text is automatically deleted and replaced by the revisions.

In both Macintosh Version 2.0 and PageMaker for the PC, you can select an individual word for revision or deletion by double clicking on it with the mouse button. Triple clicking selects a complete sentence.

Direct Keyboard Control

The second reason that PageMaker makes text editing easy is that it allows you to you use the numeric keypad on your computer's keyboard to move around text documents. This means you can edit and revise text without removing your hands from the keyboard.

For example, the PC version of PageMaker permits you either to move the text insertion point by using the numeric keypad plus the "up/down" and "left/right" cursor keys, as well as the Home, End, Page Up, and Page Down keys. Using the same keys in conjunction with the Shift key permits you to select type for deletion of replacement.

The Home key moves the cursor to the beginning of a line, while the End key moves the cursor to the end of one. Control-Home moves to the beginning of a sentence, Control-End moves to the end. The "up" arrow moves the insertion point up a line, the "down" arrow down a line.

Control-"up arrow" advances the cursor up a paragraph. Page Up and Page Down advance the screen up or down.

Version 2.0 of the Macintosh version of Pagemaker offers similar keyboard control flexibility, when used with the Macintosh Plus or Macintosh SE (or Macintosh II). The "7" key moves the insertion point to the beginning of the line, "1" moves it to the end of the line. Command-7 moves the insertion point to the beginning of a sentence, Command-1 to the end of the sentence.

Command-4 or Command-"left arrow" moves the insertion point left one word, while Command-6 or Command-"right arrow" advances the insertion point one word to the right. Command-8, or Command-"up arrow" moves the insertion point up a paragraph, and Command-2 or Command-"down arrow" moves the insertion point down one. "9" advances up a screen, "3" down a screen.

As in the PC version, if these keyboard sequences are executed while the Shift key is held down, text is selected for revision or deletion.

Special Symbols

Another area in which PageMaker moves beyond conventional word-processing programs is the ready availability of special symbols such as bullets, non-breaking long and short dashes, and trademark and copyright symbols. "Open" and "closed" single- and double quotes are available with both Macintosh Version 2.0 and PageMaker for the PC.

In addition, with the Macintosh Version 2.0 of PageMaker, you can create a copyright symbol simply by typing Option-r. You can create a bullet with Option-8, and a trademark symbol with Option-g.

FILE EXPORTING

When used with Microsoft Word 3.0, the Macintosh Version 2.0 of PageMaker offers a unique feature that ensures that editing changes in text placed in PageMaker documents are reflected in the original Word document.

The File menu of Version 2.0 contains a command not found in Page-Maker for the PC. Export permits you to send back all editing changes to the original Word file, or just to export selected text blocks. For example, you can create Word 3.0 files containing only captions or headlines you created within PageMaker.

The importance of this file-export feature should not be underestimated. It ensures coherence between your original text files and your PageMaker publications. This is extremely important if you tend to use the same copy, i.e. "boilerplate," more than once. For example, if you are producing a newsletter or catalog, and made last minute product specification changes in your PageMaker publication, the Macintosh version's file exporting feature would ensure that your original files contained the latest updated specifications. The next time you used the copy, it already would have been updated.

How to Export Text

The first step in exporting text from PageMaker Version 2.0 for the Macintosh is to use PageMaker's Text tool to select (or highlight) the text you want to export. You can select just a part of a story—such as a caption or sidebar you added—or, using the Text tool in conjunction with the Select All command found under the Edit menu, you can choose an entire story (Fig. 8-4).

With the text selected, click on the Export command located in the File menu.

A dialog box (Fig. 8-5) then asks you to name the file in which you want to save the text. A scroll box appears to refresh your memory. This lists the file folder that contained the original word-processed file.

You can send the text back to its original file or you can enter a new file name. If the original text was in Microsoft Word 3.0 format, it can be sent back the same way. This will retain any any formatting changes you may have made in PageMaker. Alternatively, you can choose to export the revised copy in standard text format for use with other word processors, such as MacWrite or Write Now!

The final step in file exporting is to confirm that you want to replace the contents of an original file with the revised PageMaker text (Fig.8-6).

———

255

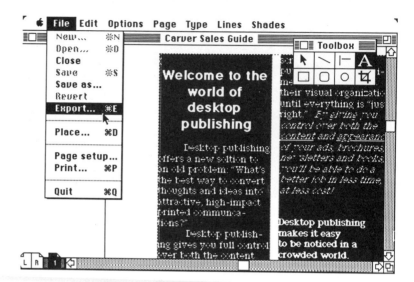

Figure 8-4

Figure 8-5

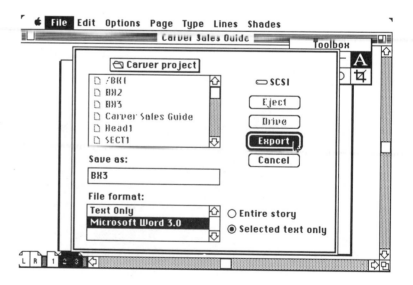

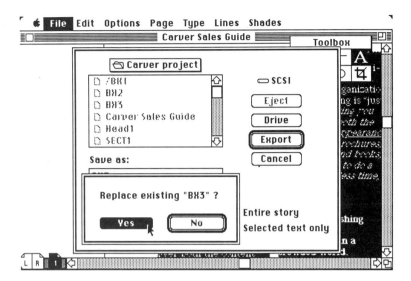

Figure 8-6

Placing Files from Other Computers

In Chapter 3, "Hardware and Software Considerations," it was emphasized how quickly the Macintosh and MS-DOS worlds are coming closer together, thanks to software such as the TOPS system. The following example shows how easy it is to place a MS-DOS word-processed into a document prepared on an Apple Macintosh.

The first step is to load the TOPS program on the MS-DOS computer, name the host computer, and define the path that contains the particularly word-processed file you want to place. In this example, the host MS-DOS computer is called "Tandon." The subdirectory is called "MSWORD" and its subdirectory is called "USINGPM."

After the MS-DOS computer has been set up as a "server," the first step on the Macintosh is to open the Apple icon and click on TOPS. You are then presented with a list of the computers presently connected to your system. Highlight "Tandon" in this list, and click on Open (Fig. 8-7).

You can then scroll through the available subdirectories until you locate the particular one containing the word-processed file you want to

257

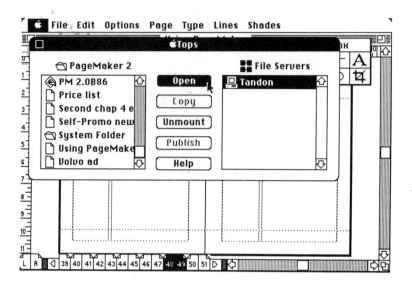

Figure 8--7

place in your PageMaker publication. When you locate it, highlight it and click on Mount (Fig. 8-8).

Then, remove the TOPS dialog box from your screen by clicking on the small box at the upper left of the screen. Your original PageMaker publication will again be visible. Click on the Place command found under the File menu, then click on Drive. A list of files contained in the selected subdirectory of your MS-DOS computer will appear on the screen of your Macintosh. Scroll through these files, highlight the file you want to place in your PageMaker publication, and click on Place as you normally would (Fig. 8-9). The MS-DOS text will then appear in your PageMaker document.

The same basic TOPS procedure is used to exchange PageMaker files between MS-DOS and Macintosh computers. This means that publications begun on PageMaker for the PC can be completed using Page-Maker Version 2.0 for the Macintosh.

You will, however, need to modify the Macintosh file header with FEdit or ResEd to change the file type to PUBF, and the file creator ALD2 to allow the Macintosh to read files created by MS-DOS.

258

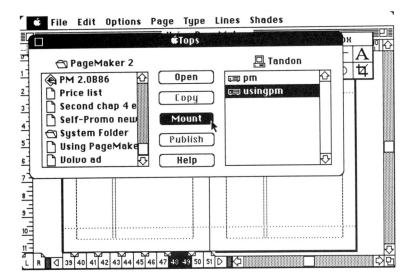

Figure 8-8

Figure 8-9

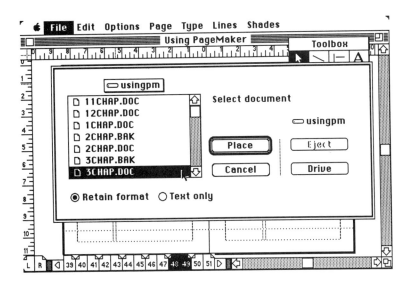

9

Working with Graphics

Enhancing Your Publications Visually

One of the most exciting aspects of desktop publishing with both the Macintosh and MS-DOS versions of Aldus PageMaker is the power it gives you to place and manipulate graphic images.

Aldus PageMaker makes it easy to add lines, rules, rectangles, squares, circles, and ovals. These images can be black, white, various shades of grey, or filled with horizontal, vertical, or diagonal lines. The outlines of these shapes can be of varying thicknesses, and can even consist of parallel lines.

PageMaker's Select and Cropping tools make it easy to change the size or shape of these graphics elements, or to move them to another part of your PageMaker document.

Equally important, PageMaker's Master Page feature makes it easy to establish formats that will automatically place identical graphic elements in the same place on each page. Thus, for example, once you have established the top, bottom and side borders you want included throughout your publication, PageMaker will automatically insert them on each page. Or, you can specify different border treatments for left- and right-hand pages.

The Extent of Graphics

It is quite difficult to define "graphics," because the term can be used to describe virtually everything that is not text (i.e., words). Yet, even words can become graphic elements when they are manipulated.

A large dropped letter at the beginning of a paragraph, for example, is both part of a word as well as a graphic element that adds character to the page. And mastheads and logos created from letters become graphic elements as well as words which can be read.

Furthermore, the basic PageMaker drawing tools can manipulate graphics images so, when they appear in a printed PageMaker document, they differ considerably from their origins.

For example, it's one thing to say: "PageMaker permits you to draw rectangles of various sizes." Yet, when you draw a rectangle and use PageMaker's Shades tool to fill it with a grey background and place words within it, the box becomes a totally different design element, especially if you add a dropped shadow box is behind it. You end up with a graphic image that bears only a superficial resemblance to its original elements.

You can use this technique to create a table of contents box or a sidebar (Fig. 9-1). Sidebars are short features that support the primary ar-

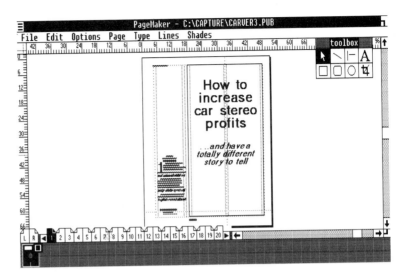

Figure 9-1

ticle on a newsletter or magazine page. You can also use it to create callouts, or pull quotes, that are excerpts from within an article and are placed on the page to break up a long article or draw attention to it.

Similarly, the Box drawing tool makes it easy to create borders of equal thickness around each page of your publication. Horizontal and vertical lines, and rectangles, can be used to separate adjacent columns and to separate topics within columns. Boxes can be used to surround photographs.

Many PageMaker tools work together to create extremely strong graphic images. For example, one of the simplest ways of calling attention to a headline is to reverse it—that is, use white type against a black background. This is accomplished in PageMaker by creating a black box and using reversed type.

This technique is extremely useful in newspaper ads. The background does not have to be black, of course. You can use PageMaker's Shades command to create different shades of grey backgrounds, from light gray to almost total black.

263

PageMaker's graphics tools can also be used to create repeating visual elements that will provide a distinctive look to your publication. For example, you can use short rectangles or squares to highlight page numbers or the first words of paragraphs that begin new topics. This technique is illustrated in Fig. 9-2.

If you are using an Apple Laserwriter Plus or QMS PS-800 Plus printer, you have access to even more graphics elements. The Zapf Dingbats font they contain consists of a series of symbols that can be used for this purpose. These include a variety of boxes, asterisks, arrows, pencils, hands with pens, and the like.

Figure 9-3 shows how the characters you can create with PageMaker's Text tool can be used to create graphic elements. The top text block shows the alphabet and numbers set in upper and lower case Times Roman. Below it are characters that are created when PageMaker's Type Specs command is used to change the Times Roman typeface to Zapf Dingbats.

Figure 9-4 shows what happens on the Macintosh when letters and numbers are typed in conjunction with the Option key. *An entirely different Times Roman typeface is created.* When this Option-created typeface is changed to Zapf Dingbats, **even more** graphics symbols become available, as the lower example shows.

With one of the graphics programs listed below, any one of these character-based graphics symbols can be enlarged or manipulated, and effectively used as part of a PageMaker publication.

Helpful Hint

Further illustrating the intimate relationship between text and graphics is the need to create a "nonsense text" file. It should contain words, sentences, and paragraphs of various lengths. Use this text file as a design tool, as you experiment with the look of various typefaces, type sizes, and spacing alternatives. You can experiment to find the correct relationship between type sizes and column widths.

Figure 9-2

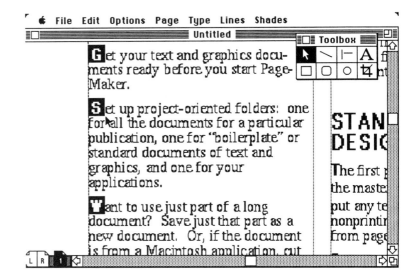

Figure 9-3

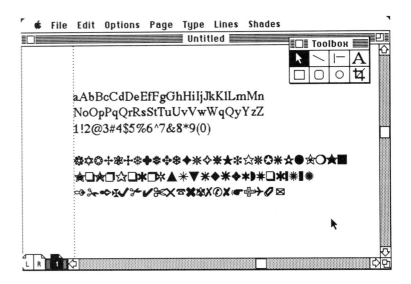

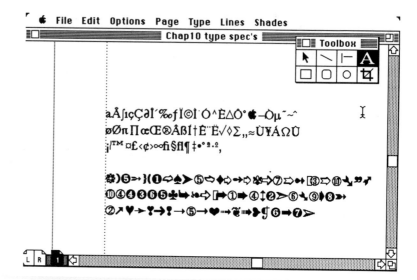

Figure 9-4

This sample file can be created with your favorite word processor's "cut and paste," or—as it's often called—"block and save" feature. Once you've created it, you can use the material it contains over and over again.

Traditional Graphics

In addition to the graphics elements that it can create itself, Page-Maker gains much of its power to generate good-looking documents from its ability to import, or place, files created by other graphics programs. These include:

- Paint-type programs
- Draw-type programs
- Charts and graphs
- Scanned images

266

PROGRAM COMPARISONS

Paint-Type Programs

In the Macintosh environment, the most popular paint-type programs are MacPaint, FullPaint, and SuperPaint. Paint-type programs create and save visual images as collections of individual dots. These dots can be greatly magnified and individually manipulated, as in the case of MacPaint's Fat Bits, or SuperPaint's LaserBits. This means you can enlarge a portion of a graphics image and modify the placement of each dot.

PC Paint, PC PaintBrush and Windows Paint are some of the popular painting programs in the MS-DOS environment. Several scanners also create files in paint formats.

The primary disadvantage of paint-type programs is that they work best when the graphic image is included in the PageMaker document at actual size. Image quality often suffers when paint-type programs are enlarged, reduced, or otherwise resized. Frequently, the image displayed on the screen is not quite the same as the one that will result when the graphic is printed. This is especially true when the paint-type programs are enlarged or reduced in size non-proportionally (stretched).

One way to get around this is to hold down the Shift key as you select a corner of the image and enlarge or reduce it in size. This maintains the correct proportions of the original drawing.

Draw-Type Programs

Draw-type programs create images as a series of mathematically defined straight and curved lines. Because of this they can be enlarged, reduced, stretched, or compressed with no deterioration in image quality. Draw-type programs are especially valuable when creating logos.

MacDraw and MacDraft are two of the most popular Macintosh programs. Windows Draw is their MS-DOS equivalent. In the MS-DOS world a variety of sophisticated drafting-type programs are also available, such as Micografix's In-a-Vision and Autodesk's AutoCAD. These programs are widely used in architectural and engineering applications.

Charts and Graphs

Many spreadsheets, such as Microsoft Excel for the Macintosh and Lotus 1-2-3 or Symphony for MS-DOS computers, are capable of creating a variety of highly detailed graphs and charts. The programs have the power to bring numbers to life by highlighting comparisons of results. These programs create draw-type files that can also be placed easily in PageMaker documents. Often, however, the fill patterns they create must be modified to be acceptable.

Scanned Images

One of the most rapidly growing aspects of desktop publishing comes from the growing interest in scanners. Scanners permit you to import photographs or line drawings to either paint- or draw-type programs—and then to place them in PageMaker documents.

Aldus and Microsoft have, together, created a TIF file format, which many scanner manufacturers have adopted as a standard. The quality of the scanned image is determined by the resolution of the scanner. Some scanners are able to scan at the same 300 dots-per-inch resolution used by laser printers. Others create coarser images, which results in larger spaces between the dots making them up.

Similar to scanners are digitizers, which convert images from a video camera into data which can be stored in your computer. When used in the closeup mode, these cameras can double as scanners, although their primary function is to capture three-dimensional images.

268

USING GRAPHICS

There are several ways to use graphics images of the types discussed above in your PageMaker documents. The simplest is to use them as guidelines for the placement and cropping of conventional photographs.

Guides for Placing Photos

At the most elementary level, you can insert shaded grey rectangles or square boxes to indicate the position of photographs or drawings, along with instructions to your printer to "Insert photo A here." This option works best if your original photograph is a square or rectangle.

A better alternative is to include a scanned image of a photograph in your PageMaker document. By including scanned images, even if they are not of publication quality, you can get a better feel for the appearance of the finished page than if you simply indicated the presence of a photograph with a grey rectangle. In addition, by resizing and cropping the photograph, you can provide your commercial printer with a detailed guide to exactly what should be included in the photograph and what should be eliminated.

Helpful Hint

When using a scanned image of a photo as a placement guide, be sure you indicate "For placement only" in the center of the scanned image. This can be done by simply typing the words over the image using PageMaker's Text tool. If you don't do this, the printer may not realize that the image was simply intended to help him enlarge or reduce the actual photograph.

Special Effects

The second way to use graphics is to use them with recognition that

269

their quality will not be equal to a halftone photograph, yet recognize that they do have an artistic quality of their own.

Often, an abstract graphic consisting of high-contrast blacks and whites adds which more drama and impact (or "character"), than a conventional photograph. Scanned photographs, because the grey areas are often missing, often resemble high-contrast, posterized images. The effect is somewhat between a carefully executed line drawing and a highly revealing photograph.

Logos and Mastheads

The final way to include graphics is to use them as logos or mastheads for your publications. You can also use graphics to create a distinct visual identity for your publication—such as using unique symbols to subdivide your newsletter and call attention to various sections—for example, upcoming events in the calendar section.

By creating your firm's logo, or the masthead of your newsletter, with a separate graphics program, you gain added control over its appearance. You can manipulate it more. You can stretch or compress it, creating new and different appearances.

Advantages

One of the reasons you will probably want to create your firm's logo using a graphics program—or to scan your existing logo and enhance it with a graphics program such as Adobe Illustrator—is the flexibility and savings in time that this will permit you to enjoy in the future.

By storing your firm's logo as a graphics file, you will be able to incorporate it easily in a variety of different projects. Once the logo has been stored as a graphics file, you can quickly place it in any Page-Maker project you're working on. This includes business cards, letterheads, brochures, newsletters, or newspaper advertisements.

If you *don't* store your logo as a graphics file, you will have to add "Insert Logo Here" in each of your projects. This will involve extra work and extra cost. You or your printer will have to enlarge or reduce the logo photographically each time it's used. You will also sacrifice the ability to see how your logo looks in conjunction with the other text and graphics elements of the page.

Retail Applications

Note that the graphics file containing your firm's logo can also contain other important information. It can include text such as your firm's motto, its address (or multiple-location addresses), and its phone number (or phone numbers).

This will prove to be a great time-saver if you produce a large number of PageMaker publications—weekly newspaper ads, for instance. Once you have arranged the "information area" of your advertisement or newsletter for maximum communicating power and visual appeal, you can place this vital information in your ads *in just one step*. This will save you time as well as ensure a good looking result.

The ability to create standing ad elements and use them easily in more than one project once again illustrates the close connection between "text" and "graphics" as used with Aldus PageMaker.

It's important to note that most graphics programs permit you to create letters larger than the point-size limitation of PageMaker. The MS-DOS version of PageMaker, for example, allows you to select a maximum type size of 72 points, and to enter sizes of up to 142 points manually. The Macintosh version allows you to set type up to 127 points. Graphics programs typically permit you to create larger type sizes.

More important, however, is that when you place text generated in graphics programs into PageMaker, you can increase its size to any dimensions desired. Text created in draw-type files placed in PageMaker documents can be stretched or compressed to any size desired.

Resizing Graphics Images

PageMaker provides several tools designed specifically for modifying graphics images placed in PageMaker documents.

One is the Select tool, which permits you to change the size and/or the proportions of any graphic image.

For example, if you select on one of the bottom handles of a graphic image and move the handle down, the graphic image will be stretched vertically (Fig. 9-5). If you select one of the side handles, the graphic image will become wider. Thus, when you pull on the middle handles of a graphic image, the proportions of the image are changed.

However, if you hold down the Shift key as you pull down the handle, the size of the image will change, while its original proportions will remain identical (Fig. 9-6).

Similarly, if you grab a corner handle and pull diagonally, the graphic image will increase in size in both the horizontal and vertical dimensions (Fig. 9-7). If you pull more to the left than downward, however, the proportions of the image will be distorted (Fig. 9-8).

Figure 9-5

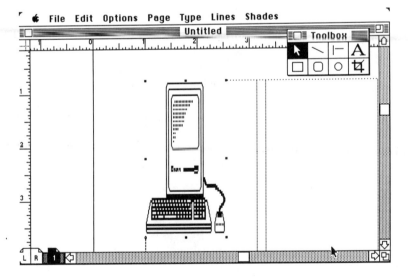

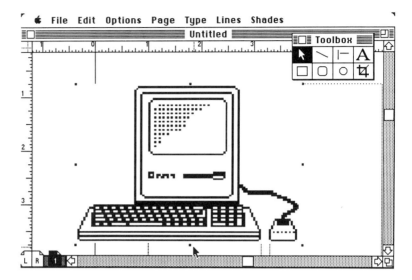

Figure 9-6

Figure 9-7

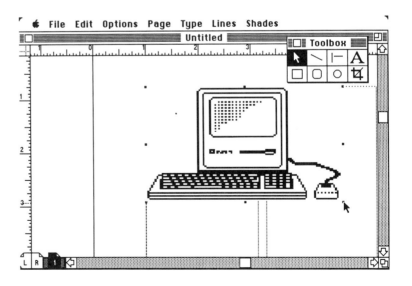

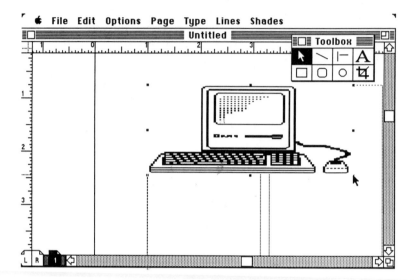

Figure 9-8

Again, however, if you hold down the Shift key as you pull the diagonal handle, the image will maintain its original proportions.

Another way to change the appearance of graphics images is to change the thickness of the lines that outline them. By selecting a graphics element such as a circle or square, you can also change its shading.

Cropping

PageMaker also makes it easy to crop graphics images, in addition to resizing them . The PageMaker Cropping tool selectively removes material from the top, bottom or sides of a graphics image. You use it like a pair of scissors. You can crop the top, sides, or both at once.

As is true for all PageMaker operations, the Undo function permits you to feel free to change your mind and restore cropped areas.

Hint

If you have cropped too much, and then selected another tool or command after you did your cropping, you can use the Select tool in conjunction with your Clear command (Backspace or Delete) to remove the graphics image, after which you can place it all over again.

Conclusion

The key to integrating graphics successfully into your PageMaker publications is to recognize that "graphics" consists of more than lines, circles, rectangles, and squares, or graphic files that you import from paint- or draw-type programs.

Graphics actually consists of the interplay of these elements *plus* your words and ideas. It is the interplay among graphics, words, and clear areas—or white space—that defines the final appearance of your PageMaker publication.

10

Looking Your Best in Print

Secrets of Effective Graphic Design

Why are some advertisements and publications better looking and easier to read than others?

Numerous books and articles have been written on the subject of graphic design. Yet, basically, effective graphic design boils down to just two elements: consistency and surprise.

The interplay of these two creates advertisements and publications that invite readership. Once you discover the ways PageMaker makes it easy to handle consistency and surprise, you'll find it easy to create powerful, result-getting advertisements and publications.

Consistency

Good looking, easy-to-read advertisements and publications reflect remarkable constant. They reflect both column-to-column and page-to-page consistency. This constancy is based on the way the following seven building blocks of graphic design are handled:

- Type
- Columns
- White space
- Organizers
- Borders
- Artwork
- Identifiers

Surprise

Consistency must never result in boredom. Surprise is an equally important element of graphic design. Surprise occurs when consistency is interrupted for emphasis. Emphasis can be added by:

- Size
- Location
- Shades and color

Style

Every publication reflects its creator's style. Style is simply a reflection of how an individual handles consistency and surprise. It reflects how the publication designer handles the diversity created by the different words and graphic images that separate each page of their brochure or each issue of their newsletter in a consistent manner.

To better understand the importance of consistency and surprise, consider what happens when you go to a newsstand to pick up a copy of the latest issue of your favorite magazine. Notice how easy it is to locate that publication quickly, even though the cover photographs and headlines differ from issue to issue.

Similarly, in the brochures and newsletters you prepare, although the specific words and photographs that make up each issue differ from those in the issue that preceded it, there should be a strong consistency that sets the publication apart from others.

PageMaker's Contribution

PageMaker makes it easy to build both consistency and surprise into your publications. The ability to establish master pages provides you with a framework for consistency. These elements include the ability to specify:

- Top, bottom and side margins

- Columns

- Repeating elements (such as titles, lines and page numbers) that appear on each page.

- Consistent spacing

At the same time, PageMaker makes it easy to modify, or even not to use, these elements whenever it is deemed necessary to create "surprise."

Within an 8½-by-11-inch newsletter page or 17-by-22-inch newspaper page there are literally tens of thousands of ways you can organize the building blocks of graphic design. Within a short time you will feel comfortable creating good looking publications that enhance the communicating power of your words and ideas, as well as reflect well on you and the firm you work for.

TYPE

Type—the appearance of the letters and numbers used in headlines and body copy—is the basic building block of graphic design.

Each typeface speaks to the reader in a different tone of voice. Each contributes a different appearance to the page. Some typefaces are formal, others informal. Some impart a heavy, or dark feel to the page, others are light and open.

There are two basic families of type faces: *serif* and *sans serif.* Serif type includes little decorations on the letters, the serifs. These assist the reader's eye movement by providing a transition from one letter to another. One of the most popular serif typefaces is Times Roman. Times Roman is a derivation of a typeface originally designed for newspapers.

Sans serif type faces are straightforward. They lack the decorations and flourishes that characterize the serif faces. Helvetica is one of the best-known sans serif faces. Sans serif typefaces are best used for headlines.

Within each typeface, there are numerous variations. Within Times Roman, for example, bold (heavier) and italic (oblique) versions are available.

Within the sans serif Helvetica family there are even more variations. There is Helvetica Black (which is even thicker than bold) and Helvetica Narrow (which compresses the width of the letters), and Helvetica Light (which is between normal Helvetica and Helvetica Bold).

PageMaker provides you with the flexibility you need to use type as a basic building block of consistency and surprise. PageMaker makes it easy to use a variety of typefaces, type sizes, and type styles. Page-Maker comes with a selection of the most popular type families built in, as can be seen in the Type Specs dialog box shown in Fig. 10-1. These are designed to complement the typefaces built into the Apple LaserWriter and Hewlett-Packard LaserJet printers.

280

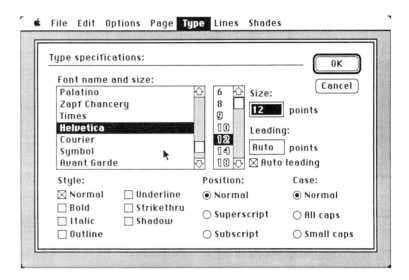

Figure 10-1

More important, PageMaker makes it easy to use downloadable type fonts. This gives you even more flexibility. You can purchase additional typefaces, such as Korinna, Avant Garde, or Lubalin, and use them as the foundation of your publication. These special typefaces will go a long way toward setting your publication apart from others.

Type flexibility for Hewlett-Packard LaserJet printers is provided by the various typefaces available as plug-in cartridges, as well as by Hewlett-Packard's downloadable typefaces. Hewlett-Packard's Desktop Publishing Kit also includes several popular typefaces.

Restraint

One of the keys to creating successful publications is consistency. Avoid the temptation to show off.

Throughout your publication, the same typeface, type size, and type style should be used in the same places. For example, you should always use the same typeface, size, and style for headlines and subheads. Similarly, the typeface, size, and style used for first-page body copy and captions should be used for page-twelve body copy and captions.

Hint

It is a good idea to prepare written style sheets for your publications. These should specify the typefaces, type sizes, type styles, and leading—or vertical spacing—for headlines, subheads, body copy, and captions, as well as other publication information.

COLUMNS

Type rarely extends the full width of a page, and is usually arranged in columns. This is because a reader's eyes move faster up and down than left and right. Columns that are too wide force his eyes to jump sideways too often. Long columns force a reader's eyes to make both horizontal and a vertical jumps from the end of one line to the beginning of the next.

Columns can be either *justified* or *unjustified* (Fig. 10-2). Columns are justified when the last letters of each line are lined up vertically with each other. Unjustified, or *ragged right*, columns are characterized by lines of irregular length, as in this book. Lines usually end where words end. Justified type permits a higher word density, but requires

Figure 10-2

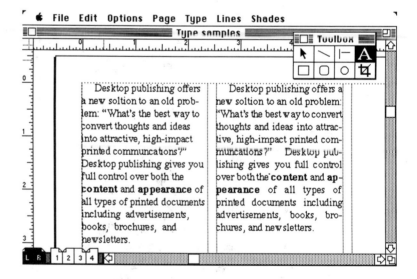

more hyphenation. Hyphenation is only rarely used in unjustified columns.

PageMaker's master-page Column Guides feature makes it easy to set up column specifications that are maintained automatically from page to page. Consistent column width will provide page-to-page consistency throughout your publication.

Type Size and Column Width

There is a close relationship between type size and column width. Small type should be set in narrow columns, and large type should be set in wide columns. eadability is compromised when type size and column width are out of proportion to each other (Fig. 10-3).

Note that all the columns on a page do not have to be the same width. You can mix narrow and wide columns. And you are not necessarily restricted to using a single column-format throughout a publication. Indeed, there may be times when you stack two columns on top of three columns. The point is to be consistent in the way you set up your columns, and to deviate from it only when there is a reason.

Figure 10-3

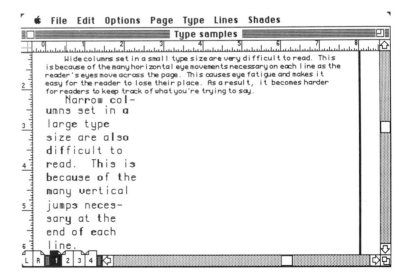

Hint

> PageMaker's Lock Guides command prevents inadvertent modification of column guides. When moving text, it's very easy to accidentally select and grab a column guide.

WHITE SPACE

> White space is one of the most important building blocks of successful graphic design. White space provides a framework for your words and ideas. It frames your words and ideas, helping them stand apart from other words and ideas competing for the reader's attention.
>
> White space provides a resting spot for the reader's eyes. It provides an opportunity for him to organize his eye travel through the page.
>
> The proper amount of white space surrounding a headline or graphic element is usually determined subjectively by the proportion and balance existing between the text or graphic and its environment.
>
> For example, Fig. 10-4 illustrates a headline dwarfed by the white space surrounding it. The words that make up the headline are not large enough to be distinguished easily from the body copy.
>
> Exactly the opposite problem exists in Fig. 10-5. Here, the headline is difficult to read because it overpowers its surrounding area. There is insufficient white space between the headline and the page borders and body copy. As a result, it is difficult to separate and read the headline.
>
> A page or advertisement gains in impact when proper proportion and balance are restored, as in Fig. 10-6. By going to a more appropriate type size and eliminating some of the leading in the headline, the page both improves in appearance and becomes easier to read.
>
> White space can also be defined in terms of spacing. Consistent spacing at the edges of your pages and between columns helps establish a distinctive look for your publication. Consistent spacing between headlines and body copy, or between photographs and captions, further reinforces your publication's visual identity.

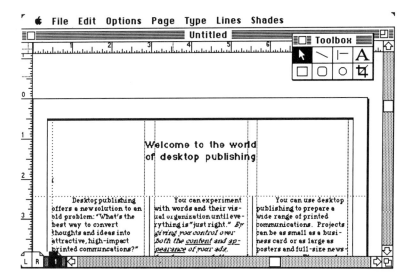

Figure 10-4

Figure 10-5

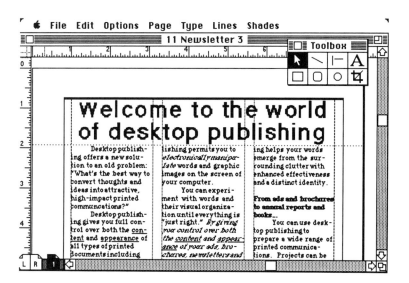

Figure 10-6

PageMaker makes it easy to maintain consistent spacing. It automatically maintains correct top, bottom, and side margins on each page. In addition, PageMaker's master pages feature permits you to add non-printing guidelines that help you align headlines, photographs, and body copy so they will always appear in the same location on each page. Columns of body copy should usually begin and end at the same point on each page.

Finally, PageMaker permits you to create spacing guides which you can use to ensure that headlines, artwork, body copy and captions are separated by the same amount of space each time they appear next to each other. These spacing guides, illustrated in Fig. 10-7, can contribute greatly to the proper appearance of your publication. They are saved as graphics images and moved wherever they are needed.

ORGANIZERS

Organizers are rules—or lines of varying thickness—and shaded boxes that direct the reader's attention to where you want it. Vertical rules are frequently used to separate columns, and horizontal rules to separate topics within the same column or adjacent columns.

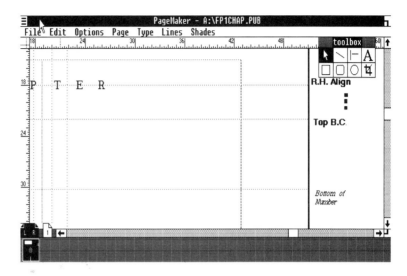

Figure 10-7

Organizers that appear on every page can be added to PageMaker's master pages, or you can draw them in when needed using PageMaker's Line and Box drawing tools. PageMaker permits you to specify lines from as thin as $1/2$-point up to 12 points. Single, double, and triple lines are available. Thicker rules can be created by creating long black boxes using PageMaker's Box drawing tool.

Distinctive rules and boxes can be created in separate graphics-software programs and inserted in PageMaker publications using either the Clipboard or PageMaker's Place command.

BORDERS

Borders provide a framework for your advertisement or publication. They focus the reader's attention on your message and isolate that message from its surroundings.

Again, PageMaker makes this easy. Borders can be set up using PageMaker's Master Pages function. These borders will appear automatically on every page. Borders can be created in several ways. They are usually thick or thin rules. Sometimes the same width of border is used on all four sides of a page; other times, thicker lines are used at the top and bottom edges of a page. Sometimes, side borders are not used at all. In this case, columns of justified type provide the vertical borders.

ARTWORK

Words are rarely enough to tell a complete story. Photographs, illustrations, and charts and graphs are usually needed to communicate your ideas fully.

PageMaker makes it easy to enhance your advertisement and publication with charts and graphs. Its Box drawing tool makes it easy to indicate where photographs will be inserted into your final publication.

More important, PageMaker's Place command makes it easy to import graphics files created by other software programs. With the Place command, you can scroll through your hard disk to find the subdirectory, or file folder, that contains the graphics file you want to import.

Or, you can create these graphics as you prepare your PageMaker publication, and use the Clipboard to transfer the graphic image from the source program into PageMaker.

Most important, PageMaker makes it easy to adjust the size of the artwork to the space that it requires, or that's available for it. Graphics images can be increased or decreased in size proportionately to fit available space. Graphics images can also be cropped, so that attention is concentrated on what's important. PageMaker's Select tool permits you to increase or decrease size proportionately, and its Cropping tool allows you to eliminate extraneous details.

IDENTIFIERS

Identifiers keep readers informed, as well as reinforcing your publication's distinct visual personality. Identifiers include the masthead, or title, of a newsletter or book and, in books, include publica-

288

tion information (title and author) as well as individual chapter and division titles. Identifiers also include page numbers.

PageMaker makes it easy to include identifiers on each page. Identifiers can be added using PageMaker's Master Page function. Separate identifiers can appear on left- and right-hand pages. In addition, Page-Maker can number each page automatically, and will renumber pages automatically when additional pages are added.

SURPRISE

The benefit of establishing a publication format based on a consistent way of handling the above seven building blocks is that emphasis can be added very easily simply by varying the way these elements are handled.

Without a consistent framework, there can be no surprise, no emphasis. At a party where everyone is talking at once, one more loud voice would likely go unnoticed. Yet, during a meditation period in a quiet church, a loud voice would attract a great deal of attention!

Once a consistent way of handling type, columns, white space, and organizers has been established, you can easily add "surprise" to your publication by varying size, location, and color.

Size

One of the easiest ways to attract attention is to increase the size of a headline or piece of artwork. Size should be in proportion to the importance of the idea you are expressing. Important headlines should be larger than supporting subheads. Photo captions should be smaller than body copy. There should be a natural progression of importance from important to supportive, with decreases in size appropriate to the subject matter.

PageMaker's numerous text and graphics resizing tools permits you to adjust text and object size to reflect its importance.

289

Location

Similarly, location should reflect importance. Important ideas should be placed in prominent locations, lesser ideas and supporting materials in less prominent ones. Just as the lead article of a newspaper reflects the most important news event of the day and unimportant happenings are relegated to the inside pages, your publication should always begin with the most important ideas.

Shades and colors

Shades and colors provide a final way of adding surprise—or diversity—to your publications. Shades can be added by using white type against a black background, or black type against a grey background. This makes it easy to call attention to features that would otherwise be lost. It also adds visual interest to the page.

PageMaker's Box drawing tool and the variety of shades available make it easy to provide gray backgrounds of varying densities to your publications.

Color can also be added at the final stage of stage reproduction, when you bring your publication to a commercial printer. Headlines, rules, and logos can be printed in a second color. This will add sparkle to your publication.

DETAILS

Details are the final element distinguishing good looking, effective communications from lesser ones.

Tiny differences can greatly affect the appearance of your publication. Powerful, good looking publications are characterized by a disciplined application of type, columns and white space. These publications reflect well on the individuals who create them, as well as the firms that publish them. Readers are presold on the contents of the publication even before they begin reading.

290

Lesser publications are characterized by pages that indiscriminately change typefaces and type sizes, have differing column lengths, irregular spacing between headlines, subheads, and body copy, and reflect other examples of sloppy workmanship.

To illustrate the way the various tools of graphic design must be consistently applied, consider the example in Fig. 10-8. It shows an easy-to-produce newsletter format based on two columns of body copy with a narrow column for headlines.

The details of this format become visible when the page is viewed at a higher magnification (Fig. 10-9). Note the "designer touch" on the top border, where the border is thicker over the two columns of body copy but thinner over the headline column. Note the dotted alignment guides, which ensure that headlines, body copy, and photograph are properly aligned with each other.

Note the style variations the format can accommodate. For example, the headlines can be centered within the narrow column (Fig. 10-10).

Or, the headlines for each topic can be set flush right against the body copy, as shown by Fig. 10-11.

The publication's neat appearance begins to fall apart when the headlines are not vertically aligned the same way with each other. Compare the neat appearance of the first example, Fig. 10-8, with Fig. 10-12. There, some headlines are placed next to the top of the accompanying body copy while the others are allowed to "float" vertically.

An even sloppier example results when headlines not only float vertically, but are aligned differently. In Fig. 10-13, some headlines are set flush left, some centered, and some flush right. The resulting disorganization presents a less professional view of the publication and the firm producing it. This cannot help but reduce the impact of the message contained in the newsletter.

Pay attention to consistency and surprise, and you'll soon develop your own style and find how easy it is to create powerful, good-looking publications with PageMaker.

291

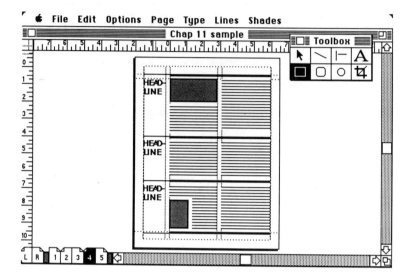

Figure 10-8

Figure 10-9

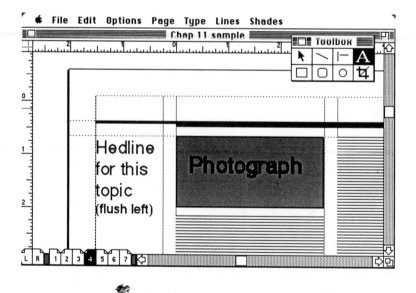

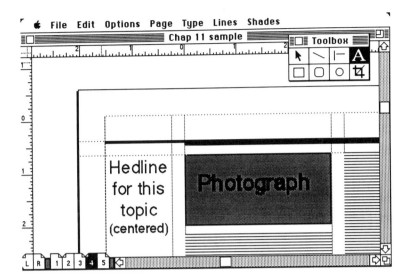

Figure 10-10

Figure 10-11

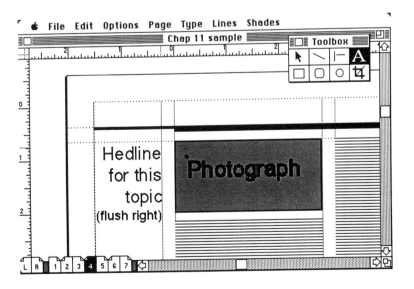

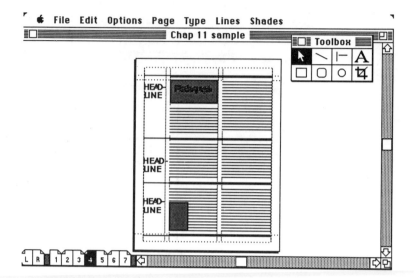

Figure 10-12

Figure 10-13

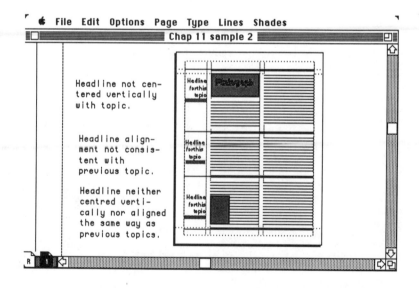

Consistency

Strive for consistency. Good looking publications result from handling type and space the same way throughout your publication or document. The following will help you produce effective, good looking publications. Here are some of the things to look for.

Headlines

All headlines should be set in the same typeface, type size, and type style, with the same leading and alignment.

Subheads

All lower-level subheads should be set in the same typeface, type size, and type style, with the same leading and alignment.

Lower-Level Subheads

All second-level subheads should be set in the same typeface, type size, and type style, leading, with the same line length and alignment.

Body Copy

All body copy should be set in the same typeface, type size, and type style, with the same leading, and alignment. Paragraphs should be uniformly indented throughout a publication. Spacing between paragraphs should be uniform.

Captions

All captions should be set in the same typeface, type size, and type style, with the same leading, line length and alignment.

Organizers

Page numbers, chapter headings, and headers and footers should be used the same way throughout your publication.

Spacing

Vertical and horizontal spacing is also crucial to the success of your publication. Equal spacing must be scrupulously maintained throughout your publication in the following areas:

Margins

The same amount of space should separate the image area of your publication from the top, bottom, and side edges of each page. The image area of your publication is the total area containing headlines, body copy, photos, and captions.

Columns

Columns should be separated from each other horizontally by the same amount of space on each page.

Body copy should be separated from headlines, subheads, captions, artwork and borders by the same amount of space on each page.

Graphic Elements

The graphics elements you use to guide the reader and emphasize important points should also be consistent throughout your publication. For example, borders should be the same throughout your publication. If different borders are used for different sections, they should remain the same within each section.

Horizontal rules used to separate articles or topics must always be the same size and surrounded by the same amount of white space.

Vertical rules between columns should be the same thickness each time, and should be surrounded by the same amount of white space.

Small boxes and bullets used to organize lists must be the same size each time they're used, and should be surrounded by the same amounts of white space.

Photographs and artwork should be separated from surrounding headlines and body copy by the same amount of space throughout your publication.

HOW TO ACHIEVE CONSISTENCY

Attention to detail in the above areas, and in others, spells the difference between an easy-to-read first-class publication and an hard-to-read, amateurish one.

Begin your search for consistency by understanding the strengths and limitations of your word processor, and making full use of its formatting capabilities. This is an example of the reason for the widespread use of Microsoft Word, beginning with Version 3.0, as the front-end word processor for desktop publishing applications in both the MS-DOS and Apple Macintosh environments.

Microsoft Word permits you to format your publication as you write or edit it, and with the convenience (on the Macintosh) of style sheets that can be instantly recalled and "retrofitted" to text. The same style sheets can be used for a variety of publications. These style sheets are also invaluable when more than one individual will be contributing to a publication. Word's style sheets can be copied and shared among documents, ensuring consistent preparation of word-processed files.

Aldus PageMaker builds on Microsoft Word's formatting capabilities with its Page Setup and Master Pages functions, as well as with the number of alignment guides PageMaker permits you to create.

PageMaker makes it easy to create master pages, which make it easy to set up a grid, or pattern of printing and non-printing lines, that will be maintained automatically from page to page. On PageMaker's master pages, you can use these alignment guides to define:

- Page borders

- Column widths

- Column spacing

- Repeating header and footer information

- Location of page numbers

- Headline location

- Position of the first line of body copy on each page

- Position of the last line of body copy on each page

- Maximum permissible photo area

These alignment guides are created by being "pulled" out of the horizontal and vertical rulers on the Pagemaker page. Once established, these guidelines can be locked in place so you will not accidentally select and grab them while trying to select and move adjacent text blocks or graphics.

Hint

Up to 40 guides per page can be added to your publication. On a complicated page, this can become somewhat confusing. There's nothing to prevent you from identifying these lines, however. Simply write notes to yourself on the pasteboard behind the PageMaker publication, outside of your publication area.

Do this on the master pages and the notes will appear automatically on each of the following pages. The type used to describe the various guidelines will usually be unreadable at normal magnifications, but it will be there for reference when needed. When needed, the page should be enlarged to 100%.

Placeholders

Another way of maintaining consistency is to create "placeholders" that will define the distance between photographs and adjacent captions or body copy. These placeholders can also be used to maintain consistent spacing between horizontal rules, headlines, subheads, and body copy.

These spaceholders can be created as shaded rectangles on the master-page pasteboard. They can be copied to the Clipboard, moved into position each time they're needed, and erased after use. Since they're part of the master pages, however, they'll remain available for reuse, whatever page you;re on..

Figure 10-14 shows one of the placeholders found in the Aldus Designs for Newsletters collection of templates. Each of the newsletter templates in the collection includes its own unique placeholders. Similar vertical and horizontal placeHolders can be created for your own publications.

Grids

Regarding column widths, it is important to remember that a five-column grid does not mean that all body copy and artwork has to be the same width. For example, the next five figures (Figs. 10-15 through 10-19) illustrate alternative body-copy variations for a five column page.

Variations on the same column building-blocks might occur on the same page. For example, photographs or copy might extend across two or more columns. What's crucial is that the artwork or copy be aligned with the original column grid forming the background for the page. Otherwise, consistency begins to be lost.

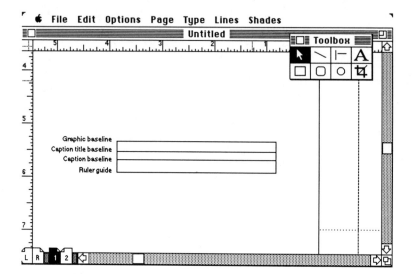

Figure 10-14

Figure 10-15

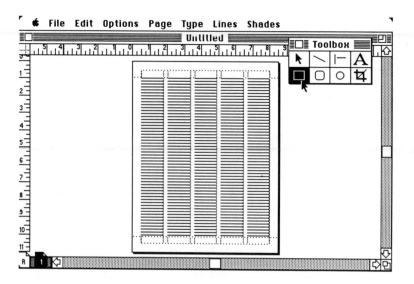

300

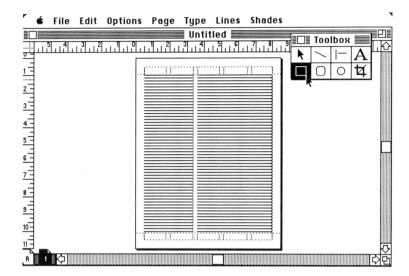

Figure 10-16

Figure 10-17

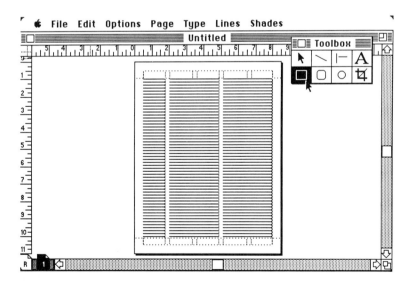

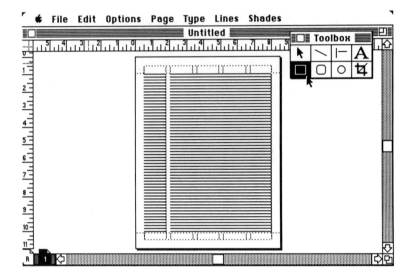

Figure 10-18

Figure 10-19

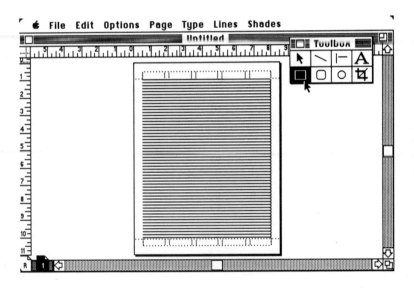

To observe the flexibility permitted by multi-column grids, look at your daily newspaper. Notice the diversity of article and advertisement widths possible, all of them based on a standard seven- or eight-column grid.

In Fig. 10-20, the photos line up with the column guides. In Fig. 10-21, however, the photographs and copy blocks extend beyond the column format.

Figure 10-22 is even more extreme, and causes a total loss of the 5 column grid. It looks messy and disorganized.

Occasionally, you may want to change column structure on the same page (Fig. 10-23). This is especially true in newsletters, where a different column arrangement could be used to separate feature articles from short topics or calendar listings.

For example, you might want to vary the bottom of your three column newsletter to include five columns containing short biographies associated with pictures.

Figure 10-20

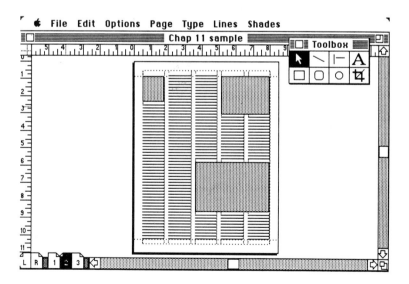

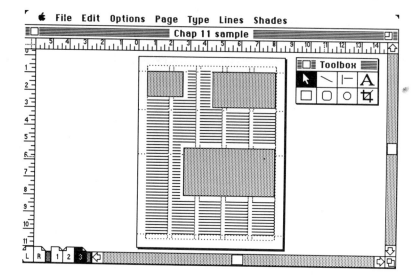

Figure 10-21

Figure 10-22

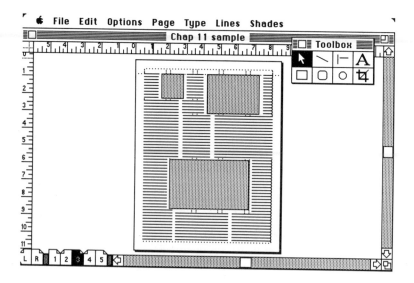

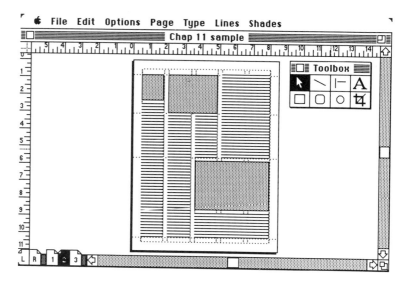

Figure 10-23

Aldus Newsletter Portfolio

For a fuller discussion of graphics and their applications to newsletters, Aldus publishes a Newsletter Portfolio that includes both software and extensive documentation. The software includes over twenty newsletter formats and grids, which you can easily modify for your own use.

By following the instructions contained in the Newsletter Portfolio, and working with the formats provided, you'll quickly gain the experience necessary to produce good looking newsletters. This knowledge can then be carried over into other types of publications, including advertisements and brochures.

C H A P T E R

11

New Directions

How to Make Even Better Use of PageMaker

Your desktop publishing system can grow with you as you become more involved in producing quality documents with Aldus PageMaker. There are numerous hardware and software additions you can make to your basic system. These add-ons can do several things for you:

a. Save you money. Services you previously had to purchase from outside firms can be provided in-house. This will save time and money. In addition, you will now be able to turn around and offer these services to others.

For example, if you have been renting time on a laser printer, at some point you will find it economically feasible to purchase your own. Similarly, if you've been using an outside scanning service, you may want to have your own image scanner. Finally, if your firm is heavily involved in high-quality desktop publishing, you may find it economically justifiable to purchase a Linotronic 300 typesetter rather than continue to bring formatted diskettes to a commercial phototypesetting service.

b. Increase your efficiency. As your productivity improves, you will be able to accomplish more work in less time. It's amazing how quickly minutes add up to hours. Big screen monitors, which eliminate the need to toggle back and forth between "fit in screen" and "actual size" views of the PageMaker document you're working on, are a good example of productivity-increasing devices.

c. Increase your flexibility. You will be able to put PageMaker to work in new ways. The quality of your output will increase, permitting you to do more things with PageMaker. You will also be able to charge higher prices for the PageMaker services you offer others.

d. Increase your security. Although not limited primarily to desktop publishing, data backup becomes increasingly important as more and more of your income becomes dependent on your desk top publishing system. If, for example, your income depends on meeting newsletter deadlines you have to anticipate, and be prepared to handle, system- and human-error problems. The issue of data backup is compounded by the large size of PageMaker files, which—if they contain many graphics—can outgrow the storage capacity of individual floppy diskettes.

Big-Screen Monitors

One of the first major add-on purchases you're likely to want to make is a big-screen monitor.

Because of the small size of most personal computer screens, you're liable to spend a great deal of time toggling back and forth between various views of the PageMaker document you're working on. Although PageMaker makes it easy to change views using either the mouse or keyboard commands, it nevertheless can become frustrating to have to switch back and forth continually between the "fit in screen" view, which permits you to look at the overall page layout, and the "actual size" or "twice actual size" views, which help you align type and graphic images accurately.

Big-screen monitors help you avoid this problem. Because you can view a full page at a time, you can work on the details as well as view the overall composition of the actual-size page or spread simultaneously.

There are two basic types of big screen monitors: single-page and double-page designs.

One of the first popular big-screen monitors to appear in the Macintosh environment was the Radius FPD—for "full page display." Many of the individuals involved in the original design of the Macintosh were also involved in the development of the Radius FPD. This perhaps accounts for the seamless integration of the FPD with the original Macintosh screen.

The Radius FPD acts as an extension of the original screen on the Macintosh. It is designed to be placed to the side of your computer, placed in such a way that the original Macintosh screen is within comfortable viewing distance.

In use, the Radius FPD displays a full 8½-by-11-inch page, while the original screen on the Macintosh displays the PageMaker toolbox plus graphic elements or text waiting to be placed in the publication. When you use this monitor with graphics programs, you can place your palettes and drawing tools on the original Macintosh screen and use the Radius for the drawing you're working on.

Integration between the Radius FPD and the Macintosh screen is extremely smooth. As you scroll the PageMaker pointer off the right-hand side of the Radius, the pointer appears at the left-hand side of your original Macintosh screen. The primary disadvantage of the FPD is the need to shift to a reduced-size display if you want to view two facing pages.

A second approach to big screen displays is exhibited by the Mega-Screen, for MS-DOS systems. The MegaScreen displays **two** full-size 8¹/₂-by-11 pages. This makes it easier to work on two-page spreads at actual size. You can see both pages at actual size, which means you will be able to read text displayed in all but the smallest type sizes.

The drawback of the MegaScreen, like most of the big screens in the PC environment, is that they **replace** your computer's original monitor. This means that part of the PageMaker document continues to be obscured by the PageMaker toolbox. It also means that there is no longer a convenient place on the PageMaker pasteboard to display text or graphics waiting to be placed in the PageMaker document.

At present, big screens are extremely expensive—in many cases their prices equal the cost of your original computer. This situation, however, will probably change and prices drop as demand increases and economies of scale reduce the costs of producing the big screens.

In most cases, these monitors require special adapter cards. To use them, you have to make sure that there are extra slots available in your computer. The Radius FPD, for example, originally required a dealer- or factory-installed modification to your Macintosh Plus. When used with the Macintosh SE, however, the necessary interface circuitry is contained on a card that is inserted in the SE's expansion slot.

NETWORKING HARDWARE AND SOFTWARE

It is becoming increasingly obvious that self-contained personal computers are, at least in some instances, starting to become obsolete. Desktop publishing quickly becomes a team effort, as articles for a company newsletter, for example, are written by several individuals. The role of the "desktop publisher," or editor, becomes one of integrating the work of others.

In the initial stages of such joint activities, it is easy enough simply to share data diskettes by transferring them from one computer to another. However, the physical transfer of diskettes takes time and increases opportunities for damaged or lost manuscripts.

Furthermore, not everybody involved in a joint effort is likely to be using the same type of computer. What happens if articles for a company newsletter are being written on a combination of Apple Macintosh and MS-DOS personal computers?

One alternative, of course, would be to purchase modems and communications programs for both computers. This alternative, however, is rarely totally satisfactory. It's time-consuming, ties up telephone lines and—in some cases—formatting information may be lost in the communications process. Frequently, a conversion process is necessary on both computers.

Several software solutions are available to expedite file transfer between Macintosh and MS-DOS personal computers. These programs include software for each computer plus a cable for hooking up a Macintosh to a MS-DOS personal computer. Two of the most popular programs of this sort are PC-To-MAC and Back and DataViz's MacLink Plus.

MacLink has proven especially popular, as it includes the sophisticated filtering necessary to overcome difficulties that may be presented by the special characters and file saving conventions built into the various word processing programs found in the Macintosh and PC environments. MacLink, for example, makes it easy to translate WordStar documents on the PC into documents usable by the Macintosh version of Microsoft Word.

The principal disadvantage of MacLink and PC-To-MAC and Back is that they are limited to connecting a single PC to a single Macintosh.

This means cumbersome cable rearranging is necessary if more than two computers are to share information.

Another disadvantage is that you have to know in advance which files you want to transfer, and have to transfer the files before you can begin placing them in PageMaker documents.

The Centram TOPS System

One of the newest and best ways to get around these problems is the Centram TOPS system. The TOPS system is based on the AppleTalk networking protocols built into every Macintosh computer.

TOPS is a combination hardware and software solution that makes it possible to connect up to thirty-two Apple Macintosh and MS-DOS computers to each other through the AppleTalk network. Hooking up the Macintoshes to each other is simple and relatively inexpensive, as both the software and cable costs are very reasonable.

Centram manufactures a plug-in expansion card for MS-DOS computers that permits them to communicate both with other MS-DOS computers and with Apple Macintosh computers through the AppleTalk network.

The TOPS system is a true file server. Any computer on the network can copy files from any other computer on the network. Once the computers are connected, there is no need to rearrange cables. Equally important, TOPS on the Macintosh is memory resident, so it is always available from whatever program you're running.

In TOPS terminology, any computer can be a "client" and any computer a "server." With the TOPS system, an Apple Macintosh running PageMaker or Microsoft Word 3.0 can search for and retrieve files hidden in any PC's subdirectories.

While working with the Apple Macintosh version of PageMaker, you can search for and directly place MS-DOS word-processed files stored anywhere on your PC's hard disk.

312

In most cases, especially when transferring Microsoft Word PC files to Macintosh Word 3.0 files, typeface, type size, and type style formatting information will be transferred. Other word processing programs vary in the amount of formatting information that can be translated.

AppleShare

The AppleShare network is an even more refined approach to sharing information among computers. The AppleShare concept is based on a dedicated Macintosh that is used as a full-time file server for all the PC's and Macintoshes connected to it. With AppleShare, basic word-processing files, for example, can be stored in the central file server, where they will be available for immediate placement in PageMaker documents without interrupting the original author's work.

Like Centram's TOPS system, Apple's AppleShare system includes a plug-in card for MS-DOS computers, which permits them to communicate with Apple Macintosh computers over the AppleTalk network.

Backing Up Your Work

TOPS and AppleShare offer an often-overlooked extra. Because they make file transfers between computers easy, it becomes just as easy to back up your work as you go along. Normally, if the hard disk on a computer malfunctions, and no backup has been made, the work is lost. On the other hand, if the computer's hard disk malfunctions, but a backup has been stored in a central file server, the file is still available for further work or placement in a PageMaker document.

Thus, although initially you may purchase a networking system to allow easy data exchange between computers, you may find it's greatest utility will come the day it instantly permits you to restore a file that otherwise would have been lost through a hardware or software failure—or even simple human error.

If you are using either a Macintosh or MS-DOS personal computer by itself, you will want to investigate the various backup alternatives available. In both the Macintosh and MS-DOS environments, there are a number of hardware and software solutions available. These solutions become more important as the size of your desktop published files grows, because in many cases the files become too large to fit on a single floppy disk.

Software solutions simply provide a directed sequence for backing up your hard disk on several floppies. During backup or file recovery you are instructed in the proper sequence of diskette insertion. Some programs back up everything, others simply back up files that have been modified since your last backup session.

Hardware solutions include tape backup units, which make a mirror image of your data on a tape cartridge similar to a standard audio cassette. Tape backups cannot be used by themselves for data storage, but they do permit the transfer of data back to the hard disk. Another alternative is offered by removable hard-disk systems, such as the Iomega Bernoulli Boxes. These are available for both Macintosh and MS-DOS computers, and consist of removable hard disks that can be backed up easily.

Additional Fonts

Laser printers such as the Apple LaserWriter and the QMS PS-800 offer a variety of built-in typefaces. These typefaces include Helvetica, a sans-serif typeface ideally-suited for headlines, as well as Times Roman, well suited for body copy and captions. The LaserWriter Plus and QMS PS-800 Plus add to these by offering additional typefaces, including Helvetica Condensed, (useful for squeezing in letters in a headline), and several distinctive body-copy faces with serifs, including Avant Garde, Bookman, New Century Schoolbook, and Palatino.

As you become more involved with desktop publishing you will probably want to expand your repertoire of fonts. Adobe is one of the leaders in producing downloadable fonts for desktop publishing use.

Adobe fonts are different from those produced by other firms in that Adobe licenses its fonts from ITC—the International Typographic Corporation, which owns the original copyrights for many of the world's most famous type fonts.

This is in contrast to other font publishers who have often chosen to create their own fonts similar, but not identical, to the "official" ITC fonts. This saves money, but sacrifices exact interchangeability between the type you set on your desktop computer and the type available from commercial typesetting firms.

The advantage of the Adobe fonts is that your work will have a closer relationship to the richness and variety of true typeset-quality publications. In addition, the fonts will perfectly complement the fonts already built into your LaserWriter or LaserWriter Plus (or QMS PS-800 or PS-800 Plus).

For example, your first add-on fonts might be Helvetica Black, (useful for short, high-impact headlines), Helvetica Light or Helvetica Condensed. Because these are designed to complement the Helvetica fonts already resident in your laser printer, you are assured of a consistent texture and a perfect visual match among these various forms of the basic Helvetica typeface.

Adobe is aggressively introducing new fonts on a continuing basis. Soon, nearly all of the ITC fonts available from commercial phototypesetting firms will be available for use on your Apple Macintosh and laser printer.

Fewer typefaces are currently available in the MS-DOS environment, especially if you are using the original Hewlett-Packard LaserJet or the new LaserJet II printers. The primary sources of font flexibility are the Hewlett-Packard plug-in font cartridges or Hewlett-Packard's downloadable fonts.

At least initially, Hewlett-Packard's desktop publishing solution, DDL, will probably lag behind the typeface offerings found in the Macintosh environment.

315

It remains to be seen how quickly the gap in typeface availability between the Macintosh and MS-DOS environments will close. Undoubtedly, more MS-DOS typefaces will become available as MS-DOS desktop publishing gains in popularity. It is likely that at some point the entire range of ITC typefaces will be available in the MS-DOS environment.

Graphics Programs

As you get further involved in desktop publishing, you will probably also grow to appreciate a greater diversity of graphics programs. In the Macintosh environment, for example, you will probably progress quickly beyond the basic MacPaint and MacDraw to more sophisticated programs the likes of FullPaint and SuperPaint.

FullPaint is valuable because it permits you to work on larger images, and you can open six files at once. SuperPaint is innovative in that it consists of "layered" software. It includes both "paint" and "draw" layers. This gives additional flexibility, especially useful when creating logos. SuperPaint also makes it easy to "nudge" graphics images from vertical to horizontal at tiny increments, for precise alignments

CricketDraw comes closest to exploiting the full potential of the Adobe PostScript page description language. CricketDraw permits you to create "shadowed" type and other three-dimensional effects.

One of the most exciting graphics programs to appear in the Macintosh environment is Adobe Illustrator. Adobe Illustrator differs from conventional programs in that it's designed to enhance graphic images entered using scanners or created with conventional paint and draw programs.

Adobe Illustrator permits you to trace a scanned image—choosing only the elements of the original drawing or photograph you decide are important. You can then use PostScript's infinite ability to scale and fill lines to come up with a revised drawing that's better than the original. Adobe Illustrator creates curves and straight lines by defining their end points and permitting you to stretch them to any shape desired. Because of the various magnifications at which you work, this method of drawing lines is far more accurate than drawing them using a mouse.

Adobe Illustrator's capabilities are so advanced that they are likely to be of interest primarily to advanced graphics professionals, yet it's nice to know such capabilities are available if needed.

In the MS-DOS environment you will probably find yourself outgrowing your initial enthusiasm for programs such as Windows Paint, and will look for graphics programs with more flexibility in terms of the types of drawings they can create as well as the speed with which they can translate your ideas into reality.

INPUT DEVICES

If you are using a Macintosh 512 Enhanced, you may want to purchase an optional Macintosh Plus keyboard. This keyboard has a separate numeric keypad, plus separate cursor control keys, which permits you to take full advantage of the editing capability built into Microsoft Word 3.0 for the Macintosh. The numeric keypad, when used in conjunction with the Option and Command keys, also makes it possible for you to move quickly through text blocks, which speeds inserting, deleting, and replacing text.

If you already have a Macintosh Plus, you may want to choose the Datatext keyboard, which has a "feel" more similar to the keyboards used in the new Macintosh SE computer. The Macintosh SE keyboard offers the same feel as the keyboards usually found on MS-DOS computers.

In the MS-DOS environment, many computer users have forsaken their IBM keyboards for the various Keytronic keyboard models. Many computer users feel these keyboards have a more comfortable key spacing and nicer "touch" than the standard IBM offering.

Keytronic's most popular, the KB5151, also has the numeric keypad that's missing on the standard IBM keyboard.

If you are heavily involved in graphics, you may want to consider a graphics tablet, such as the Koala Touch or the SummaGraphics MacTablet. These permit "freehand" drawing, in a fashion similar to using a pencil and paper. The difference is that your images appear on a screen. After creation, your "electronic pencil" sketches can be modified and improved using a standard paint- or draw-type graphics program. Graphics tablets are available for both Macintosh and MS-DOS systems.

Scanners

There are several types of graphics scanners available for inputting photographs and line drawings to your computer. There are both sheet-feed and flatbed scanners. Scanners differ in their resolution and their speed of operation. The better scanners scan at 300 dots-per-inch, which is identical to the resolution of most laser printers.

Sheet-feed scanners operate by themselves—they do not require you to move the scanning head yourself—but are limited in that you cannot scan portions of large images such as newspaper pages, and you cannot scan pages from books. Flatbed scanners are also easier on the photograph or document being scanned. There's little possibility of the photograph jamming or being warped as it passes through the scanner.

Hewlett-Packard ScanJet

One of the most interesting scanners to have appeared recently is the Hewlett-Packard ScanJet. This flatbed scanner is notable for its fast operating speed, ease of use, and—most important—the fact that it can be used with either MS-DOS computers or the Apple MacIntosh. Compatibility with both families of computers is gained through sepa-

rate software and plug-in cards that are inserted in the computer
you're using. With the Hewlett-Packard ScanJet, one scanner will
work with both types of computers in your office.

If your desktop publishing activities regularly involve preparing advertisements and catalogs that contain product photographs, you may
want to consider one of the programs that permit you to connect a
video camera to your computer to capture and store digitized images.

With such an arrangement, you could take informal "electronic photographs" of your products before you took formal (and expensive) stu-
dio-quality photographs. These scanned images would assist in the design your publication and also make it easier to take precisely the right
photograph. Instead of designing your publication around existing
photographs, you could design the photograph to include the specific
angle and perspective needed for your publication.

Additional Computer Memory

Both the Apple Macintosh and the MS-DOS "Windows" environments
help you share information easily between programs using the Clipboard feature. In addition, the Macintosh, and MS-DOS computers
running full versions of Microsoft's Windows program, permit you to
load more than one application at a time so you can switch back and
forth between them quickly.

Using the Apple Switcher, for example, both PageMaker and your favorite word processing program can be loaded at the same time, so
you can write extended text blocks and place them instantly in your
PageMaker document. Similarly, with Microsoft Windows in the MS-
DOS environment, you can prepare Windows Write word-processed
files and immediately place them in your PageMaker documents.

The down side of loading more than one program into your
computer's memory in most cases, however, is reduced operating
speed. The more programs that are active in your computer, the

slower each will run. Increased memory can eliminate many of these problems.

Besides speeding up program execution and permitting more than one program to be active at one time, increasing your computer's memory permits print spooling.

Laser printers are notoriously slow when it comes to printing complex pages—that is, pages that contain complicated graphics. A print spooler acts as a temporary holding area for data before it is sent to the printer. Thus, you can continue to use your computer—working on a second PageMaker document, for example—while the print spooler takes care of processing and printing your first PageMaker document.

Consulting and Technical Assistance

It often makes sense to hire an outside graphics consulting firm to help you with the initial formatting of your PageMaker publications. This is not to cast aspersions on your own abilities, but rather to provide you with a starting point and a head start for making the best use of your own developing talent and expertise.

A great deal of thought and many years of experience are involved in developing a visual identity for a newsletter or book good enough to withstand the test of time. An outside graphics consultant, especially one comfortable with desktop publishing, can help you develop a format for your newsletter that you will be able to maintain for many years to come. An outside consultant will know which traps to avoid and will be able to provide you with detailed style sheets to help you keep on track issue after issue.

Other Enhancements

This barely scratches the surface of the many ways you can enhance your desktop publishing system's productivity. In both the Apple

Macintosh and MS-DOS environments, a variety of spelling and grammar checkers are available that can help you write better text. Surge protectors and uninterruptable power sources can extend your computer's life and protect against data loss from power surges and outages.

Computer furniture is another area of productivity worthy of serious consideration. Your first desktop publishing system may simply be placed on your desktop. Specialized computer workstations, however, can enhance your productivity and creativity. Among other things, these workstations permit you to adjust keyboard height.

Additional comfort options include anti-glare screens to eliminate eyestrain caused by reflections from windows and overhead lights, and special chairs to eliminate back strain.

Uninterruptable Power Supplies

Brief interruptions in the power going to your computer can be extremely frustrating—as well as dangerous. Your computer's memory is instantly erased when your home or office lights flicker on and off. This is often caused by high winds, or a thunderstorm miles away.

When power is interrupted, you not only lose all the work you've done since the last time you saved your work, but the off-and-on surge of electricity can do permanent damage to your computer—especially its hard disk if it was saving or retrieving information when the power was interrupted.

Uninterruptable power supplies are the answer. They usually consist of two parts: a battery backup and a surge protector. Your computer is plugged into the uninterruptable power supply, and the power supply is plugged into the wall. When power is interrupted, your computer instantly begins to draw current from the battery. Usually a combination of lights and audible alarms will inform you that power has been interrupted. This gives you time to save your work and turn off your computer before the battery is depleted in case power is not immediately restored. The surge protector protects your computer from the voltage spike, similar to a spark, that usually follows a brief interruption of power.

Most people view uninterruptable power supplies as a luxury—until they lose an hour's work or find that their computer has been damaged through no fault of their own.

Self-Improvement

To reinforce a point made elsewhere, perhaps the most important productivity enhancement you can make is to break out of your habit of reading trade publications specific to your industry or specialty, and subscribe to visually-oriented publications such as Communications Arts, Print or U&LC.

By making a determined effort to analyze the work of others, you can inspire yourself to unleashing your hidden creative potential.

SELF-ANALYSIS WORKSHEET

Ask yourself these questions when considering whether and how to improve your basic desktop publishing system:

1) What services do you presently purchase from outside sources?

Laser printing _____

Graphic-image scanning _____

Phototypesetting _____

2) How much do you pay for those services during a typical month? _____

3) How many hours a day do you spend working with PageMaker? _____

---

4) Are you frustrated by the need to switch frequently back and forth between Actual Size and Fit In Screen views of your PageMaker document? _____

5) How many people typically contribute articles or graphic images to a typical PageMaker publication?_____

6) What types of computers do they use?

_____

7) How do file transfers currently take place in your operation? _____

8) How do you currently back up your PageMaker publications at the end of each working session?

_____

9) How many typefaces do you typically include in your PageMaker documents? _____

10) Do your PageMaker-produced documents look too much like the PageMaker-produced documents of others in your community or in your industry?

_____

11) Does your graphics software offer the flexibility you need? _____

Conclusion

As you continue to become involved with desktop publishing, you will no doubt end up designing a desktop publishing system specifically for your needs. The system you end up with will be a direct reflection of your interests and the type of desktop publishing you do.

Keep abreast of the latest advances in desktop publishing by reading the various Macintosh and MS-DOS computer publications, as well as the magazines and newsletters aimed specifically at desktop publishing. These will help you keep up-to-date about hardware and software advances that can improve your productivity and save you time and money.

EXCELLENCE THROUGH SELF IMPROVEMENT

Proofing and Evaluation

One of the most important project-management steps you can take involves building in safeguards to ensure project accuracy. This is especially important if you are working completely by yourself, doing both copywriting and layout. You must get others involved in proofreading your work.

Your eye is easily fooled, especially when called upon to review your own work. It is very easy to overlook your own typographical errors. Without your being aware of it, your eye and brain fill in missing words or overlook doubled ones.

Spell-Checking Programs

It's important to remember that, while spell-checkers are usually built into word processing programs, spell-checking is not a feature of either PageMaker 1.0 for the PC or PageMaker 2.0 for the Macintosh. This means that you, yourself, have to be sure to double check the spelling of headlines, captions and other text you type directly into PageMaker documents.

It is extremely easy, as the self-mailer shown in Fig. 11-1 illustrates, to make a simple mistake on a last-minute addition to a PageMaker document. The example shows how the author of this book succeeded in producing a perfect self-mailer with just one mistake—in his own address!

After each PageMaker project is completed and printed, you should carefully analyze it. Use the questions on the checklist that follows to make sure that everything is correct:

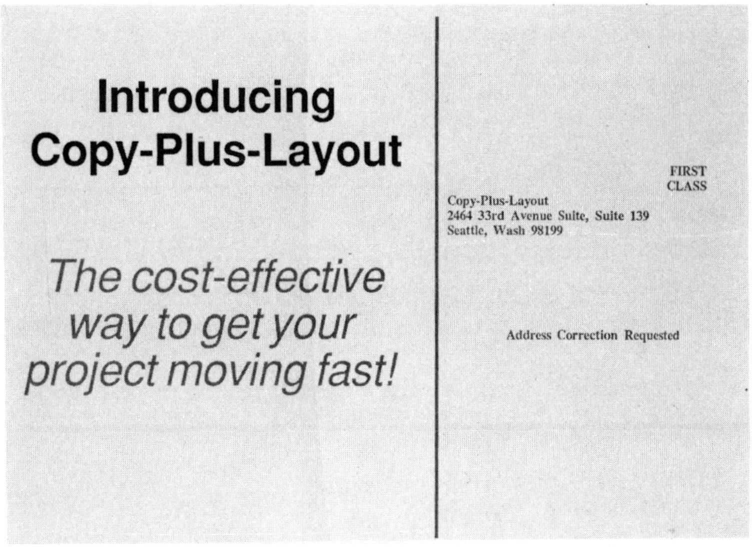

**Introducing
Copy-Plus-Layout**

FIRST
CLASS

Copy-Plus-Layout
2464 33rd Avenue Suite, Suite 139
Seattle, Wash 98199

*The cost-effective
way to get your
project moving fast!*

Address Correction Requested

Figure 11-1

LAST-MINUTE CHECKLIST

1) How many people other than myself have proofread this piece? _____

2) Did I read the publication aloud carefully, to find grammatical errors that the spelling-checker couldn't be expected to? (Words used incorrectly, etc.) _____

3) Have I double-checked the accuracy of all addresses and phone numbers? _____

4) Have I double-checked the accuracy of all model numbers and prices? (Transposed numbers are extremely difficult to detect.) _____

5) Compare your about-to-be-completed project with your personal notebook of frequently made mistakes, to make sure you haven't fallen into a familiar trap.

Then, after your publication has been printed, discipline yourself to fill-out—strictly for your own use—an evaluation sheet similar to the one below. These evaluation sheets should be kept together with the publications they refer to in a separate file, where you can review your progress. In your evaluation sheet, ask yourself questions such as:

EVALUATION SHEET

Did the project succeed in communicating the purpose of the publication visually?

How closely did the project fit into my firm's corporate identity?

How does the publication stack up against other similar publications produced by my competitors?

How consistently did I apply the tools of graphic design?

Most important, what would I do differently?

Helpful Hint

Maintain two portfolios of projects you have created with PageMaker. Use one of them for demonstration purposes, for showing off your work.

The other portfolio is strictly for your own use. Spend a lot of time with the projects in this portfolio. Evaluate them on a quarterly basis. Take a red pencil, and mark up your work. Make a list of things you would do differently. Try to discover mistakes you have made. Keep a small stenographer's notebook in this portfolio, and make a list of those mistakes.

Portfolio cases and binders are available in all sizes at local art supply stores. Binders are preferable, as you can add additional pages when needed. Most contain transparent sheet protectors with a black background that helps set off your work. Choose the size most appropriate to your work.

Improvement Through Observation

Let the work of others help you improve your own efforts. Subscribe to "inspirational" publications such as Communication Arts, Print, and other art- and design-oriented publications. At the very least, purchase the issues containing their yearly "best" categories—i.e., the best advertising, the best posters, the best letterheads, etc.

Keep these publications near your computer, where you can easily refer to them. As you review the best work in these issues, your brain will be storing away ideas for future recall.

As you review the "best" work of others, try to analyze the underlying grid structure. Try to figure out how many columns are used. Try to determine what makes the "best" work of others look so good,.

Helpful Hint

If you have a scanner, use it to scan a publication or advertisement that you like, and place the scanned image into a PageMaker document.

Then, using the Columns command and guides, try to recreate the background grid. Try to discover the underlying logic behind the advertisement or publication. You may be surprised to find how deceptively simple the foundation really is. Try to analyze the problems the original designer faced, and determine for yourself how he overcame them.

As you read your daily newspaper and weekly magazines, take note of the different ways headlines can be placed on a page. Note the different ways that mastheads and publication titles can be integrated with headlines, artwork, subheads and body copy.

Go to a large bookstore and analyze the book covers available. Take some time, too, to look at magazine covers. After you return, spend a few hours creating sample one- and two-page PageMaker documents that illustrate the various ways headlines, white space, artwork and body copy can be used.

Hint

Even better, maintain a notebook containing pencil sketches showing the basic ways you discover consistency and surprise are handled in award-winning advertisements and publications, or in those that have caught your eye. Keep this notebook handy so you can refer to it at the beginning of a project.

Books

Try to locate a bookstore specializing in art and design books, or find the "design" section of your local bookstore. Each year, several books such as The One Show, from the New York Art Directors Club, are published. These, too, can provide you with the inspiration you need to constantly improve your talents.

Educational Resources

As your confidence level rises, you may want to consider taking an evening college course, or a summer course, in publication design and layout. Like PageMaker itself, a course in design techniques could be an investment in yourself that would reward you for many years to come.

Consider joining the local advertising or art director's club in your area. These organizations frequently have presentations by outside professionals. These presentations can keep your creative juices flowing, and you'll meet new friends who share your interest in design.

Indeed, after you become familiar with PageMaker, you may want to consider teaching an evening college or "experimental college" desktop publishing course. Teachers often learn as much as their students. They learn from the act of seeing things from their student's fresh perspective, and ideas, and from the organization of material that is necessary before each class.

Outside Consultants

Outside consultants are another important resource that should be utilized to the fullest. Even if you are comfortable with using PageMaker, there may be times when you are simply stumped on a project. At times like these, when you can't find inspiration in the work of others contained in your "idea notebooks" or "Best of . . ." design book, you might consider hiring a graphics consultant to get you started.

Before you do, you should define your expectations carefully, so you can discuss your needs and use this outside professional as efficiently as possible. Ask yourself questions like these:

CONSULTANT CHECKLIST

How much assistance am I looking for?

____ Tight comprehensive design for a specific project

____ Formatting for future projects that I will complete myself

____ Rough layout ideas

____ Someone with whom to discuss alternative design strategies

What are the qualifications I'm looking for?

____ Proven design excellence

____ Previous desktop publishing experience

____ Experience in my field

How much money do I want to invest?

Am I looking for assistance on new projects or constructive criticism on previously finished projects?

Experimentation

However, a willingness to solicit the advice of outside professionals should not detract from the importance of cultivating your own talents.

It should never be forgotten that trial-and-error forms the basis of successful graphic design . . . and that you learn by doing. This is an aspect of design most designers are curiously reticent about.

It's interesting that most photographers freely admit that they take hundreds of pictures for every prize-winner that gets published. Yet, the mounds of scrap paper containing discarded layout sketches next to an experienced designer's desk is rarely discussed. Use PageMaker's "electronic scratch pad" to try out various design solutions constantly in your quest for the "best" design.

Experimenting with PageMaker

Remember that the file menu in both PageMaker for the PC and the Macintosh Version 2.0 of PageMaker contains a Save As feature. This makes it easy for you to save different versions of your project as you work on them.

For example, let's say you're working on a newsletter layout. You have been using a three-column format, but want to experiment with a four-column one for a page containing numerous short topics. You have been saving your newsletter under the file name "NEWSJUNE" on the PC.

Make a final save of your work, and then modify your column structure. Use Save As to save your revised four-column format under a different name, such as "REVJUNE".

Hint

The Save As command can also be used to make backup copies of your work. Many experienced PageMaker users always keep a floppy disk in their computer, even if they are working from a hard disk. Every so often, they save their work to it. That way, if the hard disk should fail hey have an backup copy. At the end of the day, final "saves" are made to both the hard disk and the floppy backup.

There is a secondary benefit to this. Because projects are saved on both floppy disks and your computer's hard disk, after a publication has been printed, you can erase it from your hard disk and keep an "archive" copy on floppies. This will prevent your hard disk from becoming overloaded as well as speed up hard disk access time.

The only limiting factor to floppy disk backups is that conventional PC floppy disks can hold only 360K of information. This means that the length of PageMaker files containing lots of complex graphics may exceed the capacity of a single disk. The MS-DOS BACKUP utility will allow you to save part of the file on one disk, and the remainder on another. (This is less of a problem with 800K Macintosh disks.) If your PC AT contains both a 360K drive and a 1.2 megabyte drive, make sure you use the high-capacity one. PageMaker files can quickly grow beyond the 360K limitation of most floppy disks.

MAXIMIZING YOUR INVESTMENT

Should you consider becoming a PageMaker entrepreneur? Once you have mastered the basic PageMaker skills and have put them to work successfully in your primary business, you may want to consider selling your services to others.There are several benefits to be gained from this:

1) Your investment in hardware, software and learning becomes an extra profit center. You can earn extra money for yourself or for your business.

2) You can justify the purchase of a laser printer, or speed up purchasing one if you don't already own one.

3) You can afford system enhancements that would otherwise be beyond your reach, such as big-screen monitors, expanded memory or hard disk storage capacity, extra type fonts, an image scanner, or hardware and software to connect two or more computers.

---

4) Most important, since "practice makes perfect," you can earn extra money while enhancing your skills and becoming even more proficient with PageMaker. This will improve both the speed and quality of your PageMaker projects. Whether or not soliciting extra business makes sense for you depends on the amount of extra time you and your staff can comfortably devote to additional PageMaker projects, and on the nature of the market and competition in your area.

Here are some guidelines for determining whether or not it makes sense to offer PageMaker services in your area. Begin by considering the services you can offer:

Hardware Rentals

Many PageMaker users do not own their own laser printers. If you own one, you can rent time on it to those who want to output their already formatted diskettes but are without the means to do so on their own.

Similarly, many PageMaker users in your area can probably use scanning services, but are unable (or unwilling) to invest in their own scanners. By purchasing scanning services from you, these individuals can help you expand your system's capabilities even if you could not otherwise justify the purchase of a scanner.

- Time requirement: Low

- Profit potential: Low

- Flexibility: Low. You must be available when clients need you.

- Potential clients: Individuals and small firms.

- Limitations: Time, competition, accessibility (you must be located where people can find you; parking is important).

Teaching and Consulting

If you have untapped teaching abilities searching for an outlet, you may enjoy helping others get started with Aldus PageMaker. As a PageMaker user, you probably have already had more hands-on experience with PageMaker than most computer store salespeople. As such, your opinions and recommendations can be extremely valuable to people buying their first computer.

Your duties might include helping newcomers to desktop publishing choose the right hardware and software, as well as helping them to integrate desktop publishing into their overall communications objectives. Your recommendations as an unbiased "outsider" rather than "salesperson" are liable to carry a lot of weight.

Teaching and consulting also provide you with an opportunity to share "tricks of the trade" you have picked up during your own experience with PageMaker.

- Time requirement: Low to medium
- Flexibility: Medium—evenings possible
- Profit potential: Medium to high
- Potential clients: Individuals, small-to-medium firms
- Limitations: Time, skill, and your ability to market your services.

Newsletter Editing and Production

If you enjoy writing and working with others, you could offer a newsletter editing and formatting service. You could become as involved in the writing process as you and your clients desired.

At the start you could limit your activities simply to formatting their newsletters and assembling their word-processed articles into completed newsletters.

Later, you could become actively involved and improve their newsletters by editing their copy and rewriting their stories. Articles would be submitted to you on word-processed diskettes. You would edit and rewrite these articles as needed, and place them into PageMaker documents.

- Time requirement: Medium to high
- Flexibility: High. Except for occasional client meetings, work can be done evenings, weekends, or between your own projects.
- Profit potential: Medium, sensitive to competition.
- Potential clients: Businesses of all sizes, including trade and non-profit organizations.
- Limitations: Time, ability to market and service your clients.

Project Management

If you are a multi-talented individual, you can offer complete project management for those interested in producing newsletters and brochures. This activity could become as large as you wanted it to be. Good writing is always in demand, especially when accompanied by strong art direction, consistent on-time performance, and attention to detail. You could take total responsibility for the production of your client's newsletters and brochures—from the initial concept and research through delivery of the final printed product.

The areas you could become involved in include: interviewing and research, copywriting, art direction and photography. Your responsibilities might include choosing and supervising commercial printers—

which opens the profit possibility of marking up the printer's bills by 15 to 17 percent, a legitimate source of advertising agency income.

If you also own database management software and can produce mailing labels, you could even become involved in fulfillment: maintaining your client's mailing list, applying address labels, and bringing the newsletters to the post office.

From a beginning in newsletters, you could undertake assignments in other areas of corporate communications, such as writing speeches, or preparing handout materials including brochures and public relations press kits, as well as other projects requiring a combination of writing and PageMaker talents.

Your purchase of Aldus PageMaker could be the first step in developing a profitable second career!

- Time requirement: High

- Flexibility: Low—you must schedule your time around the client's convenience. Client deadlines must be met.

- Profit potential: High, limited primarily by your selling, writing and marketing skills.

- Potential clients: Local firms of any size, nonprofit organizations.

- Limitations: Time and your ability to market yourself and service your clients.

Analyzing Your Time Resources

One of he first things you'll want to do when considering whether or not to become a PageMaker entrepreneur is to define your goals and your resources. You'll have to determine exactly how much time you have available to devote to outside business, and define exactly what you expect to gain by offering PageMaker services to others. Some of the questions you'll want to ask yourself appear in the following worksheet.

GOAL-DEFINITION AND RESOURCE ANALYSIS WORKSHEET

1) How badly do I want (or need) extra income?

2) How much extra income do I want (or need) to earn each month? $_____

3) What PageMaker services do I want to offer?

Hardware rentals _____

Training or consulting _____

Newsletter editing and production _____

Total project management _____

4) How many hours, during normal business hours, do I have available each month to devote to outside business? _____

5) Am I willing to work evenings and weekends to earn extra money? _____

6) How many evening and weekend hours do I have available each month to devote to outside business?

_____

7) Do I prefer working with:

Entrepreneurs _____   Service firms _____

Large corporations _____   Retailers _____

Small corporations _____   Trade and non-profit organizations _____

> 8) If I presently work for someone else, will he allow me to use his computer and software to earn extra money for myself, on my own time? _____
>
> How much will he charge to rent me time on his computer? $_____
>
> 9) If more computer time than personal time is available, am I willing to hire and train someone to assist me?
>
> 10) Are there other benefits to offering PageMaker services in my area? Such as introduction to clients who are prospects for other services.)

In some cases, the last point may be your best reason to offer Page-Maker services! Similarly, your "at home" second job could lead to a new, more lucrative, position within your present firm, or at another company.

Analyzing Your Competition

The presence of existing and potential competition will have a great deal of influence on the feasibility of your offering PageMaker services in your area. Market research is an important step in determining whether or not to offer PageMaker services.

To determine whether it will be profitable for you to offer PageMaker services, use the following worksheet.

> ### COMPETITIVE ANALYSIS FORM
>
> 1) Who presently offers PageMaker services in your area? List names, addresses, and phone numbers.
>
> 2) What services do these firms offer?
>
> Equipment rentals _____
>
> Training and consulting _____

Newsletter formatting _____

Editorial and project management _____

3) Are your competitors in full-time or part-time operation? If part-time, with what types of businesses are they
affiliated (ad agencies, printers, typesetters)?

4) Which of these do existing competitors do correctly?

Convenient locations _____

Adequate parking _____

Convenient hours_____

What have you heard about the quality of their work?

_____

5) Which of these do existing firms do badly?

Location _____   Quality _____

Attitude _____   Cost _____

6) Who are the present clients of these firms?

Entrepreneurs _____ Large firms _____

Small firms _____   Non-profit organizations _____

7) How do these firms promote themselves?

Word of mouth _____ Personal sales calls _____

Direct mail_____   Advertisements _____

Where do they run these advertisements? _____

_____

8) How do existing firms charge for their PageMaker services?

By the page ____By the hour ____By project ____

9) Are there any new firms likely to offer PageMaker services in your area? If so, who?

_____

Most important, you must determine what you can do to make you offering different from the competition's. What will set you apart from the competition? What services can you offer that your competition doesn't?

Lower prices ____

Free pickup and delivery ____

Higher quality ____

Faster service ____

Higher visibility ____

Other (specify) _____

Before you begin offering PageMaker services to others, you should have a convincing answer to the question: "Why should prospective clients purchase their services from me instead of from my existing and potential competition?"

Marketing Considerations

Analyze the market for your PageMaker services and determine how much it will cost you to reach that market. Start by asking yourself: "Who publishes newsletters in my area?" It helps to break your answer into categories:

Large firms ____   Service firms ____

Small firms ____   Trade associations ____

Retailers ____   Non-profit groups ____

After you have identified the types of firms, you should try to identify the department or individual responsible in each for producing newsletters and other printed communications. It's important that you identify the specific individuals as accurately as possible.

Begin by preparing a prospect list of specific firms and individuals who are good candidates for purchasing your services. The information you assemble about each of your potential clients should include:

PROSPECT PLANNER

Name of firm _____

Street address

_____

Mailing address

_____

Department most likely to need your services

_____

Person in charge:

Name _____

Position _____

Phone (including extension)

_____

Services likely needed

_____

How and where are these services presently being acquired?_____

How much do they currently cost (estimate)_____

What is the likelihood of doing business with this firm (rate on a scale of 1-10)?

_____

Date of first contact _____

Your Prospect Planner can be as simple as pages in a three-ring binder, or you can organize the information on your computer using a database management program. The important thing is that you *immediately* begin to look at your market in an organized way.

The more effort you put into targeting potential buyers of your PageMaker services, the greater the likelihood that you will succeed in attaining your goals.

Advertising

You must determine how you will reach potential clients. Start by making a list of newspapers and business publications in your area. Ask them to send you rate cards. Set up a filing system similar to your Prospect Management system.

Publication _____

Cost per column inch _____

Circulation _____

Representative _____

Phone _____

Next, ask yourself: "Are there other ways of reaching potential clients?" Let your imagination roam free. Don't forget the value of "free" advertising through public relations efforts. Consider delivering a desktop publishing presentation to local business groups such as the Chamber of Commerce, or service organizations such as Kiwanis and Rotary Clubs.

Visit the information section of your public library. You may be able to locate a list of non-profit business and trade associations in your area. These groups are often interested in outside speakers. Make a list of these organizations, and the names of their program directors.

Association _____

Address _____

Program director _____

Phone _____

Consider submitting a short article on desktop publishing to a local publication. Or, prepare an article for a national publication describing how you solved a particular communications problem. These articles, more than anything else, will increase your visibility and establish your credibility.

Profitability Analysis

The income-planning worksheet below will help you gain a rough idea of the feasibility of offering PageMaker services to other firms in your area.

INCOME PLANNING WORKSHEET

Start by listing the desired monthly income you hope to earn from providing PageMaker services to others:

Income goal: $_____

Next, add the estimated costs of providing these services:

Additional supply expense: +$ _____

Additional labor expense: +$ _____

Advertising and promotional costs: +$ _____

Describe in detail where money will be spent:

Brochures $_____

Printing $_____

Postage $_____

Advertisements $_____

Selling expenses (if any):

Travel/gas +$_____

Parking +$_____

Telephone +$_____

Commissions (if any) +$_____

Miscellaneous expenses (business license, accounting, etc.): +$_____

Adjusted Income Goal: $_____

Feasibility

Finally, divide your adjusted income goal by the number of hours you have available each month to earn that income (see "Analyzing Your Resources," above).

$_____ (income goal)

_____

$\dfrac{}{} = \$_____ (hourly rate)

_____ (hours available)

This figure should be close to the hourly rate currently being paid for PageMaker services in your area.If it is equal to, or less than, the current rate for PageMaker services in your area, you have a good chance of meeting your income goal.

If, however, it is greater than the current rate being charged in your area for PageMaker services, you will possibly have difficulty in meeting your income goal. In this case, you should either be more conservative in your income expectations or find ways to cut expenses. Or, plan on spending more time offering PageMaker services.

Conclusion

Competence is not enough to succeed in business. Your ability to succeed as a PageMaker entrepreneur is based on realistically matching your expectations, talents and resources with the market and competition realities in your area.

If your expectations and resources are in line with your market and your competition, you will probably succeed in developing a profitable, PageMaker-based, source of income. This can pay great dividends in terms of income as well as the satisfaction and enhanced self-confidence that comes from entrepreneurial success.

Bibliography

Books

The Aldus Guide to Basic Design, by Roger C. Parker. Aldus Corporation, 1987.

A 68-page volume sent free to all PageMaker buyers who register their software. It reviews the graphic elements that contribute to good-looking publications.

The Chicago Manual of Style: The 13th Edition of a Manual of Style, Revised and Expanded, the University of Chicago Press, 1982.

A comprehensive look at the technical aspects of preparing book-length publications.

The Copywriter's Handbook: A Step-by-Step Guide to Writing Copy That Sells, by Robert W. Bly. Dodd, Mead & Company, 1985.

An excellent companion to accompany the power that desktop publishing gives you in creating good-looking brochures, newsletters, and other print communications.

Create the Perfect Sales Piece: A Do-It-Yourself Guide to Producing Brochures, Catalogs, Fliers, and Pamphlets, by Robert W. Bly. John Wiley & Sons, Inc., 1985.

An excellent catalyst for ideas, this book shows how to plan and get started producing the various types of projects the typical business needs. Provides a framework for relating your desktop publishing skills to your specific business applications.

Designs for Newsletters, Aldus Corporation, 1986.

Includes Macintosh disk plus 118 page workbook. The disk contains 21 newsletter templates, a self-paced tutorial, and text and graphics files for creating your own newsletter. The workbook describes the basics of newsletter design and shows how to modify the templates for your own use.

The Design of Advertising, by Roy Paul Nelson. Wm. C. Brown Company, 1984.

An in-depth look at integrating art and copy.

Editing by Design: A Guide To Effective Word-and-Picture Communication for Editors And Designers, by Jan V. White. R.R. Bowker, Company, 1982.

This book communicates a tremendous amount of information in an informal, easy-to-read style. Numerous examples show how to construct grids to hold your publication together.

How to Do Leaflets, Newsletters and Newspapers, by Nancy Brigham with Ann Raszmann and Dick Cluster. Hastings House Publishers, 1982.

Although written in pre-desktop-publishing days, this down-to-earth guide contains numerous useful tips and suggestions.

PostScript Language Tutorial and Cookbook and **PostScript Language Reference Manual,** Adobe Systems, Inc. Addison-Wesley Publishing Company, 1985.

For advanced users only, these technical volumes describe the Page Description Language that forms the basis of PageMaker's power.

Publication Design, by Roy Paul Nelson. W. C. Brown Company, 1984.

Detailed descriptions of newsletter, magazine, newspaper, and book design principles. Special attention is devoted to masthead and front-page design principles, and to the integration of art and copy.

Periodicals

Communication Arts, Palo Alto, California.

Thumbing through past issues is an excellent way to break design stalemates and restore your creative energies. Annual issues are devoted to the year's best advertisements and corporate publications.

Personal Publishing, Renegade Company, Itasca, IL.

Reviews the latest hardware and software and contains practical applications stories.

Print. RC Publications, New York, NY

Another idea generator, this publication emphasizes the visual aspects of contemporary advertising and marketing. Focuses on the practical issues design as well as highlighting outstanding examples of work produced each year.

Publish! The How-To Magazine Of Desktop Publishing. PCW Communications, San Francisco, CA.

Covers both Macintosh and MS-DOS based desktop publishing systems. Focuses on the latest hardware and software as well as on the human and design aspects of desktop publishing.

Index

"none," 142

percent of shading, 141

"white," 142

Snap-to Guides, 125-126

Target Printer command, 114-115

Toolbox command, 129

Type Menu commands, 134-139

aligning text, 138

Bold command, 134

Indents/tabs command, 137

Italics command, 134

Justification of text, 138-139

Normal command, 134

Paragraph command, 137

Reverse type, 139

short cuts, function keys, 136

Spacing command, 138

Strikethru command, 135

Type Specs command, 135-136

Underline command, 135

Zero lock command, 123

Consistency, tools for

alignment guides, 298

grids, 22, 303

placeholders, 299

Consulting assistance, 320

Copy command, 117

Copy Master Guides command, 133

Cricket Draw, 316

Cropping

graphics, 274

Cropping tool

Toolbox, 90, 92

Customization, presentations, 196-197

Cut command, 116

D

Design elements

borders, 150

thickness of line, 150-151

Desktop publishing

advantages of, 9

added control, 10

communicating power, 11-12

font cartridges, 67

Hewlett-Packard LaserJet printers, 67-69, 72

Laser Connection, 71

LaserWriter Plus, 69, 71

limitations, 67

MacEnhancer, 68

PostScript, 69, 71

QMS PS-800, 71

speed factors, 320

Leading

letter spacing, 166

line spacing, 165

Letter spacing, 165-166

Lines

diagonal line, 86

lines Menu, helpful hints, 141

line spacing, 165

perpendicular lines, 86-87

Lock Guides, 126

Logos, 270-271

M

MacEnhancer, 68

Macintosh screen, 75-76

MacLink, 311

Margins, setting of, 146

Master pages, 34-35

left-hand/right-hand pages, 97

non-printing elements, 95

presentations, 184-185

printing elements, 95, 97

problems with, 147-148

Mastheads, 270

MegaScreen, 310

Memory, 319-320

Menu Bar, screen, 77-78

Microsoft Mach 10 board, 50

Microsoft Windows, 49, 67

Microsoft Word 3.1, 59-60

Monitors, 50

big screen, 308-310

MegaScreen, 310

PageMaker, 43

Special effects, 269-270

Spelling/grammar checkers, 321, 324

Squares, 90

Strikethru command, 135

Super Paint, 316

Surprise (adding)

   colors/shades, 290

   location factors, 290

   size factors, 289

Switcher command, 98

T

Target Printer command, 114-115

Templates, newspaper ads, 198, 199

Text

   "#" and, 85

   highlighting text, 87-88

   rolling up, 85

   selection of, 82, 85-86

   "+" and, 85

   Toolbox, 87

   width of, 86

Text operations

   column rules, 170-172

   column width, 157

   graphics adding, 169-170

   headlines, 160-165

   interrupting text, 166-169

   letter spacing, 165-166

   line spacing, 165

   long text, 156

   placing text, 153-156

      for Macintosh, 156

      for PC, 153-156

      for TOPS system, 156

   "+" in, 155, 166

   "#" in, 155

   printing, 173-174

   reformatting text, 157, 159-160

   Retain format option, 154

   saving, 173

   Text only option, 154

   thumbnail feature, presentations, 196

Tiling, large visuals, 196

For better-looking newsletters...
Aldus Corporation introduces
PageMaker Portfolio :
Designs for Newsletters

PageMaker Portfolio: Designs for Newsletters is a set of 21 newsletter templates developed by Aldus Corporation to help PageMaker users produce visually exciting publications. Now you can use *PageMaker Portfolio* to produce your own newsletters by placing your text and graphics in pages already designed by a professional. To customize a template format, you simply apply our advanced design techniques to suit your needs.

Here's what you get with PageMaker Portfolio.

PageMaker Portfolio: Designs for Newsletters includes 21 newsletter formats on disk, a 114-page instructional workbook, a step-by-step tutorial, advanced design tips, and more.

Return this card for a $10 discount on PageMaker Portfolio.

PageMaker Portfolio: Designs for Newsletters retails for $79. But you can buy it for only $69 by returning this order form with your check or credit card authorization.

———————————— FOLD HERE ————————————

☐ Yes!

I want to order *PageMaker Portfolio: Designs for Newsletters* for only $69.

Send me _____ copies. I want PageMaker Portfolio for the

☐ Macintosh   ☐ PC AT or compatible (available May 1)

Ship to:

Name _____

Company name _____

Street address (no P.O. box) _____

City _____ State _____ Zip _____

Phone (   ) _____

Payment:

☐ Check payable to Aldus Corporation enclosed

☐ VISA   ☐ MasterCard   ☐ American Express

Card number _____ Expiration date _____

Total amount of order _____
(Add 7.9% sales tax in Washington state)

Products are shipped by UPS within the continental United States, and by airmail elsewhere. Foreign orders must be prepaid in United States currency. Allow four weeks for delivery.

Thank you for your order!

BUSINESS REPLY MAIL

FIRST CLASS MAIL   PERMIT NO. 1049   SEATTLE, WA.

POSTAGE WILL BE PAID BY ADDRESSEE

Aldus Corporation
PageMaker Portfolio Order Department
411 First Avenue South
Suite 200
Seattle, Washington 98104